Many changes have oc[...] tion of *The Hiker's hip* [...] *to the Humboldt Coast* in 1988. This completely revised second edition reports all the important changes in the parks, trails, facilities and access.

We have added more than 100 miles of new trails, represented in nine trail reports and twelve new **OTHER SUGGESTIONS**. This second edition explores new trails around Lake Earl, a vast area of ancient dunes and wetlands; the remarkable climb from climax redwood forest to upland Jeffrey pine forest on Little Bald Hills Trail at Jedediah Smith Redwoods State Park; new segments of the California Coastal Trail; pretty Dolason Prairie Trail and new and expanded bike loops in Redwood National Park; and expanded trails in King Range National Conservation Area.

These new trails join updated reports of our fifty original hikes, offering 600 miles to explore on foot, bike or horse. You will find more information on Native Americans, plants and history. plus changes you need to know for a safe and rewarding trip. With this book you can start planning your next trip to explore the wild, untrammeled beauty of California's marvelous North Coast.

UPDATES & CORRECTIONS THROUGH APRIL 1996
BY TRAIL NUMBER (#) & PAGE (P)

Please note the following changes, not reflected in the trail reports, which have occurred since Second Edition 1993 printing.

#6. DeMartin Trail will be rerouted in Autumn 1996. Total distance will be about 6¾ miles instead of current 5¼. Rerouted to east from around 1¾-mile point to DeMartin Campground.

#12 – #17. Elk Prairie Parkway renamed N. B. Drury Parkway.

#35. Arcata's Redwood Park now has a handicap-accessible trail.

#40. The "immense slide of mucky mud" described as north of Oil Creek is actually between Fleener Creek and Guthrie Creek, around 1½ miles. You must climb over the slide to reach Guthrie Creek. If you do, stay off flat areas of slide — deep, oozing mud — and don't go during storms.

#44. P163. The Flatiron Tree fell during a January 1995 storm.

#47 – #53. Bureau of Land Management has new phone numbers. Arcata BLM: (707) 825-2300. Ukiah BLM: (707) 468-4000. Permits now required for overnight trips for groups over 10 and groups with pack animals. Call for info.

#53. Starting from Wailaki or Nadelos Campground shortens the trail by 2¼ miles, not 1¼ miles.

P196. Sinkyone's Needle Rock Visitor Center no longer rents sleeping space.

On every stump and fallen log, and on every fork and bulge of living tree, little elves' gardens of small plants and fungi were growing—dainty sprays of vaccinium, red and orange toadstools, barberry, gaultheria; and the roadside banks were set with myriads of ferns, while mosses grew to such size that I sometimes mistook them for a young growth of some stiff, heathery plant.

—J. Smeaton Chase at Prairie Creek, 1913,
California Coastal Trails

The
HIKER'S
hip
pocket
GUIDE
to the
Humboldt
Coast

by
Bob Lorentzen

BORED FEET PUBLICATIONS
MENDOCINO, CALIFORNIA
Second Edition
1996

© 1988, 1993, 1996 by Robert S. Lorentzen
Second edition, July 1993
Printed in the United States of America on 85% recycled
paper (15% post-consumer)

Illustrations by Joshua Edelman
Symbols by Jann Patterson-Watters and Taylor Cranney
Maps by Bob Lorentzen and USGS
Design by Judy Detrick
Additional design and production by Elizabeth Petersen
Edited by Anne Fox

Published by Bored Feet Publications
Post Office Box 1832
Mendocino, California 95460
(707) 964-6629

Library of Congress Cataloging-in-Publication Data
Lorentzen, Bob, 1949-
The hiker's hip pocket guide to the Humboldt coast, second edition.
        / by Bob Lorentzen.
    pp. 224
    Bibliography: p. 219
    Includes index
    ISBN 0-939431-13-0
        1. Hiking-California-Humboldt County (Calif.)-Guide-books.
2. Hiking-California-Del Norte County (Calif.)-Guide-books.
3. Humboldt County (Calif.)-Description and travel-Guide-books.
4. Del Norte County (Calif.)-Description and travel-Guide-books.
I. Title.
GV199.42.C22H865   1988 917.94'11—dc19   88-22293
                                          CIP

ISBN 0-939431-13-0

10 9 8 7 6 5

Dedicated to Patricia Priano, who provided invaluable support and encouragement from the beginning.

This book is also dedicated to California Ocean Sanctuary, the movement to prevent the degradation and destruction that would result if oil exploration and development were allowed on the Northern California Coast. Save the coast for future generations, whether of people, fish, birds, whales or other life.

NO OFFSHORE OIL!
OCEAN SANCTUARY NOW!

For more information, write:
OCEAN SANCTUARY COORDINATING COMMITTEE
  P.O. Box 498
  Mendocino, CA 95460

In memoriam,
Samuel Harman
Eris Rasmussen Harman
Glenn Watters
Sam Watnick
Zia Dancer Zuma

ACKNOWLEDGMENTS

I wish to express my hearty thanks to all who helped create this book. In particular, I thank Anne Fox for her enthusiasm and sensitive editing; Joshua Edelman for his great illustrations; May Edelman for her brainstorming; Jann Patterson-Watters for her marvelous symbols and infectious excitement; Margaret Fox for her early feedback, support and copying machine; Judy Detrick for the time at her kitchen table and her superb design.

For their early support, enthusiasm and pithy comments, I thank Humboldt County booksellers, especially Carlos Benemann and Shar Evans, and Alan and Barbara Wilkinson of Prairie Creek Redwoods State Park. For resourceful and constructive comments, I thank Douglas Warnock, Anne Smith and John Sacklin of Redwood National Park; Bruce Cann of Bureau of Land Management; Joe Hardcastle and co-workers at Humboldt Redwoods State Park; David Hull and Mark Andre of the City of Arcata; Noelle Imperatore of Wilderness Press; and many others at the various state parks of Humboldt and Del Norte counties.

Thanks also to my dedicated proofreaders, Judith Becker, Ruth Dobberpuhl, Carole Raye, Amanda Avery, Chris Hock, Bill Brown, Carol Goodwin-Blick, Maureen Oliva, Karen Timmer, Caitlin Bean, Marsha Green, Gina Salamone; Linda Pack for creative scheduling; Anthony Miksak of the Gallery Bookshop for his outspoken enthusiasm; Jeffery Garcia for companionship on the trails; Taylor Cranney for her help with the symbols. Special thanks to Paul Smith, his family and friends for their generosity and caring; and to the readers of my other *Hiker's hip pocket Guides* who have provided constructive criticism, without which this book might never have been completed.

For help with trail changes and new trails in the second edition, I thank Jim Baird and Jack Rundell of Humboldt Redwoods State Park, Dick Mayle and Beth Koltun of Redwood National Park, Dick Goss of Lake Earl State Park, Carl Knapp and Brian Cahill of Prairie Creek Redwoods State Park, Bruce Cann of BLM, Alan Wilkinson and Don Beers of Coast Redwood District, State Parks. Special thanks to Loren Bommelyn for information about Tolowa culture, Syd Hammill for his fastidious altimeter readings along the New Lost Coast Trail, and Liz Petersen for her meticulous plant identification, patience and perseverance under pressure, and design innovations.

CONTENTS

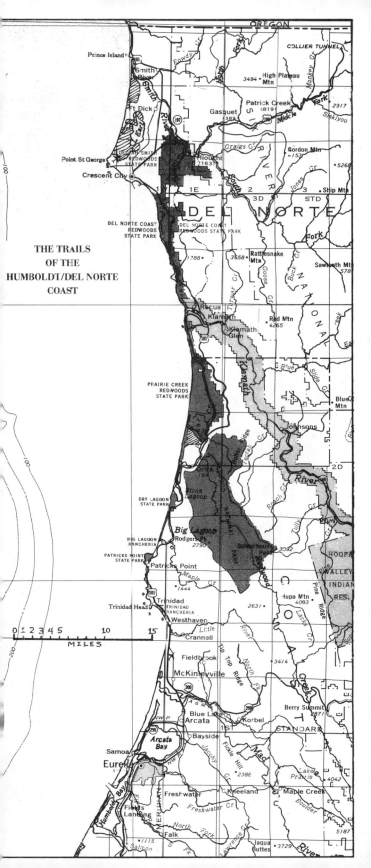

THE TRAILS
OF THE
HUMBOLDT/DEL NORTE
COAST

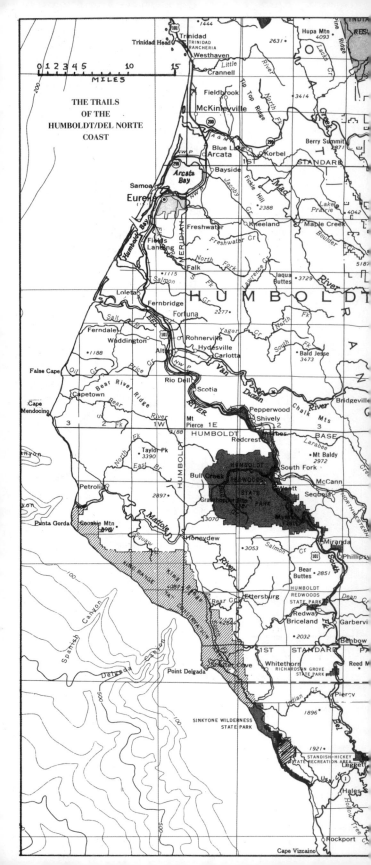

THE TRAILS
OF THE
HUMBOLDT/DEL NORTE
COAST

INTRODUCTION

Humboldt and Del Norte Counties comprise a vast wild land of forests, mountains, rivers and shores in the northwestern corner of California. The area's 165-mile coastline varies greatly from north to south. From Crescent City north, the shore consists of sandy beaches backed by marine terraces. South of Crescent City, the rugged rocky shore lies below high, eroded cliffs that stretch to the Humboldt County line. Humboldt County's coast north of Trinidad is characterized by dark sand beaches with high bluffs, rocky coves and tidepools, three large lagoons and vast forests. Then the coast turns more gentle, with long, dune-backed beaches adjacent to fertile river flood plains and the lowlands of Humboldt Bay. South of Ferndale, high coastal mountains drop steeply to the narrow, secluded beaches of California's Lost Coast.

Highway 101 crosses the heart of this rugged land from north to south, providing access to hundreds of miles of trails. Although the highway stays within 25 miles of the shore, roads to the coast are few, except in the vicinity of Humboldt Bay.

This book tells you how to find and walk, hike or ride more than 400 miles of trails through this wild, scenic land. The trails range from easy walks to difficult backpacks, with choices to fit the taste of every nature lover. The hikes will lead you to the highest peak on the Northern California Coast, the world's tallest trees, the broad mouths of wild rivers, marshes and estuaries rich in bird and plant life, pristine ponds and streams, city parks, vast wild beaches, meadows and prairies sprinkled with wildflowers, and jagged rock outcrops.

So get out of your car and use feet, bicycle, horse or wheelchair to explore the Humboldt/Del Norte Coast.

HOW TO USE THIS BOOK

The trails in this book are organized from the north to the south. Highway 101 is the starting point for the directions to every trailhead. No trail is more than two hours from Eureka or Arcata.

You will find a milepost number on Highway 101 in the directions to each trail. These numbers refer to the white highway mileposts placed frequently (but at irregular intervals) along Highway 101 by CalTrans, the State Department of Transportation. You can quickly determine the location of a trail (and where it is in relation to you) by referring to its milepost number. The detailed directions to each trailhead may include other mileposts on secondary roads.

You do not have to start at the beginning of the book. Simply turn to the trail nearest your location and you will be on your way. Neighboring trails will be on adjacent pages.

For each trail in the book you will find a map (top is north unless noted otherwise), specific directions to the trailhead, the best time to go, appropriate warnings, and a detailed trail description with some history and/or natural history.

You will find a group of symbols below the access information for each trail. They tell you at a glance the level of difficulty, type of trail, whether there is a fee, and whether dogs are allowed. The list of symbols follows.

At the end of the book are appendices that list the trails most suitable for a particular type of recreation: mountain bikes, equestrians, backpacking and handicapped access. Another appendix details the California Coastal Trail as it currently runs through Del Norte and Humboldt Counties.

THE DANGERS
TEN COASTAL COMMANDMENTS

When on the trail, *always* keep your senses wide open so that you can best appreciate nature's pleasures as well as her dangers. Don't let nature lull you into complacency. Here are ten rules to keep you out of danger and enhance your journey so that you may safely enjoy the beauty of the coast.

1. DON'T LITTER. Most of these places are unspoiled. Do your part to keep them that way. Show your appreciation for Mother Nature by hiking with a trash bag which you can fill with any trash you find in otherwise pristine places, even cigarette butts, matches and bottle caps.

2. NO TRESPASSING. Property owners have a right to privacy. Stay off private property. There are enough public places without walking through someone's yard.

3. NEVER TURN YOUR BACK ON THE OCEAN. Oversized rogue waves can strike the coast at anytime. They are especially common in winter. They have killed people; watch for them. More subtle are the changes of the tides: don't let rising tides strand you against steep cliffs or on a submerged tidal island. The ocean is icy and unforgiving, generally unsafe for swimming without a wetsuit.

4. STAY BACK FROM CLIFFS. Coastal soils are often unstable. You wouldn't want to fall 40 feet into the icy sea, would you? Don't get too close to the cliff's edge, and never climb on cliffs unless there is a safe trail.

THE SYMBOLS

WALK:
Less than 2 miles
Easy Terrain

EASY HIKE:
2 to 10 miles
Easy terrain

MODERATE HIKE:
2 to 10 miles
Rougher terrain

DIFFICULT HIKE:
Strenuous terrain
Backpacking possible

**MOUNTAIN BIKE
TRAIL**

BIKE TRAIL

HANDICAP ACCESS

**TRAIL FOR
EQUESTRIANS**

CAR CAMPING

**WALK-IN OR
BIKE-IN CAMPING:**
Environmental camps

13

**DOGS ALLOWED
ON LEASH**

**INTERPRETIVE
NATURE TRAIL**

TIDEPOOL ACCESS

**RECOMMENDED
FOR FAMILIES**

**PICNIC SPOT
May be tables or just a
good blanket spot**

**RESTROOMS
AVAILABLE**

WATER AVAILABLE

FEE AREA

FISHING ACCESS

**NO OIL EXPLORATION
OR DRILLING**

5. WILD THINGS: ANIMAL. Most of the animal pests of the Humboldt Coast are small, unless a bear goes after your food (keep camp clean and food put safely away) or you get chased by a Roosevelt elk (generally they will not chase you unless you get too close). Watch out for ticks, wasps, mosquitoes, biting spiders, scorpions and rattlesnakes. Human animals are easily the most dangerous, especially in deer hunting season (from the first week in August until the end of September). Always listen for gunfire, especially outside state parks. *Never* (even in a vehicle) enter an area where logging is in progress. UNDERWATER ANIMALS: When tidepooling or at the beach, always watch for sea urchins and jellyfish. Both have stinging spines that are painful. Remember that mussels are quarantined each year from May through October; at that time they contain deadly poison.

6. WILD THINGS: PLANT. These mean business too, especially poison oak and stinging nettles, which can get you with the slightest touch. Many other plants are poisonous. It is best to not touch any plants unless you know by positive identification that they are safe; this is most important with mushrooms.

7. POT GARDENS. Don't even think about messing with one, no matter whose side you are on. If you ever stumble onto a pot patch (not likely if you stay on the trails in this book), leave more quietly than you came. Take only memories.

8. TRAFFIC. Coast roads are difficult and often overcrowded. Drive carefully and courteously. Please turn out for faster traffic. You will enjoy the coast more if you do. If you stop, pull safely off the road.

9. CRIME. Be sure to lock your car when you leave it at the trailhead. Leave valuables out of sight, or better yet, back at your lodging.

10. ALWAYS TAKE RESPONSIBILITY FOR YOURSELF AND YOUR PARTY. This is a trail guide, not a nursery school. The author cannot and will not be responsible for you in the wilds. Information contained in this book is correct to the best of the author's knowledge. Author and publisher assume no liability for damages arising from errors or omissions. **You must take the responsibility for your safety and health while on these trails.** These are wild places. Trails may change over time and safety conditions may vary with seasons and tides. Be cautious, heed the above warnings and the warnings for each trail, and always check on local conditions. It is always better to hike with a friend. Know where you can get help in case of emergency.

THE HISTORY

Native Americans have lived along the Humboldt Coast for at least 1000 years, perhaps as long as 5000 years. The cultures of the Tolowa, Yurok, Chilula, Wiyot, Mattole and Sinkyone prospered with the coast's abundant natural resources.

Spanish galleons sailed along the coast beginning in the sixteenth century. The first recorded European visitors came in 1775 when Spanish explorers sailed into Trinidad Bay, met the local Yuroks, and erected a cross on Trinidad Head. Their mapping of Trinidad as a safe harbor brought later explorers. In 1806 an American named Jonathan Winship discovered Humboldt Bay as his ship explored the coast for the Russian-American Fur Company. His discovery was forgotten because he deemed the bay unnavigable for large ships.

In the 1820s and 1830s, fur trappers and explorers made the first overland journeys through Humboldt County. Jedediah Smith, Stephen Meek, Ewing Young, Peter Ogden and three others named McLeod, Mofras and LaFrambois stayed briefly without recording much information about the area.

In July 1848 gold was discovered first on the Trinity River, then on the Klamath. The difficult inland route to these mines provoked the search for safe harbors along the North Coast.

On November 5, 1849, a party of eight explorers left the Trinity mines seeking the Trinidad Bay shown on Spanish maps. They were led by Dr. Josiah Gregg, writer and frontiersman, who made the first extensive record of a visit to Humboldt County. The Indians told Gregg it was an eight-day journey to the coast, so the party set out with enough food for a ten-day trek. Lacking guides, they lost the Indian trail in a snowstorm and struggled through rugged country. The snow turned to rain. By the seventh day they were reduced to eating the flour paste that formed inside their packs. On their journey, they had to cut their way through immense quantities of fallen timber in the vast forests, often progressing only two miles a day. They traveled four and a half weeks to reach the coast.

The starving party arrived at Trinidad Bay on December 7. They traded with the Indians for provisions, then headed south. Crossing the Mad River in Indian canoes, they named it for an argument they had there. They found Humboldt Bay the next evening, and by Christmas Day they camped at the future location of Arcata, feasting on elk and clams provided by the friendly Wiyots.

They headed south to tell California of their discoveries. They named the Eel River as they met Indians fishing for eels (actually lampreys). They named the Van Duzen River for one of their members. Then the eight men separated into two groups. Gregg's group sought a route along the coast, but the rugged country forced them to turn inland south of Cape Mendocino. Gregg died of starvation near Clear Lake. The other group, led by L. K. Wood, followed the Eel River south, faring little better. Wood was mauled by grizzly bears and crippled for life. But they reached Sonoma to report their discoveries on February 17, 1850.

Several ships immediately left San Francisco searching for Humboldt and Trinidad Bays. Settlement began at Trinidad in March, at Humboldt Bay in April. By that summer a trail was completed to the Klamath and Trinity mines. In September the first sawmill opened at Eureka. By 1853 nine mills along Humboldt Bay shipped 20 million board feet of lumber to San Francisco. By 1856 the packing business to the northern mines had 5000 mules in service.

The towns of Eureka, Arcata and Trinidad grew and prospered, but not without hostilities from the Indians and natural hardships caused by the wild, rugged country. Eureka became the county seat in May 1856. Humboldt County remained accessible primarily by ship until 1911, when an all-weather road was established to San Francisco.

THE CLIMATE

The climate of the Humboldt Coast is cool, but mild enough for you to hike year round, if you are prepared for varying conditions. In planning your excursions, keep in mind the following about the seasons along the Humboldt Coast: November to March are the rainy months, time to bring rain coats and rubber boots. Still, there are often fine sunny days between storms.

April and May are often windy, with occasional rainstorms. The wind may be gentle, or fierce and unrelenting. The landscape is at its most lush and beautiful. Bring layered clothing and hats.

June, July and August bring sunny summer days, alternating with thick fog. You may be comfortable in shorts, but bring layered clothing in case the fog comes in. Sometimes you can beat the fog by heading a few miles inland. (This is the most crowded season, especially August.)

September and October are a beautiful time. Fog is less common. Though there may be rainstorms, most of the days are calm and warm. The land is dry, the hills golden, and the sunsets often spectacular.

GET READY, GET SET, HIKE!

You must be chomping at the bit to get out on the trail by now. Here are a few suggestions of what you need to take on your hike: layered clothing—sweater, sweatshirt, hat, windbreaker or rain coat; insect repellent; sunscreen; sunglasses; and small first-aid kit including moleskin for blisters. Highly recommended for all but the shortest walks: water container, extra food, pocket knife, flashlight or headlamp and extra batteries, matches and fire starter, map, compass (helps if you know how to use it), and of course your *Hiker's hip pocket Guide*!

Additional suggestions: spare socks, toilet paper and plastic trowel, binoculars, camera, field guides to birds, wildflowers and/or trees. If you are backpacking, you should consult an equipment list for that purpose.

When you are on the trail, remember to slow down, open your senses and enjoy. Most people hike at a rate of 2 to 3 miles per hour. But beach sand or steep terrain may slow all but the most hardy to as little as one mile per hour. Leave ample time to do the hike you plan at a pleasant pace. Hike not to count the miles, but to enjoy and appreciate nature. Happy trails to you!

LAKE EARL STATE PARK & WILDLIFE AREA

This new State Park and the adjacent Wildlife Area (managed by Department of Fish and Game) together comprise about 10,000 acres of lagoon, marsh and beach surrounded by vegetated dunes with wooded ridges and flowered meadows. Lying between the Smith River Delta and Crescent City, the large natural tract offers diverse plant and animal life in a fascinating array of habitats. Up to half of this acreage may be covered with water during the wet season, providing a rich habitat for migratory and resident birds. More than 250 avian species use the area; during migration you might see as many as 100,000 birds here. Wild-flowers present spectacular displays from late March through summer. Lakes Earl and Tolowa, joined by the deep slender channel called the Narrows, were once a part of the Smith River drainage, but the mighty river bypasses them to the east and north today. Lake Earl, fed by Jordan Creek, is mostly freshwater, while Lake Tolowa to the west is somewhat saline. Being joined, however, they exist in a fluid, shifting balance that supports a striking diversity of fish and aquatic vegetation.

You can explore the area on an expanding network of trails. They provide access to this wondrous world of ancient sand dunes and changing bodies of water where a wide variety of ecological communities, each with a varied assortment of flora and fauna, exist in a relatively small area.

1.

NORTH TO YONTOCKET & THE MOUTH OF SMITH RIVER
CENTER OF THE TOLOWA WORLD

When the Tolowa world was new, there was nothing. Then, the first three people, Thunder, Baby Sender and Daylight, and their sweat house came into existence. It was extremely cold in the void. One day Baby Sender got up. That is how the cold was chased out. He thought, "A first place, like this one, shall come into existence."

Daylight said, "Yes" and opened the door of the sweat house. In that way, daylight came into existence.

Baby Sender then spat downward and the ocean came into being. He parted the waters and underneath he could see earth. "What is it that looks this way? It's a world for people, I suppose,"

19

NORTH TO YONTOCKET &
THE MOUTH OF SMITH RIVER:

DISTANCE: 5¾-mile loop, plus 6¼-mile option to Smith River mouth; 2⅝ miles to Yontocket, 3¼ miles to Horse Camp.

TIME: Three hours to full day.

TERRAIN: Through gently rolling vegetated dunes to a Tolowa village site near mouth of Smith River, returning past several ponds.

ELEVATION GAIN/LOSS: Loop: 300 feet +/-. One way to Yontocket: 200 feet +/180 feet -; to River: 200 feet +/220 feet -.

BEST TIME: Spring, early summer for wildflowers. Autumn for best weather.

WARNINGS: Watch for poison oak. Portions of trail may be wet in winter and spring.

DIRECTIONS TO TRAILHEAD: Turn west off Highway 101 at M.31.2 onto Elk Valley Road (.6 mile north of Highway 199 interchange). Turn right on Lake Earl Drive in .9 mile. At 2.9 miles from Highway 101, turn left on Lower Lake Road. At 5.5 miles go left on Kellogg Road for .75 mile to trailhead parking on right.

FEES: Environmental Camp: $7-9/night. Hike/bike/horse Camp: $3/person/night.

FURTHER INFO: Lake Earl State Park & Wildlife Area (707)464-2523, 464-9533.

OTHER SUGGESTION: Six pleasant ENVIRONMENTAL CAMPS are located .6 mile along Kellogg Road; you must call first. A HIKE/BIKE/HORSE CAMP is located near Yontocket. For a SHORTER ROUTE TO YONTOCKET & THE HORSE CAMP, drive north to the end of Lake Earl Drive, then west on Pala Road for one mile to trailhead at a white gate; it is ¼ to Yontocket, ⅞ mile to the Horse Camp, 3⅛ miles to river mouth.

Baby Sender said. "Everything will come forth and bloom."

Historically the Tolowa were a small, prosperous Athapascan culture, the bridge between the magnificent Athapascan cultures of the Pacific Northwest coast and tribes of Northern California. Archaeological evidence shows that the Tolowa have inhabited what is now Del Norte County for at least 2300 years. Before the invasion of white people seeking gold in the 1850s, the Tolowa had eight large villages of 100 to 300 people each. Tolowa culture and religion are similar to those of the Yuroks in many ways, although the Yurok are an Algonkian people. There has been considerable intermarriage between these ethnically different, culturally related groups.

The Tolowa and their neighbors considered the Tolowa village of Yontakit, which was located at the north end of this hike, to be the center of the world, the place where the First People created this world. Every year Yurok from the south and Chetco and Tututnu from the north would journey to Yontakit for a ten-day world renewal ceremony, believed essential for the continuance of the cycle of life. During one of these ceremonies in 1853, a tragic slaughter occurred at Yontakit. White vigilantes came at the height of the ceremony, setting the village on fire and massacring hundreds of residents and visitors.

The Tolowa believed heaven was just behind the sun, somehow fitting for the people who lived in this mist-shrouded world.

Walk through the gate at the north end of the parking area and follow the level double track heading north. You cross grasslands abundant with lupine, yellow mat, knotweed, beach strawberry, sea thrift and coast buckwheat. A willow thicket lies on your left, wooded dunes on the right. Your path winds to the right at ⅛ mile. You pass two side trails on the right. Our described loop returns by the second one.

Head north again by ¼ mile, where yellow Del Norte wallflower grows on nearby dunes, with silverweed and silver-laced phacelia in the grasslands. Around ½ mile you pass through a low area with several tiny seasonal ponds. The trail may be wet here in winter and spring. Your trail skirts a forest where wind-shaped shore pines shelter Oregon grape and the manzanita ground cover known as bearberry or kinnikinnick.

Beyond ¾ mile Sitka spruce dominate the nearby forest as you traverse prairie with clumps of elderberry and huckleberry. Pass the tiny yellow and white flowers of cream cup and johnny tuck around one mile as you climb slightly to top a wooded dune, then descend into a wooded valley.

Beyond 1¼ miles you climb to meet a gravel double track. You can see a large seasonal pond to the east. Follow the gravel track north, rolling over and through dunes as grand fir joins the pines and spruces, with wax myrtle, coyote brush, salmonberry, twinberry, salal, coast silktassel, hairy honeysuckle and red-flowering currant in the understory.

From 1½ miles you follow the crest of a dune. To the west you can see across valley and dune to the Pacific, with Point St. George Lighthouse seven miles offshore. To the east a large pond is backed by the marshy Smith River Delta, the Coast Range rising beyond. Old stumps to five feet in diameter

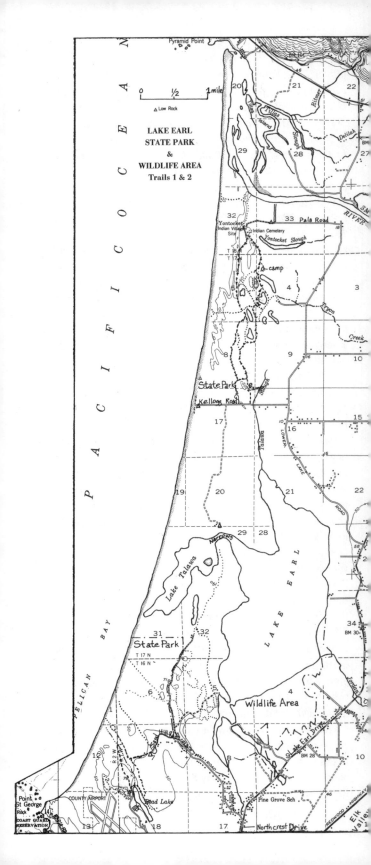

indicate the size of the original forest in this unusual plant community.

Your trail soon descends gently. Ignore a spur on the right, then meet one on the left at 1¾ miles. It heads west through dune and marsh, coming to the beach in ½ mile. Descend north on the gravel track, passing checker lilies in spring. By 1⅞ miles your road follows a valley between two vegetated dunes. Common juniper grows as a sprawling ground cover and coastal nemophila offers delicate white flowers in spring.

Beyond 2⅛ miles the track returns to the ridgetop where three-foot-diameter spruce grow. You descend along mossy slopes where calypso orchids and violets thrive in spring, then drop through two grassy valleys lined with conifers.

Ascend gradually for ¼ mile, coming to a junction at the top of a hill at 2⅝ miles. This is Yontocket, anglicized name for the native village of Yon'takit, center of the Tolowa world. The fenced cemetery on the right marks the site of the 1853 massacre of hundreds of Tolowa by vigilante settlers, another tragic cataclysm in the conquering of California. A bench east of the cemetery surveys the magical land where river and ancient dunes meet. Yontocket Slough lies in the flood plain to the east. A picnic table sits nearby.

Our described loop heads southeast from here. (You may also return the way you came for a 5¼-mile round trip.) Before you return however, consider a side trip north to extend your trek.

The double track north descends past pioneer apple, cypress and eucalyptus trees to meet Pala Road (see OTHER SUGGESTION), with an outhouse near the junction. Take the grassy track north, contouring between dunes to another fork at ¼ mile. If you go right, you come to the Smith River at ½ mile. The left fork heads west to the beach at 1⅛ miles. From there it is about 2 miles north to the mouth of Smith River.

Heading south from Yontocket our described loop returns by the left fork. Climb briefly, then descend past spruces with roots like stilts. Around 2¾ miles the grassy double track crosses the edge of the flood plain, where the trail may be flooded in winter. You can detour to the right on a single track along the base of the grassy dune. By 3 miles the trails become one and head southwest through the dunes.

Just beyond 3⅛ miles a signed trail forks left for the hike/ bike/horse camp (⅛ mile), with tables, toilets, non-potable water, a fireplace and corral at the eastern edge of the dunes overlooking the flood plain. The main trail, a distinct double track, turns west, then south, passing another spur to the camp before 3⅜ miles (Port Orford cedar and Indian plum grow along the spur).

Your double track makes a winding ascent south through forest to a view of a long pond, the most permanent of the seasonal ponds in the area. The trail meanders through grassy hills north, then west of the pond. Before 3½ miles an arrow points right for a single track winding south, but our described loop stays on the double track, soon following a lake shore on your right.

Turn right onto a second arrow-marked track before 3⅝ miles and descend south between two ponds. You follow an enchanting, twisting path that reveals views of the lake on the right, then the one on the left. Watch for head-high poison oak. Iris hunker, entwined with honeysuckle and native blackberry. Melodic bird song and the distant rumble of surf punctuate a pervading quiet.

The path winds, ducks, twists, then hides in verdant tunnels, passing cattails, then foxgloves beside a small lily pond. All too soon your path turns south through grasslands, where hummingbirds dart from one flowering currant to the next in spring.

Meet a graveled double track at 3⅞ miles. Walk 150 feet west on the gravel, then turn left on a single sandy track south through conifer forest. You soon make a winding climb into grasslands for views of a pond on the right. Dense hardwood forest fills a deep depression on your left.

Your sandy track rolls and dips, winding in and out of forest. Beyond 4⅜ miles you have brief glimpses of a second pond on your right, then views of the Smith River flood plain on the left. Climb to a last view of the pond at 4⅝ miles. Then your path turns west to meet a gravel road.

Turn left and wind south to meet another gravel track. Go left again, winding through patchy forest and grasslands. Around 5 miles alders fill a gully on your right. Continue south to a hitching post beside a honey house on the left before 5⅜ miles. In 250 feet a trail on the right is marked horses OK. (The gravel road—no horses—continues to the Environmental Camps.) Take the horse path 400 feet, then go left on the double track, returning to the trailhead at 5¾ miles.

vaV./93

2.
DEAD LAKE LOOP
SCENE OF THE TOLOWA LEGEND OF THE FALL

*In ancient Tolowa mythology, Dead Lake was the scene of the
People's fall from grace. After Baby Sender created the world, a
numerous tribe dwelt just inland from Tagian-te, what we today
call Point St. George. Many summers they lived in peace. The
waters abounded with fish, the forests with game, and the
peoples' hearts were glad. Then came the time of sorrow. One day
in council the chief became angry at one of the elders and struck
him to the ground. This blow led to the destruction of the
harmony that had existed. Some of the People began to doubt
their leaders, others cried for vengeance. While many remained
loyal, the discord allowed one dark-hearted person to practice
evil. The heavens covered with menacing clouds of terrible
darkness and the wind roared over the shifting sands, blinding
everyone. Suddenly a deafening sound broke upon the ears of the
people. Like the jaws of a dragon, the earth opened beneath their
feet and swallowed them. The gaping abyss opened where Dead
Lake is today. The storm broke in wild fury and torrents filled the
sepulcher. To this day the Tolowa consider the lake bottomless,
infested with enormous serpents, and they will not go there.*

*This mysterious lake has no inlet, and yet despite the ceaseless
outpouring of Sweetwater Creek from it, retains a constant water
level. You might carry angelica root or other protection from evil
if you visit Dead Lake today. Or you can steer clear of the lake and
head for the miles of open beach to which this trail provides
access. It is due to another reason, the sensitive habitat surrounding the lake, that state parks people have closed the area to
equestrians. Horseback riders are allowed on the trail to the
beach.*

Behind a locked gate, a level double track heads southwest. You

DEAD LAKE LOOP:

DISTANCE: 2½-mile loop, plus 2½-mile side trip to beach, where you can go south 1½ miles to Point St. George or north up to 6 miles to Smith River mouth.

TIME: One or 2 hours for loop.

ELEVATION GAIN/LOSS: Loop: 120 feet +/120 feet-.

TERRAIN: Contours through grasslands and wooded dunes, ascends along creek to Dead Lake, then returns.

BEST TIME: Spring, early summer for wildflowers.

WARNINGS: Watch for poison oak.

DIRECTIONS TO TRAILHEAD: Turn off Highway 101 at M.27.0 (north end of Crescent City) onto Northcrest Drive for 1.3 miles, then go left on Old Mill Road for 1.5 miles, then left on Sand Hill Road .5 mile to its end and the trailhead.

FURTHER INFO: Lake Earl State Park & Wildlife Area (707) 464-2523 or 464-9533.

OTHER SUGGESTION: CADRE POINT/MCLAUGHLIN POND LOOP (3¾ miles, fee: $2.50 or current fishing or hunting license) explores the south shore of Lake Earl, then heads north to the pond, where beaver and river otters live. From Mclaughlin Pond you can walk 1½ miles north to THE NARROWS, the deep channel connecting Lake Earl with Lake Tolowa. The entire area, accessible from the trailhead at the end of Old Mill Road, provides excellent wildlife viewing. Be aware that hunting is allowed on most of these Department of Fish and Game lands.

cross grasslands surrounded by coastal fir forest. Around ⅛ mile the trail can be very wet in winter and spring. A spur on the right leads to a picnic area on an old house site surrounded by cypress trees.

The main trail contours to another picnic table by ¼ mile. Climb a short hill as your path bends left, passing shore pine, wax myrtle, Oregon grape, evergreen huckleberry, coast buckwheat and lupine. Walk sandy tread past Del Norte wallflower in a depression in the dunes on your left.

Your track bends right, coming to a junction at ⅜ mile. The trail on the left, signed "Dead Lake" (closed to horses), will be your return path. Go right and head northwest through grasslands, then into forest as Sitka spruce, Douglas fir and grand fir join the pines. Look for false lily of the valley, iris, checker lily and calypso orchid in spring. Red huckleberry and rattlesnake plantain also grow along the route.

At ⅝ mile a faint trail on the left (closed to equestrians) climbs northwest. The main double track (open to horses) continues north-northwest, coming to the beach at 1¼ miles. From there hikers and equestrians can go south 1½ miles to Point St. George, or north up to 6 miles to the mouth of Smith River.

Our described loop goes left on the faint trail at ⅝ mile. It quickly descends into forest, then crosses tiny Sweetwater Creek on one of two logs. (The crossing, particularly in winter, may not be advisable to people with unsure footing.) Shaded by alders, the creek is jammed with skunk cabbage and crowded by tall salmonberry and low waterleaf.

Pick up the faint trail heading south through lush, dense vegetation. At ¾ mile the path climbs above the creek on a mossy roadbed, passing an escaped holly bush on the left. You leave the forest and meet a sandy trail.

Follow the sandy track south-southeast along the crest of a vegetated dune, climbing gradually. Beyond one mile you ascend to a view southwest across expansive dunes to offshore rocks near Point St. George. You can also see Dead Lake to the south.

At 1⅛ miles your trail drops off the dune's crest to its west face, leaving the conifer forest. Go left as the trail forks, soon heading south through the dunes. The path becomes extremely vague beyond 1¼ miles, but continue south through the dunes until you look out over Dead Lake. The trail reappears, dropping off the dune to approach the lake shore. (The Riverside Street access is to the south.)

Take the trail that heads west along Dead Lake's north shore. Look beyond the alders for pond lilies on the lake. The yellow flowers bloom in spring. Cross Sweetwater Creek on the driftwood logs jammed in the lake's outlet.

Once you cross the creek your trail improves. Around 1⅜ miles it turns south through the alder forest along the shore. Then climb through grasslands to a junction at 1½ miles. Continue along the lake shore 300 feet to a second junction, where your return trail is on the left. (The shoreline trail continues for ⅛ mile to a large dune area.)

Go left on the path that heads north briefly, then follows the crest of a dune northwest. Pass a side trail, staying on the clearly marked path. At the next junction a spur heads north to Dead Lake Dune in ⅛ mile. Go left for the trailhead, heading northwest on the obvious path through dense vegetation.

At 2 miles the trail bends right and descends east to meet the main double track. Turn right and retrace your steps to the trailhead.

REDWOOD NATIONAL PARK

Redwood National Park comprises 108,000 acres of virgin forests, rugged coastal cliffs and beaches, meadows and streams. In its boundaries are three separately administered redwood state parks: Jedediah Smith, Del Norte Coast and Prairie Creek. Redwood National Park stretches for almost 50 miles from Crescent City in the north to Orick in the south. It includes the traditional territories of three Native American groups who have lived here for centuries: the Tolowa, Yurok and Chilula.

The virgin forests of the park are among the greatest on earth. The redwoods endure from ancient times: as a species they have survived dinosaurs, the Ice Age, and the creation of mountain ranges. Today they stand in awesome silence, catching clouds and fog on their sweeping branches and filtering sunlight with stunning effect. Be forewarned: a walk among these ancient beings will have you craving more.

Redwood National Park was created in 1968 after 50 years of effort. In 1917 the founders of Save-the-Redwoods League toured the groves along newly opened Highway 101 and began to lobby Congress for a park. In 1920 the House of Representatives passed a bill to create a Redwood National Park. But when the bill was defeated in the Senate, efforts turned to creating California state parks. In 1964 a National Geographic article rekindled national park efforts after a survey team from the magazine found the world's tallest tree on private timber land on Redwood Creek. The protracted struggle between logging companies and conservationists ended with the creation of a park of 58,000 acres, the largest national park ever created from privately held lands.

The Tall Tree was saved, but logging continued upstream. Resulting erosion threatened the trees in the new parklands. Another bitter battle led to the expansion of Redwood National Park by 48,000 acres in 1978. Since most of those lands had been clearcut, extensive rehabilitation began in the drainage of Redwood Creek. More than 200 miles of roads and 2000 miles of tractor trails are being removed, the natural contours of the land reshaped, extenvsive acreage replanted.

The young trail system of the park, already with several fine trails, will be greatly expanded before the year 2000.

JEDEDIAH SMITH
REDWOODS STATE PARK

This northernmost of the redwood parks straddles the confluence of Mill Creek and the Smith River. The river, the largest wild and undammed river remaining in California, was named for mountain man Jedediah Strong Smith, who camped here in 1828 while leading an expedition north to Oregon. The Smith River is renowned for its exceptional salmon and steelhead fishing, which peaks during the very rainy period from October through February.

The park, one of three state owned and managed units of Redwood National Park, comprises 9792 rugged, wooded acres. Lying a few miles inland from the coast, in summer the park offers some of the most sunny and warm weather to be found in the northern end of the redwood belt. This inland location also provides hikers the opportunity to observe the transition zone from the immense redwood groves to the Jeffrey pine forests of the upland interior.

SMITH RIVER NATIONAL RECREATION AREA

Bordering Jedediah Smith Redwoods State Park on the east is the newly designated Smith River National Recreation Area, a 305,000-acre area with about 70 miles of trails. Conservationists sought National Park status for this spectacularly diverse, rugged landscape, but Congress compromised on a multiple-use classification, bowing to pressure from timber companies. Nonetheless, the NRA designation does offer some protection for the 315 pristine miles of the Smith River which drain this wild country.

The NRA also encompasses about one fourth of the 249,000-acre Siskiyou Wilderness. Among the state park, the NRA and the wilderness area, hikers can explore a rich and complex series of habitats spanning from near-coastal redwood forest to 7000-foot Coast Range crest.

3.

LITTLE BALD HILLS
TRANSITION FROM REDWOODS TO JEFFREY PINES

This trail begins in climax redwood forest beside the Smith River, then climbs into the very different world of upland Jeffrey pine forest in native grasslands, passing through a botanically rich transition zone. A phenomenal variety of plant species occur on Little Bald Hills Ridge. In addition to the many species noted in the trail description, the area supports 22 native grasses, five manzanitas and the uncommon deer and huckleberry oaks. More than 100 flowering species grow here, including four *brodiaeas, four violets and two uncommon irises. The ridge also offers great opportunities for spotting raptors.*

The 9½-mile trail begins in Jedediah Smith Redwoods State Park, climbs through Redwood National Park to a trail camp, then enters Smith River National Recreation Area. This is the only trail in Redwood National Park open to hikers, mountain bikers and equestrians. Watch for traffic, especially at blind corners, and please yield to horses. This trail description starts at Howland Hill Road, although you can drive the first 250 feet to more parking.

Your trail starts in Sitka spruce forest, climbing southwest into a grove of large redwoods where you come to additional parking beside a locked gate. The tread narrows, soon turning south on a gentle climb through typical redwood habitat. The understory consists of sword, lady and deer ferns, evergreen and red huckleberries, rhododendron, salal and redwood sorrel. Beyond ⅛ mile these are joined by thimbleberry, salmonberry, bear grass, clintonia and trail plant, as alder, hemlock, tanoak and bay laurel join the forest. Where the path turns southeast beyond ¼ mile, look for vanilla leaf, wood rose, trillium, coast lily, evergreen violet and yerba de selva.

Before ½ mile your trail begins a moderate, winding climb. You begin to see Douglas fir and young Port Orford cedar more frequently in the redwood forest, with hazel in the understory. Ascend steeply, then switchback to the right at one mile. The forest thins as twisted stalk and solomon's seal line the path.

Your ascent turns gentle again by 1¼ miles. As you leave state park land for Redwood National Park proper, the original forest has been logged. Young redwoods and alders allow occasional glimpses east over the deep canyons of the Smith River.

From 1½ miles your trail ascends south moderately, passing red-flowering currant, foxglove and horsetail fern. The path steepens as it crosses several small gullies. You pass a sign for the "Earth Peoples Garden," where a spur heads east to a small pond. The last redwoods on your route grow just above the pond.

Your trail climbs gradually beyond the pond. You see the first Jeffrey pines mingling with Douglas firs around 1¾ miles. The path soon becomes rocky on a moderate, winding ascent. Your climb eases around 2 miles, soon passing through small grassy clearings alternating with second-growth forest.

After a steep hill, climb gradually through forest around 2¼ miles where Port Orford cedars to four feet in diameter grow beside seasonal springs. Azalea, coffeeberry and ocean spray grow in the understory. You may also see the tiny California lace fern, with lacy foliage on chestnut stalks. Make a steady ascent

LITTLE BALD HILLS:

DISTANCE: 9½ miles one way to South Fork Road; 3⅛ miles to camp, 4½ miles to National Recreation Area boundary.

TIME: Full day or overnight.

TERRAIN: Climbs steeply, then contours through open prairies rimmed by forest before descending to eastern trailhead.

ELEVATION GAIN/LOSS: North-South: 2240 feet+/1800- To camp: 1600 feet+/100 feet-; to NRA boundary: 1940 feet+/100 feet-.

BEST TIME: Late spring for wildflowers, summer also good.

WARNINGS: Steep trail. Horses have right of way. Mountain bikers use caution, slow to walking speed on curves. Watch for rattlesnakes and poison oak.

DIRECTIONS TO TRAILHEAD: Exit Highway 101 onto Highway 199 (M.30.6). Go east 7.2 miles, then right on South Fork Road. In .45 mile go right on Douglas Park Road 1.6 miles to main trailhead. EASTERN TRAILHEAD: Go 7.9 miles on South Fork Road, then right on rough, rocky forest service road for one mile to trailhead at Rock Creek Camp.

FURTHER INFO: Jedediah Smith Redwoods State Park (707) 464-9533. Redwood National Park (707) 464-6101, Smith River National Recreation Area, Gasquet Ranger District (707) 457-3131.

OTHER SUGGESTION: Many other trails, both short and long, explore this wonderful state park. STOUT GROVE TRAIL, across the road from Little Bald Hills Trailhead, is a ½-mile walk through park's most impressive redwood grove. HIOUCHI TRAIL (2 miles) is an easy hike along the Smith River. The moderate BOY SCOUT TRAIL (7⅜ miles round trip) climbs through mature redwood forest to Fern Falls.

southeast until the trail veers left, leaving the old ranch road at a glade closed to allow the vegetation to recover from years of trampling.

Ascend moderately northeast through mixed forest. Beyond 2⅝ miles your rocky, red-dirt path winds past Douglas firs to six feet in diameter. Calypso orchids thrive here in spring.

By 2⅞ miles your trail gains the ridgetop. Turn east on a winding gentle ascent past more areas closed for rehabilitation.

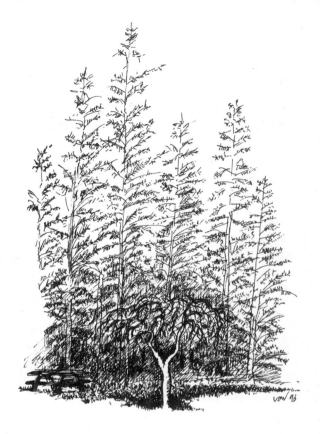

Patchy forest provides plenty of room for the spreading ground covers ceanothus prostratus and pinemat manzanita along with taller manzanita and Oregon grape. You may also see shooting star, fairy bells and columbine in spring and early summer. Ascend through forest to a junction at 3⅛ miles.

The left fork descends for 400 feet to Little Bald Hills Camp. You can camp for free at five sites with tables, fire rings and bear-proof food boxes on a gentle slope at the edge of forest and prairie. The camp also has a corral and piped water that should be purified before drinking. A lone pioneer apple tree stands beside site #3.

Little Bald Hills Trail ascends gradually east from the junction. Snowberry and western wood anemone grow beneath Douglas firs and scattered Jeffrey pines. At 3¼ miles a glade of native grasses beneath large pines offers views south over the canyons of the forks of Mill Creek to 2330-foot Childs Hill. Look for the yellow-white flowers of death camas here in spring. Your trail contours briefly, then climbs moderately along the ridgetop. The ascent turns gentle around 3½ miles, passing through ridgetop grasslands where club mosses thrive nestled amidst the rocks.

You soon return to the old ranch track and contour southeast through more pine-rich prairies. Climb gently south to a ridge-top knob at 4 miles. The tiny scythe-leaved onion grows here. Then your track contours east through more native grasslands along the ridgetop. Ascend moderately to the trail's highest point (1956') at 4¼ miles, where creeping snowberry grows.

The trail turns east, contouring along the crest through dense forest, then through scattered forest in native-grass prairies. Leave the ridgetop and descend gradually to the park boundary at 4½ miles. Your trail enters Smith River National Recreation Area, meaning you may camp wherever you like. (A campfire permit is required to have a fire; please be careful if you do.)

Your trail drops over a tank trap, then contours southeast through glades and forest where you encounter deer oak. Dip through a depression where the trail can be wet in spring, then come to a large clump of sprawling common juniper on your left. Knobcone pines grow nearby.

At 4¾ miles you come to another fork. The right fork, signed "Bummer Lake Way," climbs south. Take the left fork to descend southeast away from the ridge. A campsite sits just east of the junction, with a seasonal water source nearby (treat before drinking). The trail begins a winding descent. In spring look for the nodding white and pink flowers of the uncommon creek trillium. Your path descends across several seasonal creeks, dropping through Douglas fir-dominated forest on a north

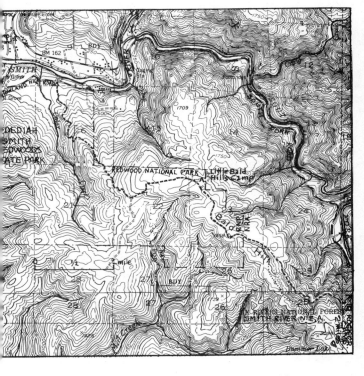

slope. The dense, brushy understory includes rhododendron, bear grass, chinquapin and common juniper. Around 5 miles you have a view southeast to the Siskiyou crest around Sawtooth Mountain (5781').

Little Bald Hills Trail continues its winding descent east and south, descending 1250 feet in 4½ miles to reach Rock Creek Camp and the southern trailhead (elevation 500 feet). Unless you have arranged a car shuttle, it is best to turn back before descending much more.

4.

ENDERTS BEACH LAST CHANCE SECTION COASTAL TRAIL

WALK OLD HIGHWAY ABOVE RUGGED COAST

Enderts Beach Road leaves the west side of Highway 101 about two miles south of Crescent City. Today the quiet side road dead-ends at the Enderts Beach Trailhead after just 2.3 miles. But this narrow, winding road was once busy Highway 101, the main artery connecting Del Norte County to the rest of California. Enderts Beach Road and most of the Last Chance Section of the Coastal Trail was the main highway until 1935. It was drivable as a scenic route until about 1970. Part of the old road south of Nickel Creek is on the National Register of Historic Places.

Enderts Beach Road parallels the broad curve of Crescent Beach, which extends for 4 miles south of Crescent City Harbor. It then climbs to Crescent Beach Overlook, a picnic area with a grand view of the rugged coast. Just beyond the Overlook, the road ends at the start of the Enderts Beach/Last Chance Trail. Use this trail for a one mile round trip to Enderts Beach as a day hike, an easy overnight to Nickel Creek Camp or the longer strenuous hike along the Last Chance Section of the Coastal Trail. (For more about the Coastal Trail, see appendix.) The Last Chance Section of the Coastal Trail is now open to bicycles, providing a steep but scenic alternative to busy Highway 101.

Head south from the trailhead on the now grassy old coast highway, descending gradually. After you pass an old quarry in the cliff to your left, magnificent views appear to the north along Crescent Head and beyond to Crescent City and Point St. George. Beyond ⅛ mile you come to an excellent view south to Enderts Beach.

Rock slides cover portions of the road as you descend south.

ENDERTS BEACH/LAST CHANCE SECTION COASTAL TRAIL:

DISTANCE: 1 mile round trip to beach or Nickel Creek Camp, 7⅜ miles one way on Coastal Trail.

TIME: One hour for beach; 3-4 hours, whole trail (one way).

TERRAIN: Follows old highway along steep cliffs above coast, then climbs steep hill into virgin forest at headwaters of Damnation Creek.

ELEVATION GAIN/LOSS: To beach: 160 feet+/160 feet-. Coastal Trail, one way: 1400 feet+/650 feet-.

BEST TIME: Spring, early summer for wildflowers. When it is not foggy for views.

WARNINGS: Watch for ticks, especially in spring. Trail beyond Nickel Creek is extremely steep. Parking not allowed at southern trailhead (OK at Damnation Creek). Mountain bikers must watch for, yield to hikers.

DIRECTIONS TO TRAILHEAD: NORTH END: Turn west off Highway 101 at M.23.8 (Del Norte) onto Enderts Beach Road. Drive 2.3 miles to end of road where trail begins.

SOUTH END: At M.15.6 (Del Norte) on Highway 101 (no parking allowed; park at Damnation Creek Trailhead and walk south).

FURTHER INFO: Redwood National Park (707) 464-6101.

OTHER SUGGESTION: CRESCENT BEACH extends for 4 miles from just south of Crescent City to just north of Crescent Beach Overlook. A new 1¾-mile segment of the COASTAL TRAIL runs between new Interpretive Center on Enderts Beach Road and Crescent Beach Overlook, passing a picnic area in a beautiful spot beside Cushing Creek.

Just beyond ¼ mile, a side trail on the right descends to Enderts Beach. The surf-scoured, sandy pocket beach is small but pretty. At low tide you can explore tidepools here. Park Service naturalists conduct guided walks in summer.

The Coastal Trail descends southeast on the old road. Dense vegetation grows here where coastal scrub and forest mingle: Douglas fir, Sitka spruce and red alder mix with silktassel, redflowering currant, Indian plum, coyote brush and berry vines. The trees have been sculptured by the prevailing winds.

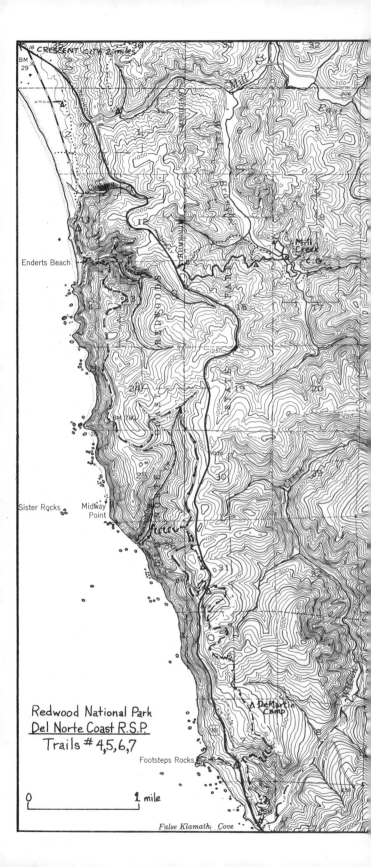

Redwood National Park
<u>Del Norte Coast R.S.P.</u>
Trails # 4,5,6,7

Before ⅜ mile, your path bends left and descends into Nickel Creek Canyon. Before you cross the creek, the side trail to the campground heads west to five campsites overlooking Enderts Beach. You must purify water from the stream. Another side trail heads east from the junction, exploring the lush creek canyon.

Beyond the creek your trail leaves the old highway, turning left and climbing southeast above the creek. Pace yourself for a long steep hill. This most strenuous portion of the trail climbs 900 feet in the next 1¼ miles. Your path turns away from the creek at ⅝ mile, continuing the steep climb. Pass the first redwoods around ¾ mile. At ⅞ mile you come to a flat spot at a big west bend. This good picnic spot has views down to Enderts Beach. Then head east, climbing moderately to the one-mile point, with views into Nickel Creek Canyon.

Turn south before 1⅛ miles, passing ocean spray, Oregon grape, salmonberry, huckleberry and salal, then redwood sorrel, evergreen violet and trillium. Your climb steepens briefly, then becomes moderate again. Rejoin the old highway at 1¼ miles and continue to climb south, following a ridge with steep drops on both sides. Wild ginger, with large, fragrant, heart-shaped leaves, grows along the trail.

Reach the first summit beyond 1½ miles. A healthy young redwood forest grows in an area logged years ago. Descend briefly before a gentle ascent brings you to a second top at 1⅞ miles, where you may get a glimpse down to the rugged coast. The surf roars from below.

Begin a steady descent south, dropping 400 feet in the next ⅝ mile. Beyond a sign, the trail enters old-growth redwood forest and Del Norte Coast Redwoods State Park around 2⅛ miles. At 2½ miles you can look southwest through alders to the breakers and offshore rocks below. Your trail begins a gradual climb. A fragment of the old highway pavement survives here.

Your ascending trail passes under the power line beyond 2⅞ miles, offering a view north to Lake Earl. Your trail turns east at a spot where the old roadbed survives intact. Your easy climb quickly brings you under the power line again.

At 3 miles an old brass plaque marks Anson Grove. The redwoods grow large as you approach the headwaters of Damnation Creek. Your trail winds south, then east, climbing gradually. Beyond 3¼ miles redwood, fir and Sitka spruce grow to ten feet in diameter along the trail.

You quickly come to a sloughing of the roadbed. Here the powerful geologic forces that shape this coast have toyed with the old road. Your trail bends left, entering primeval forest. The trail contours, curving left, then right, to cross a fern-filled gully. Rhododendrons and redwood giants thrive in the moist habitat.

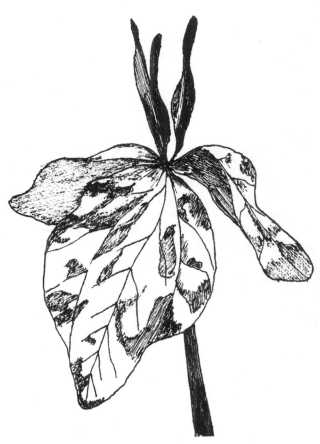

Descend gradually, crossing more gullies and spring-fed streams. Climb briefly around 4⅛ miles. An immense redwood crowds the road's left shoulder at 4⅜ miles. The path bends left and descends gently to Damnation Creek at 4½ miles. Where the road is washed out, you once crossed the creek on a slippery log. Now a short bypass crosses a sturdy new bridge.

Rejoin the old road and climb south paralleling the creek to 4¾ miles. Your trail contours through primeval forest, passing several old highway markers. Before 5¼ miles you pass a 14-foot-diameter redwood on your right with a leather fern growing on its south side. You can hear the roar of traffic on Highway 101 less than ¼ mile away. Your path winds somewhat as it contours south.

After a short climb, you meet the Damnation Creek Trail at 6⅛ miles. It heads west-southwest from a big bend in the old road, descending 1½ miles to the mouth of the creek (see Trail #5). The trail to the Damnation Creek Trailhead is 50 feet beyond, climbing east-southeast. Your trail continues southeast on the old road, descending moderately through a virgin forest of massive trees. At 6¼ miles you can glimpse the ocean through the trees.

Where you reach a big bend at 6½ miles, the roar of the surf and the barking of sea lions rise from the isolated coast below. The road turns southeast for a winding contour. Between 7 and 7⅛ miles, the forest below the road thins, providing views of the steep, wild coastline.

At 7¼ miles steps lead uphill away from the old road. Take this narrow footpath over a small ridge, coming to Highway 101 at milepost 15.6, 7⅜ miles from the trailhead. If you continue on the Coastal Trail, be careful crossing the busy road. A "CT" sign across the highway marks the DeMartin Section of the Coastal Trail (see Trail #6).

5.

DAMNATION CREEK
ANCIENT TRAIL TO A HIDDEN COAST

The well-beaten trail climbs northwest into a dense forest of large redwoods and Douglas firs. Ascend gradually for ¼ mile through a lush understory of salal, redwood sorrel, sword and deer ferns, evergreen and red huckleberries, rhododendrons, inside-out flower and wild ginger.

Your trail tops the coastal ridge, then begins a winding descent. At ½ mile, as you descend steeply by three switchbacks, you can see the ocean through the forest. Descend gradually again, paralleling the old highway below to your west. After a short uphill stretch at ⅝ mile, you descend to the old road, now the Last Chance Section of the Coastal Trail (see Trail #4).

The Damnation Creek Trail follows the roadbed north for 50 feet before turning west-southwest at a marked junction. The trail descends gradually west, winding among large, fire-scarred redwoods. Your path levels briefly at ¾ mile, where Douglas firs to eight feet in diameter mix with the giant redwoods.

You then begin a steady but well-graded descent with frequent switchbacks. The sound of the crashing surf rises from below. At ⅞ mile the deep, rugged canyon of Damnation Creek is visible to the northwest. Continue your switchbacking descent into the canyon.

Beyond one mile, as the trail switches sharply right, you get your best glimpse yet of the ocean below. Lady and five-finger fern thrive in this moist habitat, along with gooseberry, ocean spray, fairy bells, bleeding heart, iris and trail plant. Descend steeply to 1¼ miles, then contour briefly before more switchbacks.

At 1½ miles Sitka spruce begin to dominate the forest, with scattered large redwoods. A spruce on the left is eight feet in

39

```
┌─────────────────────────────────────────────┐
│              DAMNATION CREEK:                │
├─────────────────────────────────────────────┤
```

DISTANCE: 4¼ miles round trip.

TIME: Two hours minimum.

TERRAIN: Descends steeply to beach at mouth of creek, with steep return.

ELEVATION GAIN/LOSS: 1100 feet+/1100 feet-.

BEST TIME: Low tide, spring, late afternoon.

WARNINGS: Steep trail. Take it easy. Do not get trapped on the beach by rising tides.

DIRECTIONS TO TRAILHEAD: On Highway 101, a wide turnout is at M.16.0 (Del Norte), on west side of road. Signed trail leaves from upper end of turnout.

FURTHER INFO: Redwood National Park (707) 464-6101, Del Norte Coast Redwoods State Park (707) 464-9533.

OTHER SUGGESTION: Del Norte Coast Redwoods State Park has other trails around Mill Creek Campground. Turn east off Highway 101 at M.20.25 (Del Norte). HOBBS WALL TRAIL (3¾ miles, moderate) can be reached just after you turn off the highway. ALDER BASIN and MILL CREEK TRAILS (1 mile each, easy) start near the entrance to Mill Creek Campground.

diameter. Standing beside it, you can look down to the mouth of Damnation Creek Canyon, your destination.

After a short level stretch, you descend by two switchbacks followed by steep steps. As you continue descending by switchbacks, step carefully over the slippery spruce roots in the trail. You come to a stretch of trail disrupted by a small landslide, where saxifrage grows profusely. Watch your footing in this spot.

After three more switchbacks, your trail turns south-southwest, paralleling the creek. You are 1¾ miles from the trailhead. Salmon- and thimbleberries grow in a dense thicket between you and the rushing creek. Red alders are the dominant tree in this moist habitat. You can hear the breakers crashing on the rocky beach below.

Your descent steepens at 1⅞ miles. Then your trail bends left and climbs into a side canyon, crossing a small creek on a sturdy bridge. More big spruce roots disrupt the trail bed. Descend gradually through a thicket of alders, willows and berry vines.

At 2 miles you enter a second side canyon, crossing its creek on a bridge below twisted Sitka spruce. Pass under a power line as you climb to a bright green one-acre clearing of coastal scrub. As the trail levels, you can see the breakers ahead. The botanically rich wild garden around you includes cow parsnip, angelica, silver beachweed, iris, mitrewort, coltsfoot, yarrow, yerba de selva, false lily of the valley, miners lettuce, bedstraw, false solomon's seal, giant trillium and abundant checker lily in spring.

The trail then forks. If you continue straight, you cross over a small natural arch onto a narrow promontory above the beach where hen and chicks cling to the cliffs. To descend to the mouth of Damnation Creek and the beach, take the right fork before the arch and descend steeply, using caution on the steep drop to the beach.

If you get here at a high tide of +5.0 feet or more, the beach is almost completely submerged. Do not venture onto the beach at such a high tide. If you are trapped by the rising tide on this rugged, isolated coast, there is no escape! If the tide is low enough (+2.0 feet or less) and ebbing, you can walk 200 feet north along the rocky beach and about ⅛ mile south. During a minus tide you can reach rocky tidepools near the mouth of the creek. The Tolowa used an earlier version of Damnation Creek Trail to come here to harvest shellfish and seaweed at low tide. The Yuroks may have visited as well.

You can find shelter from the harsh wind in the mouth of the rocky creek canyon. Amidst a pile of huge logs jammed into the creek is the rusted piece of an old ship, remnant of one of the many shipwrecks along this wild coast.

From the bluff above the mouth of the creek, you can look northwest to Sister Rocks. To the south are other rocks, including onshore Footsteps Rocks (247 feet; see Trail #7) and offshore False Klamath Rock (209 feet). Gazing at the razor-edged cliffs along the coast, you might marvel that a trail leads to this special place.

Remember to leave adequate time to climb the 2⅛ miles back to the trailhead (an elevation gain of 1100 feet). Fortunately, the trail is well graded. The steepest portions lie in the first mile from the beach.

6.

DEMARTIN SECTION
COASTAL TRAIL

FORESTS AND GLADES WITH COASTAL VIEWS

This section of the Coastal Trail climbs through virgin forest to follow the ridge between the rugged coast to the west and the steep canyon of Wilson Creek to the east. While the route seldom wanders farther than ½ mile from Highway 101, ridge-hugging DeMartin Primitive Campground offers a lovely, secluded retreat where the sun often shines even when dense fog shrouds the coast. If you prefer beds, hot water and fellowship, the DeMartin Redwood Hostel occupies a turn-of-the-century pioneer homestead at the south end of this trail. Reservations are advised in summer, when travelers from all corners of the globe stop there.

The trail heads east from Highway 101 at M.15.6, where a sign reads "CT." Descend through fern-filled forest by steps and switchbacks to a bridge over a skunk-cabbage-filled tributary of Wilson Creek at ⅛ mile. Then climb away from the highway, zigzagging east past redwoods and Sitka spruce up to 12 feet in diameter. The trail turns south, ascending through the lush forest understory by switchbacks. Before ¼ mile your winding climb becomes gradual.

At ½ mile you come to a series of rough steps. Your ascent continues to the top of a ridge at ¾ mile. Your trail, lined with rhododendrons, bends right and heads south, following the ridge on your right, with a steep, verdant canyon on the left. Follow the winding ridge around a gulch at one mile.

The trail passes through a walk-through redwood and winds southwest to meet a power line at 1¼ miles. Descend briefly to a spectacular view down to the rocky coast nearly 1000 feet below. Your trail climbs away from the coast. At 1⅜ miles you come to another saddle with a coastal view.

You again turn away from the coast, returning to the forest. Climb gradually, then steeply to 1½ miles, where a "CT" sign confirms that you are still on the Coastal Trail. The path descends along the coastal ridge, as the pounding of surf rises from far below.

At 1⅝ miles you climb along the power line, heading generally south. Around 1¾ miles you climb steadily to reach the peak marked 1118 feet on the topo map.

Continue along the power line, making a steep descent to 2 miles, where you pass through a stand of alder. The forest thins as your steady descent passes bleeding heart and Douglas iris amidst dense berry thickets. The coastal scrub offers views of the spectacular coast, including False Klamath Cove and False Klamath Rock. Descend steeply along the power line to 2¼ miles, with views all the way.

You come to level ground, then descend gradually southeast through alder forest and coastal prairie, passing a sign, "Entering Redwood National Park, DeMartin Campground - ½ mile." In 200 feet turn left and climb east (the trail has been rerouted to pass the edge of the campground). Pass California buckeye and ascend through grasslands scattered with coastal scrub.

DEMARTIN SECTION, COASTAL TRAIL:

DISTANCE: 5¼ miles one way.

TIME: Two to 3 hours one way, 5 to 6 hours round trip.

TERRAIN: Climbs through mixed forest, then descends through coastal prairie with sweeping views. Finally descends into deep Wilson Creek Canyon.

ELEVATION GAIN/LOSS: North-South: 650 feet+/1450 feet -.

BEST TIME: Spring for wildflowers.

WARNINGS: Watch for poison oak.

DIRECTIONS TO TRAILHEAD: NORTH END: On Highway 101 at M.15.6 (Del Norte). Look for signpost marked **CT**. Additional parking at M.16.0.

SOUTH END: At M.12.8 (Del Norte) on Highway 101, at north end of DeMartin Bridge over Wilson Creek, east side of highway.

FURTHER INFO: Redwood National Park (707) 464-6101, Del Norte Redwoods State Park (707) 464-9533.

Your trail forks at 2½ miles. The left fork climbs to the camp on the eastern edge of DeMartin Prairie, where the remote ambience is punctuated by crashing surf rising on heavy, salt-scented air. The ten sites offer tables, fire rings, bear boxes, a composting toilet and tapped drinking water. No open fires are permitted.

The main trail ascends briefly through spruce/alder forest. After passing campsites 9 and 10, your route descends southeast, soon leaving the forest to cross the heart of DeMartin Prairie, a lush grassland dense with coastal scrub. You pass lupine, canyon gooseberry, coyote brush and clumps of sword ferns. The path bends right to cross an old road lined with alders, then left to descend through more prairie. In winter and spring you may see a seasonal pond below on your right.

At 2¾ miles you descend south through forest with the prairie on your right. The path descends through the prairie, then through fir/spruce forest. Pass a water tank on your left surrounded by spruce and alder beyond 2⅞ miles.

Descend gradually to 3 miles, where you come dramatically upon the edge of steep Wilson Creek Canyon. Though the canyon has been logged, the view is spectacular. The trail switches right and makes a winding descent through forest. A private residence lies below the trail beyond 3¼ miles.

Your trail descends south by 11 switchbacks for the next ¼ mile. The path levels briefly beyond 3½ miles, then switches right and climbs to gain a narrow ridgetop not far from the highway. Climb gradually along this ridgetop, which has broad views of the ocean through the trees around 3¾ miles.

Your trail switches left and ascends steeply to a magnificent view of Footsteps Rocks on the coast to the northwest. Then two more switchbacks bring you back to the edge of Wilson Creek Canyon beyond 3⅞ miles.

Make a winding climb to a level stretch of trail beyond 4 miles where you pass a big rock outcrop on your left. Make a steady descent southeast around 4⅛ miles. Then descend by more switchbacks to 4¼ miles. Your trail turns south-southeast for a relatively straight stretch through more coastal scrub with scattered alders and large spruces.

As you trail bends sharply right to meet an old road, notice claw marks left by bears on alders beside the path. Follow the road northwest for just 150 feet. Then fork right to continue northwest on a footpath through a dense thicket of coastal scrub.

Beyond 4⅜ miles your trail switches left and heads southeast, paralleling the power line. Continue your descent through open country, with views of False Klamath and Wilson Rocks offshore. At 4½ miles, descend through prairie, cross under the power line and wind through a berry thicket. Descend a series of long switchbacks through the coastal prairie and scrub, Highway 101 not far below.

Enter the forest at 4¾ miles, where your trail levels briefly. After the path bends left, begin a winding descent, crossing eight small boardwalks. The trail levels at 5⅛ miles, coming to an overgrown stretch of old highway and a trail junction. Here you have a decision. In summer you can take the footpath on the far side of the old road. This leads to a bridgeless crossing of Wilson Creek in ⅛ mile, below the highway bridge. But in winter you must turn right and follow the old highway uphill for 500 feet to meet Highway 101 at M.12.8. Then, if you are going to the hostel across the creek or continuing on the Coastal Trail, use extreme caution as you cross the narrow highway bridge. The hostel is located in the beautiful old two-story house south of the creek and east of the highway.

7.

FOOTSTEPS ROCKS
TOWERING OUTCROPS AT THE SEA'S EDGE

The Footsteps Rocks Trail is easily overlooked in the rush of traffic on Highway 101 at Childs Hill. Yet this short trail provides easy access to views of this rugged and isolated coast at a

FOOTSTEPS ROCKS:

DISTANCE: 1 mile round trip.
TIME: Thirty to 60 minutes.
TERRAIN: Descends gently across coastal prairie to base of
impressive rock outcrop.
ELEVATION GAIN/LOSS: 280 feet-/280 feet+ round trip.
BEST TIME: Spring for wildflowers, great at sunset.
DIRECTIONS TO TRAILHEAD: On west side of Highway 101,
first turnout north of Wilson Creek at M.13.44.
FURTHER INFO: Del Norte Coast Redwoods State Park
(707) 464-9533.

spectacular spot.

Your trail heads west from the tiny sign marking the trailhead.
You descend gradually through a tangle of berry thickets and
coastal scrub with scattered alders. At ⅛ mile your trail levels
briefly, then descends again, passing alders 3 feet in diameter.

After a short steep section, the tops of Footsteps Rocks appear
ahead. Angle northwest at ¼ mile, continuing your descent.
You cross a small bridge and continue to descend as more of the
towering rocks come into view. At ⅜ mile your trail levels, then
climbs briefly. On your right is another rock outcrop; a garden
of succulents hangs from the top of its sheer face. The terrain
is open and grassy here, with more room for wildflowers.
Poppies, lupines and irises dominate.

Your trail levels and turns west, heading straight for the base
of the massive outcrops of dark Franciscan stone. In another
200 feet you are directly below towering rocks rising to 247 feet
above sea level. The official trail ends here, but two rough foot
trails continue. The left fork descends to meet the rocky shore
to the south, accessible only at low tide. The right fork winds
around to the immense pile of boulders on the north side of the
rocks. A few Sitka spruce struggle to grow in this harsh environment.

The right fork continues another 200 feet before ending atop
a pile of jagged dark boulders that seem to have dropped from
the imposing cliff above. The north face of Footsteps Rocks rises
vertically from this spot. Succulents and coastal scrub dangle
precariously from the overhang at the top. Gulls soar on the
fierce wind currents around the rocks.

You could sit for hours in this wild place and forget you are

only ½ mile from a major highway. Immense breakers roll in from the open ocean, smashing against the base of these rocks. The incredibly turbulent waters warn you from approaching too close to shore. One large wave could easily sweep away anyone standing on the lower rocks. Stay back!

Spectacular, rewarding views lie at the trail's end. To the north razor ridges plunge to the sea. The deep canyon of Damnation Creek is the only breach in the vertical coastline. Sisters Rocks cluster offshore. To the south you can see False Klamath Cove, with False Klamath Rock offshore. South of there the coastline near Hidden Beach hides the mouth of the Klamath River. The high ridges above Big Lagoon rise far to the south. Patrick's Point extends west from there.

If you are here at sunset, be sure to leave 20 minutes of daylight to return to the trailhead.

8.

HOSTEL/TREES OF MYSTERY SECTION, COASTAL TRAIL

NEW COASTAL TRAIL LINK AT TREES OF MYSTERY

This new segment of the Coastal Trail offers through hikers or guests at Redwood Hostel a 2 ½-mile link between the DeMartin and Hidden Beach sections of the Coastal Trail, an alternative to the old route along the beach of False Klamath Cove. (The alternate route is often impassable in winter, when storm waves cover or carry away the sand.) The new Coastal Trail segment also offers two pleasant day hikes that can be made from Trees of

DISTANCE: 2½ miles one way. From Trees of Mystery: two
round trips of 3¾ and 1¼ miles.

TIME: One or two hours.

TERRAIN: Climbs from hostel into forest, follows mostly level
road, then trail, descending to Trees of Mystery; nearly level
to beach.

ELEVATION GAIN/LOSS: Entire trail, north-south: 300 feet+/
340 feet-. Round trip, Hostel to Trees: 360 feet+/360 feet-;
Trees to beach: 280 feet-/280 feet+.

BEST TIME: Spring for wildflowers. Nice anytime.

WARNINGS: Watch for ticks in spring, poison oak year round.
When crossing Highway 101, use crosswalk and be careful.

DIRECTIONS TO TRAILHEAD: NORTH END: Turn east off
Highway 101 onto Wilson Creek Road (M.12.53). Immediately veer right to Redwood Hostel. Trail leaves from hostel
parking lot.

SOUTH END: On Highway 101 at M.10.9 (Del Norte), Trees
of Mystery has a gift shop and museum east of highway,
motel and restaurant on west. Signed trail to Hidden Beach
heads west just north of motel. Trail to hostel climbs east
directly across highway.

FURTHER INFO: Redwood National Park (707) 464-6101.

*Mystery: the short, rewarding walk to secluded Hidden Beach, or
the longer walk north through the narrowest part of Redwood
National Park to Redwood Hostel and Wilson Creek. (The latter
day hike follows the first two miles of the described hike, but in
the opposite direction.)*

*Trees of Mystery is one of those curious California roadside
attractions that sprung up in the early days of automotive travel.
Owned by the same family since 1940, they gave the old-fashioned
tourist stop is current name and built the gargantuan Paul
Bunyan and Babe that have become a landmark on Highway
101. Trees of Mystery has its own trail (fee) which meanders for
nearly a mile through ancient forest. Most noteworthy is the
collection of Native American artifacts in their museum.*

Walk east 150 feet from the base of the hostel's front steps to
find the trail's signed north end. Your route climbs moderately
west, then south on a gravel road. Your ascent through forest of
spruce and alder soon turns gradual. After crossing a seasonal
creek at ¼ mile, your winding road offers views north along the
coast to onshore Footsteps Rocks, with offshore Sisters Rocks

beyond, and west to immense False Klamath Rock.

The road contours beyond ⅜ mile. The lush forest understory includes salal, salmonberry, sword fern, California buckeye, cow parsnip, coltsfoot and angelica. Beyond ½ mile your road becomes less traveled, a winding double track through the forest.

Cross a cascading stream at ¾ mile and wind south, passing

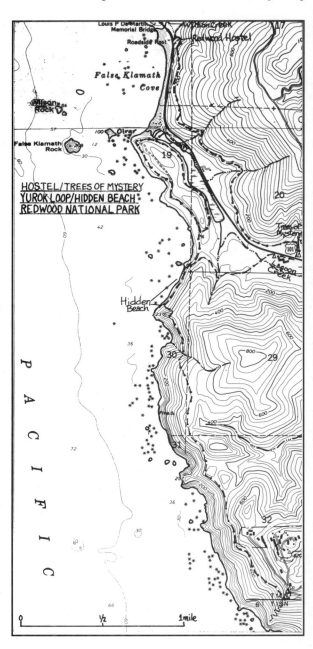

a lush patch of saxifrage and skunk cabbage. At one mile a trail sign confirms you are on track. Your road turns east as dense huckleberry bushes tower fifteen feet overhead.

Where the winding track descends to cross two creeks, the pristine beauty of the route is marred by a view of the charred clearcut on the steep slope above. This recent cut just beyond the park boundary reminds us that only the virgin forests within park boundaries are protected. Beyond the second creek at 1⅛ miles, the road becomes a grassy track through lush growth, in sharp contrast to the ugly scar above.

Climb gently to 1⅜ miles, then contour south, winding away from the clearcut. From 1½ miles your path narrows and descends gently through luxuriant growth. Cross a seasonal creek with abundant skunk cabbage as you near Highway 101. The path contours east to 1¾ miles, then descends to the Trees of Mystery parking lot. Unless you crave pavement, veer left on the footpath above the lot. It leads to the Trees Gift Shop at 1⅞ miles. Restrooms and a pay phone are on your left.

Head south to cautiously cross Highway 101 at the crosswalk, then turn west, paralleling the highway in front of the restaurant and motel. The Coastal Trail continues on a gravel footpath beyond the motel.

Walk 75 feet west from Room #25 of the motel to find the marked trail to Hidden Beach. The gravel path descends southwest through dense young forest of red alders and Sitka spruce. You cross a bridge over Lagoon Creek, where skunk cabbage and salmonberry are plentiful. Contour across a swampy area, an ancient riverbed carved when the mighty Klamath River emptied into the Pacific where Lagoon Creek does today.

By ⅛ mile you ascend gently to higher ground. The trail soon steepens to climb over a small ridge, then undulates beneath the power line to ¼ mile. Veer west over another small ridge where deer fern grows. A large spruce on your right grows precariously atop a rotting stump.

The trail contours northwest through dense undergrowth beneath mixed forest. Dip across a tributary of Lagoon Creek, then climb to meet the Hidden Beach Section, Coastal Trail at ½ mile (2½ miles from Redwood Hostel). To get to Hidden Beach, go right for 75 feet, then left on the side trail that descends to the jewel of a beach, tucked in the crook of the rocky point to the south.

9

YUROK LOOP/HIDDEN BEACH SECTION, COASTAL TRAIL

ENCHANTED COAST NORTH OF KLAMATH

The Yurok tribe of the Klamath River country has always been one of the largest tribes of Native Americans in Northern California. Their territory stretched from Wilson Creek on the north to Little River (south of Trinidad) on the south, and up the Klamath River to Weitchpec.

The Yuroks controlled a land abundant with food along the shore and in the sea and river. This abundance helped them to achieve a complex civilization. They built sturdy houses of split redwood. They carved canoes from whole redwood logs: short, agile boats to navigate the rivers; larger vessels with sails for the powerful ocean. The ocean-going canoes were up to 40 feet long and five to ten feet wide. Karok and Hupa peoples traded for the valuable Yurok canoes. The Yurok leaders accumulated property—land, slaves and other wealth. They used a 13-month calendar based on the moon and had a monetary system based on dentalium shells. The Yuroks traded with the Tolowas for these shells, which originated far to the north around Puget Sound.

Evidence of Yurok civilization has been traced back at least 1000 years along this coast. They greeted the Spanish galleons that landed at Trinidad in 1775. When fur trapper and mountain man Jedediah Smith explored this country in 1828, his party camped at Wilson Creek and probably received food and other help from the Yuroks. But when hordes of white men arrived in the 1850s, inevitable conflicts occurred and the Yuroks were displaced. Still, a large number of Yuroks survived by retreating into the heart of their rugged country. In spite of the conflicts, the Yurok tribe retained a viable culture and is currently growing in number. The south end of this hike ends at Klamath Overlook, within the present boundary of Yurok land.

The Yurok Loop Trail is a one-mile interpretive trail introducing you to the Yurok culture as it follows an ancient Yurok path along the sea's edge. This short easy loop connects with the Hidden Beach Section of the Coastal Trail.

You can follow the Coastal Trail south for 4 miles to an overlook above the mouth of the Klamath River, the lifeblood of Yurok civilization. (The Coastal Trail also leads north for 16 miles. See Trails #4,6 and 8.)

The trail heads northwest from the north end of the parking area, following the shore of the freshwater pond on Lagoon

YUROK LOOP/HIDDEN BEACH SECTION
COASTAL TRAIL:

DISTANCE: 1-mile loop/3⅞ miles one way.

TIME: Thirty minutes/ 2 to 3 hours.

TERRAIN: Easy loop follows coast and lagoon shore. Easy hike to Hidden Beach, then climbs steeply and descends through forest along rugged coast, coming to steep, grassy headlands above mouth of Klamath River.

ELEVATION GAIN/LOSS: Yurok Loop or Hidden Beach: 150 feet+/150 feet-. Coastal Trail, north to south: 980 feet+/320 feet-.

BEST TIME: Spring, early summer for wildflowers.

WARNINGS: Poison oak along trail. Watch for ticks, especially in spring.

DIRECTIONS TO TRAILHEAD: NORTH END: Park at the Lagoon Creek Parking Area at M.11.8 (Del Norte) on the west side of Highway 101.

SOUTH END: Turn west off Highway 101 at M.7.1 onto Requa Road. Go 2.5 miles to Klamath Overlook. Trailhead is on south end of parking area.

FURTHER INFO: Redwood National Park (707) 464-6101.

Creek. This pond was enlarged in 1940 as a log pond for a sawmill. Today the pond is stocked with rainbow trout; its surface provides a home for yellow pond lilies and native and migrating birds. Your trail passes through a thicket of alders and willows, then forks. The right fork leads to Wilson Creek Beach and a branch of the Coastal Trail north (see Trail #6). Take the left fork and cross a bridge over Lagoon Creek. Get a brochure for the Yurok Loop at the dispenser west of the bridge.

The trail soon heads west, climbing a moderate hill along the edge of the forest. You come to a clearing overlooking the ocean and the mouth of Lagoon Creek. The original Yurok trail south along the bluffs was widened by the U.S. Army in the 1850s. Pioneer settler Peter Louis DeMartin upgraded the trail to a wagon road in 1889.

As you follow the trail along the shore, coastal grasslands alternate with coastal scrub of salal, ferns, lupine, berry vines

and ceanothus. At ¼ mile you come to item #4 in the brochure and a grassy clearing. Offshore a jagged rock pinnacle rises 100 feet from the ocean. The Yuroks referred to it as "the place where bald eagle rests." With luck you might see a bald eagle somewhere along this hike. Farther offshore is the 209-foot-tall sea stack called False Klamath Rock. To the Yuroks it was *olrgr* meaning "digging place." Yuroks went there to harvest edible brodiaea bulbs.

A short hill brings you to #6 before ⅜ mile. You then enter a forest of alder and spruce, climbing to a rest bench and #7. The Yuroks considered their trails to be living things that could become resentful if travelers did not treat them with respect. An Indian hiker would ask, "May I come this way again?" Along each major trail the Yuroks designated pleasant spots as special resting places. For travelers to pass such spots without taking off their load to rest showed disrespect for the trail.

The trail soon descends gently, paralleling the shore. False Klamath Rock dwarfs the many other rocks offshore. At ½ mile, the trail forks. To complete the Yurok Loop, go left up a short hill, then descend to the Lagoon Creek pond. As you follow the shore, look for river otters, beavers, herons, egrets and ducks that forage here. Where the trail meets the start of the loop, turn right to return to the parking area.

You take the right fork to get to Hidden Beach or continue south along the Coastal Trail. The trail descends slightly, then levels in dense forest. At ⅝ mile you climb gradually. Leave the forest for a spectacular view of Hidden Beach and the rocky coast. Contour through grasslands at the edge of the forest. Your path tunnels through a stand of young spruce at ¾ mile.

The trail contours along the level, open bluff. Beyond ⅞ mile, the trail returns to forest. At one mile you meet the side trail to Hidden Beach. The spur makes a short descent to the secluded beach.

The Coastal Trail continues southeast, passing the trail to Trees of Mystery (see Trail #8). Go straight, climbing moderately into dense, dark forest. After a view of the coast and False Klamath Rock, start a steep climb around the high, rocky promontory to the south. Climb steeply to 1¼ miles, then moderately. At 1⅜ miles you approach the 223-foot-high point on your right.

Your trail climbs sporadically through the forest, with superb views of False Klamath Cove and the rocky coast. Salmon- and huckleberries provide a dense undercover. A silk-tassel-shrouded rock outcrop on the left has ocean spray growing at its base. You climb again, with the sound of the surf rising from a cove hiding 200 feet below.

At 1⅝ miles you pass iris and bleeding heart along rough, slide-prone tread, then climb again. The trail veers east into a wooded gulch, then turns back toward the coast. After a short descent, your trail contours along the steep hillside, where leather ferns grow profusely on the trees.

Climb 22 steep steps to reach the top of the coastal ridge at 2⅛ miles. Your trail contours along the ridgetop through a lush patch of false lily of the valley. Only the chattering of birds and the distant roar of surf break the silence of the forest. You descend briefly, then climb to 2⅜ mile.

Contour through spruce/alder forest on or near the ridgetop to 2½ miles, then descend moderately to a saddle. To the east is the northwest corner boundary of the reservation the Yuroks were left with after the invading settlers took the rest of their land.

You climb steeply through several twists in the trail, then leave the forest for grasslands around 2¾ miles. You are rewarded with a marvelous view. On a clear day you can see Patrick's Point, 30 miles to the south. The mouth of the Klamath is hidden, but the rest of the rugged coast lies before you. You may hear sea lions barking to the west, 400 feet below. In spring western dog violets grow at your feet.

Your trail contours through grasslands with coastal scrub. Regain the ridgetop briefly at the head of a north-flowing stream. A knot of irises here is surrounded by a whole field of Siberian miners lettuce, or candyflower. Contour through lush alder forest near the ridgetop, passing a rock outcrop shrouded in scrub. At the head of another stream, a small pond on your left supports lush vegetation.

The trail climbs for ⅛ mile, then contours across lush, steep slopes where red-flowering currants grow to the size of small fruit trees. Ascend to 3¼ miles, where a fence on the left marks the boundary of the Redwood National Park maintenance center. You quickly come to an overlook with a guard rail and rest bench. The land here is sinking gradually into the Pacific, unlike the coast south of Cape Mendocino, which is still rising from the ocean. You can see the broad mouth of the Klamath River.

Your last stretch of trail contours the steep, scrub-choked grasslands above the mouth of the Klamath, a prime spot for spring and summer wildflowers. Before 3½ miles you pass through a stand of spruce and cross a small creek on a board-walk. Returning to grasslands, your trail ascends sporadically, angling southeast toward the Klamath Overlook Parking Area.

Before 3⅞ miles a bench on the right provides a view of the outlet of the Klamath and the three large sea stacks guarding its mouth. The largest of these is called Oregos after the Yurok spirit who lives there. Yurok legend says that Oregos told the fish when to enter the river and what route to follow upstream.

In another 250 feet, a spur trail on the right winds down to Klamath Overlook in about ½ mile, right above the rock Oregos (no ocean access). The main trail climbs to its end at the parking area.

The Coastal Trail continues on the south side of the Klamath, but you need a car to get there, unless you can convince a fisherman with a boat to ferry you across the river. It is 7 miles by road, about 3 miles by the river to Flint Ridge Trailhead.

10.

FLINT RIDGE SECTION COASTAL TRAIL

VIRGIN FOREST ABOVE THE KLAMATH

The mighty Klamath River empties into the Pacific just 3 miles downstream from the Douglas Bridge parking area, the eastern trailhead for Flint Ridge. The Klamath, second only to the Sacramento River in size of California rivers, winds 260 miles from southern Oregon to its broad mouth. The Klamath River has the largest runs of salmon and steelhead in the state, making it a popular destination for sport fishermen. In fact, the banks near the mouth of the river have several resorts catering to anglers.

The Klamath River is the heart of Yurok culture. Three dozen Yurok villages once lay along the lower 40 miles of the river. The influence of the river was so great upon the culture that the Yurok language expresses directions in terms of upstream and downstream rather than the cardinal points used by most cul-

tures. *Today many Yuroks live on the Hoopa Valley Indian
Reservation, which lies up the river.*

*After gold was discovered at Gold Bluffs in 1850, prospectors
invaded the Klamath, taking much of the Yuroks' land. The forty-
niners established the town of Klamath in 1851. The original
town, located on the south bank near here, clustered around an
iron house that provided protection when angry natives raided
the invaders. The town lasted only a year before the gold seekers
moved elsewhere.*

*Later another settlement called Klamath grew across the river.
A ferry shuttled travelers for a fee until the Douglas Memorial
Bridge opened in 1926. The original bridge and the town of
Klamath were destroyed by the 1964 flood. The south portal of the
old bridge, marked by two golden grizzly bears, is north of the
parking area.*

The trail descends northeast into a dense forest of red alders,
then turns left to cross a bridge over Richardson Creek. Your
trail parallels the creek, heading upstream to Marshall Pond.
The trail veers right and follows the shore of this old mill pond.
Keep an eye out for gnawed logs, a sign of the beavers living in
the pond. Sometimes if you sit quietly at the pond's northeast
corner (around ¼ mile), you will see a beaver break the surface
of the still waters. But be forewarned: it takes patience, silence
and luck.

After veering away from the pond, you meet a gravel road.
This promptly makes two left turns, coming to a trail sign

directing you back toward the pond. Follow its northern shore west on the old road. Climb gradually above the shore, passing a piece of old mill machinery at ½ mile.

Just before ¾ mile, your narrowing path suddenly switchbacks right and climbs away from the pond. Ascend into the dense forest, crossing a bridge over a tiny creek. Redwood sorrel, wild ginger, salal, huckleberry, and deer and sword ferns blanket the forest floor. After another bridge, you climb by several switchbacks into a forest of larger redwoods mixed with Douglas firs. The trail steepens at one mile, climbing by many switchbacks toward Flint Ridge. After more bridges and some steps, turn north at 1¼ miles and continue a steady but gradual climb through the dense redwood forest.

Just before 2 miles, the trail turns left as it gains the ridgetop. You get a glimpse of the deep Klamath River Canyon to the north. Then climb southwest with the ridge. Redwoods here range to 12 feet in diameter, but most of the trees have broken tops, being exposed to harsh coastal winds that roar in at the mouth of the Klamath.

Your trail winds near the top of the ridge, with short up and down stretches. Beyond 2½ miles a very steep drop lies on your left, with Richardson Creek far below. You stay south of the ridgetop. The trail passes under a big fallen log at 2¾ miles. Descend to 3 miles, passing between a leaning fir and a rock outcrop.

Continue your winding descent to 3¼ miles. Then your trail levels as alders start to mix with the virgin redwood forest. Ascend to a second summit at 3¾ miles. Now alders dominate the forest; the sounds of pounding surf rise from 850 feet below.

At 3⅞ miles your trail switches left and descends by a series of switchbacks toward the coast. The vegetation becomes more lush: buttercup, coltsfoot and yellow skunk cabbage grow along the trail. Lichens droop from the alders.

Your steady descent passes under a power line at 4¼ miles. In 250 feet the side trail to Flint Ridge Campground branches right. Ten sites in a grassy clearing provide tables, metal food lockers, water and a composting toilet.

Continue your descent north to cross a boardwalk at 4⅜ miles. The trail climbs briefly before it descends and switchbacks left. Cross another bridge and come to a side road at 4½ miles, where a trail sign posts the distances in the opposite direction. Turn right and make a short descent to the western trailhead on the Coastal Drive.

11

COASTAL DRIVE
AND SHORT TRAILS
DRIVE/WALK A WILD COAST

*The Coastal Drive hugs a rugged, steep section of coast between
the mouth of the Klamath River and the north edge of Prairie
Creek Redwoods State Park. The road provides the only opportunity (other than by boat) to see this wild stretch of coast. The
drive is described from north to south.*

Exit Highway 101 onto Klamath Beach Road, which follows the
south bank of the broad river. In 1.7 miles from the highway, you
come to Alder Camp Road and the parking area for the Flint
Ridge Trail (see Trail #10). Vehicles with trailers should turn
left on Alder Camp Road, bypassing the narrow, steep and
winding portion of Klamath Beach Road.

Continuing along Klamath Beach Road, you wind along the
flat on the south side of the river, passing several seasonal
fishing resorts and campgrounds. Immediately after the road
starts to climb above the river flat, you come to South Klamath
Overlook, four miles from Highway 101. From here you have a

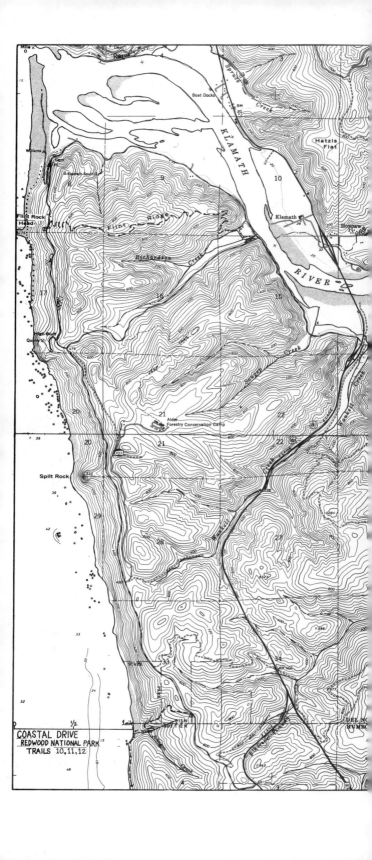

COASTAL DRIVE
REDWOOD NATIONAL PARK
TRAILS 10, 11, 12

COASTAL DRIVE AND SHORT TRAILS:

DISTANCE: Road is 10 miles long.
  Klamath beach access: 1 to 5 miles.
  Flint Ridge Trail to campground: ½ mile round trip.
  Radar station trail: ¼ mile round trip.
  High Bluff trail: 1 mile round trip.
TIME: At least one hour.
TERRAIN: Road follows the Klamath River to its mouth, then climbs to high bluffs overlooking a wild and isolated coast, returning to redwood forest before ending at Elk Prairie Parkway.
ELEVATION GAIN/LOSS: Radar station trail: 40 feet-/40 feet+. Flint Ridge Trail to camp: 400 feet+/feet-. High Bluff trail to beach, round trip: 320 feet-/320 feet+.
BEST TIME: A clear day; when it's foggy, you do not see much here. Spring for wildflowers.
WARNINGS: Drive carefully on the winding, occasionally steep road. No trailers allowed on Klamath Beach Road west of Alder Camp Road. Watch for poison oak when walking coastal grasslands.
DIRECTIONS TO TRAILHEAD: Exit Highway 101 onto Klamath Beach Road at M.3.5 (Del Norte) from south, M.3.7 from north.
FEES: Klamath Beach access at Dad's Camp: $2.50/carload ($2 for seniors, less for walk-in).
FURTHER INFO: Redwood National Park (707) 464-6101; Dad's Camp (707) 482-3415.

view of the mouth of the river. Nearby, Dad's Camp controls access to the gated road to the beach. To drive to the beach, you must pay $2.50 at Dad's. (It is $2 for seniors, less to walk in.) You can walk a mile north to the river mouth or, depending on the tide, up to 1½ miles south at the base of steep bluffs.

The gravel road climbs the steep, twisting grade. At 4.5 miles from the highway, you come to the parking area for the west end of the Flint Ridge Trail. From here you can look down to the 175-foot pinnacle of Flint Rock Head on the sandy beach below. To the east, a ¼-mile climb leads to Flint Ridge Primitive Campground, where water is available.

At 4.9 miles on the road, you come to wide spot where a trail descends to a World-War-II-vintage radar station in ⅛ mile. The station was disguised as a typical coastal ranch house to fool possible invaders from the Pacific.

Continuing along the Coastal Drive, at 5.6 miles you come to a short road on your right. The road descends to High Bluff Picnic Area, with wheelchair-accessible picnic tables and toilet. A short paved path leads to a nearby overlook, where you look down a cliff to the crashing breakers 300 feet below. If it is clear enough, you have one of the best views of the rugged coast to the south, all the way to Patrick's Point (25 miles). A steep trail winds ½ mile down to the beach.

One mile south stands the massive rock outcrop called Split Rock, sacred to the Yuroks. Composed of metamorphosed volcanic rock called greenstone, it rises 533 feet from the Pacific. Traditional Yurok belief considers rock outcrops the last dwelling places of immortals on this earth. Split Rock has a 100-foot-deep cleft down the middle (not visible from here). Yurok legend says that an ancestral fisherman anchored his net on the rock. When the Spirit of the West Wind filled the net with an enormous catch of salmon, the load split the rock in two.

Just .1 mile beyond the High Bluff access, Klamath Beach Road ends at Alder Camp Road. Turn right to continue the Coastal Drive. Two turnouts with views of Split Rock are at 6.3 and 6.5 miles. At 7.4 and 7.7 miles, two more turnouts provide views of the precipitous coast 550 feet below.

Another turnout is eight miles from the highway. A steep, short trail descends to an eagle's perch with spectacular views of the coast. Continuing south along the rough, roller-coaster drive, you come to yet another turnout at 8.5 miles. This one, with a sturdy stone wall, is known as Carruthers Cove Overlook. It features fine, bird's-eye views from an elevation of 600 feet south to Carruthers Cove, Ossagon Rocks, and Gold Bluffs Beach, and north to Split Rock.

You come to the trailhead for Carruthers Cove at 9.1 miles (see Trail #12). You then cross the boundary into Prairie Creek Redwoods State Park and turn inland, immediately coming to large redwoods. The road brings you to Elk Prairie Parkway (old Highway 101) after one more mile.

PRAIRIE CREEK
REDWOODS STATE PARK

On a moonlit night in Prairie Creek Campground, the silhouette of the land takes quintessential wilderness form. The tall forest parades atop the rolling ridges and along the very edge of the glistening, dewy prairie. The distant crashing of waves punctuates the profound silence, joined sometimes by the howl of a coyote, the piercing cry of a night bird, the crackle of a campfire, the soft crunching of elk grazing.

Prairie Creek Redwoods State Park comprises 14,523 acres of friendly wilderness (except when the weather turns fierce). Somehow nature graced it with an absence of the bane of hikers, poison oak. Its charms include vast virgin forests, verdant canyons with crystalline streams, herds of magnificent elk, and a wild, rugged coast of cliffs, waterfalls, wildflower-dappled dunes and gold-flecked beaches extending for miles. It is one of my favorite places on earth.

In 1992 this paradise became even better. The new freeway bypassing the park to the east has alleviated congestion on Elk Prairie Parkway, making it easier and more pleasant to stop for a walk or look for the majestic elk.

12.

CARRUTHERS COVE
SECLUDED BEACH BACKED BY SPECTACULAR ROCKS

While the Coastal Drive provides spectacular views of the rugged shoreline south of the Klamath River's mouth at almost every turnout, the only trail down to this "Little Lost Coast" is the Carruthers Cove Trail. It leaves the Coastal Drive one mile from

CARRUTHERS COVE:

DISTANCE: ⅞ mile to beach (1¾ miles round trip). To West Ridge Trail & Butler Creek Backpack Camp: 3⅛ miles one way.

TIME: One hour to all day.

TERRAIN: Descends steeply through alder/spruce forest to small cove on isolated stretch of beach. Coastal Trail south is on sand, may be impassable at high tide.

ELEVATION GAIN/LOSS: Round trip: 560 feet-/560 feet+.

BEST TIME: Low tide. Marvelous for sunsets. Anytime OK.

WARNINGS: Watch for poison oak in the tangle of coastal vegetation near the beach. No camping here. Do not walk south more than ½ mile from the rocks when the tide is rising, or you may be cut off. Watch for oversize waves as you walk on the beach.

DIRECTIONS TO TRAILHEAD: Turn west off Highway 101 at M.137.45 from south, M.0.3 (Del Norte) from north onto Elk Prairie Parkway. Go south 0.9 mile to Coastal Drive (M.134.2). Trailhead is 1.0 mile from the Parkway, beside the sign marking the entrance to Redwood National Park.

FURTHER INFO: Prairie Creek Redwoods State Park (707) 488-2171.

OTHER SUGGESTION: Can be used as a portion of the continuous Coastal Trail: after the Flint Ridge Section, walk south along the mostly gravel Coastal Drive. Then take Carruthers Cove Trail (at low tide) to continue the Coastal Trail (see also Trail #19).

the road's south end, near the national park boundary sign. The steep, well-graded trail drops nearly 600 feet in ¾ mile to reach a pristine, driftwood-strewn beach with large rocks at the mouth of Johnson Creek. Unless it is high tide, you can walk south to Ossagon Creek and Gold Bluffs Beach. Though the trail is highly recommended, keep in mind that the steep climb out will be the hardest part.

The trail takes a few steep steps to drop onto the old roadbed that you follow to the beach. Head generally west on the old road, descending through mixed Sitka spruce and alder forest with a lush green understory. The forest obscures all views of the coast as your track curves right, then left. You descend southwest at ¼ mile.

Continue your steady descent toward the beach, passing iris, fairy bells and bleeding heart. Around ½ mile your trail twists west, then south before returning to a southwest bearing. You get a glimpse of the coastline to the north through the dense forest. Its full grandeur, however, still lies hidden.

Your trail steepens approaching the ⅝-mile point. Swing left for your first good look at the beach below. The path soon bends left again, paralleling the deep canyon of Johnson Creek. Notice how the winds have sculpted the forest.

Descend west above the canyon, heading toward the beach. Your trail comes to a level spot where two cabins stood until the 1970s, marked by bricks and dense clumps of daffodils. Where the path turns sharply right at ¾ mile, you can see the mouth of the creek beyond the bramble thicket below. Pause to absorb your first clear view of the magnificent rock outcrop at the mouth of the creek.

Then you plunge steeply to the beach by a series of short switchbacks. This stretch of trail offers occasionally precarious footing, so proceed with caution. At the base of the switchbacks, make your way over a pile of driftwood. You reach firm footing on the beach sand before ⅞ mile.

It is ⅛ mile south across level, sand-filled Carruthers Cove to the base of the spectacular rock outcrops. Sea rocket and salal hunker beneath the imposing cliff. A crevice at the base of these rocks shelters you from the wind. You can snack or picnic here. Previous visitors have built driftwood fires in the shelter of the rock, but camping is not allowed. It is well worth a rest to contemplate the wild isolation of this coast.

To the north and south, the pristine beach stretches along the base of steep cliffs. Less than ¾ mile north, the sandy beach ends at the base of a rocky cliff. Two miles north stands imposing Split Rock, rising 533 feet from the edge of the sea. This greenstone dome has a shape reminiscent of Yosemite's Half Dome when viewed from here.

If the tide is below +3.0 feet and ebbing, you can walk south along the beach to the mouth of Ossagon Creek and beyond. It is ⅛ mile south to the tallest of several offshore rocks, a pointed spire. From the 1⅛-mile point, the beach gradually narrows. Beyond 1⅜ miles you pass medium- to large-sized rocks scattered along the tide line. At 1⅝ miles you come to the crucial narrow spot, impassable at high tide. Here you must scramble around a protruding rock outcrop that is somewhat protected from large waves by the tall rocks offshore. You then hop over a thigh-high rock ledge, after which the beach becomes wider again. At 1¾ miles you pass another narrow spot, but it is nothing compared to the first one.

Continue south on the broadening beach. Tracks of elk, raccoon and occasionally mountain lion may be seen in the fine sand. Keep an eye out for the herd of elk that grazes Gold Bluffs Beach; they are frequently seen this far north.

At 2¼ miles from your trailhead, you come to the Ossagon Rocks, which are on the beach as well as offshore. Go another ¼ mile and you are west of the place where the Ossagon Trail comes down to the coastal plain. You can head east to find the trail, which is marked by a sign where it rises from the flat beside Ossagon Creek. If you loop back on the Ossagon Trail, be sure to have arranged a car shuttle to return you to the Carruthers Cove Trailhead. If you head south along the Coastal Trail, it is ½ mile to Butler Creek Camp and West Ridge Trail, 2¾ miles to Fern Canyon and the end of the dirt road, 4¼ miles to the hike/bike camp at Gold Bluffs Beach.

13.

OSSAGON
OLD ROAD TO HEART OF WILDERNESS BEACH

This trail follows an old road through redwood, spruce and alder forest. It makes a steep but short descent to the wildest portion of Gold Bluffs Beach, passing sites of an old homestead and a Yurok village. At the shore it meets the Coastal Trail, which goes south past Butler Creek to Fern Canyon Trailhead. If you time your

DISTANCE: 1¾ miles to beach (3½ miles round trip), 4⅜
miles to Fern Canyon Trailhead; part of 19-mile bike loop.

TIME: At least 2 hours for trail, half to full day for bike loop.

TERRAIN: Descends old road through forest to beach.

ELEVATION GAIN/LOSS: To beach: 120 feet+/720 feet-. Round
trip: 840 feet+/840 feet-. Bike loop: 1480 feet-/1480 feet+.

BEST TIME: Spring for wildflowers, but nice anytime.

WARNINGS: Do not approach wild elk on beach. Mountain
bikers: please stay on designated route and watch for
hikers.

DIRECTIONS TO TRAILHEAD: Exit Highway 101 at M.137.45
from north, M.125.9 from south onto Elk Prairie Parkway.
Trail heads west from M.132.87. Better parking just south
at Hope Creek Trailhead, M.132.74.

FURTHER INFO: Prairie Creek Redwoods State Park
(707) 488-2171.

OTHER SUGGESTION: BIKE LOOP (total distance: 19 miles)
allows two-wheel exploration of the park's backcountry. No
other trails at Prairie Creek are open to biking. From park
entrance, bike north on Elk Prairie Parkway for 5¾ miles.
Go west 1¾ miles on Ossagon Trail to the beach. Take
Coastal Trail south 3 miles. Then follow Gold Bluffs Road
4½ miles to its summit, where you meet Jogging Trail.
Follow this 2¾ miles, then complete loop with 1¼ miles on
campground road.

visit with the tides, you can also walk north to Carruthers Cove.
Bikers can also use the Ossagon Trail, part of a 19-mile desig-
nated bike loop (see OTHER SUGGESTION).

The trail climbs south-southwest from the parkway amidst
large redwoods. The old roadbed climbs steeply at first, then
gradually as you head west. An old bronze plaque beside the
road marks a memorial grove.

Your trail levels at ⅛ mile as the roar of the surf overtakes
the sound of road traffic. Climb gradually to ¼ mile where large
Sitka spruce mingle with the redwoods. One last easy uphill
stretch brings you to ⅜ mile.

You now start a steady descent toward the coast. The road
makes a big bend to the right, descending steeply. As your track
bends back to the left, a stand of immense redwoods lines the
path. These quickly give way to a forest of alders as you drop

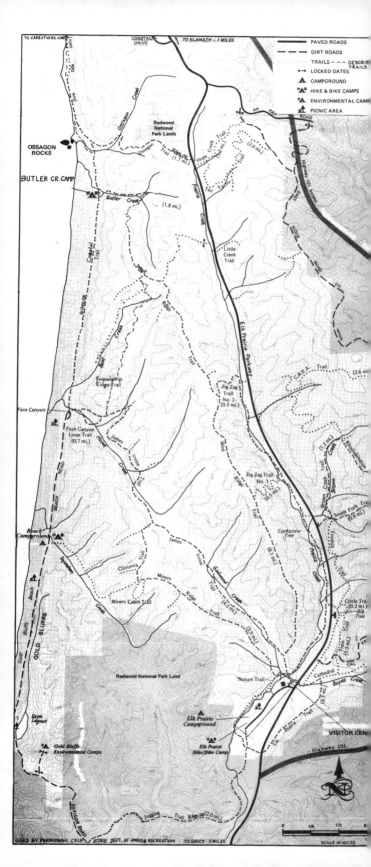

southwest. The trail turns west at ½ mile. You can glimpse the ocean through the trees, though the view is best in winter when the alders have dropped their leaves.

At ⅝ mile the trail bends left, then right. Evergreen violets grow in the roadbed. The steady descent wraps around another big bend. At ⅞ mile your trail makes another big swing to the right, approaching a crossing of Ossagon Creek at one mile. A grassy clearing on the left marks the site of an old homestead.

Descend to cross the creek on a sturdy bridge, then climb 21 steps to return to the roadbed. The trail contours to 1⅜ miles. As you descend again, you can see the broad beach ahead. On your right is Ossagon Prairie, once the site of the small Yurok hamlet of Osegen. Several side trails lead up to the large, steeply sloping prairie with a pleasant southern exposure.

The main trail descends steeply from here, passing two overgrown side trails on the right. At the second of these, the old road turns sharply left and makes its last descent to level beside Ossagon Creek. (A sign at the base of the hill marks the trail back to the highway.) You are 1½ miles from the trailhead.

A faint trail leads northwest from this spot, though it quickly becomes overgrown and hard to follow, leading into a swampy area. You should follow the main trail southwest to a crossing of the creek in ⅛ mile. Notice the elk wallow just downstream from the crossing. On the other side of the creek you leave the alder forest for flat coastal prairie. Keep your eyes open for the herd of elk that frequents this area.

The Coastal Trail leads south to Butler Creek in ½ mile, where you meet the north end of the West Ridge Trail. Fern Canyon Trailhead is 2¼ miles beyond. See Trails #15 and 19.

The Coastal Trail also follows the beach north to Carruthers Cove, passable at a tide of +3.0 feet or lower. It is 1¾ miles to where Carruthers Cove Trail meets the beach (see Trail #12). To get to the beach from the creek crossing, you can either follow the meandering creek to its outlet or take a shorter route. For the latter, a well-beaten path leads west from the ford. The tread turns sandy beyond ⅛ mile, as Ossagon Rocks come into view to the north. You come to a second crossing of the creek, where the water is deeper. You may be able to construct a makeshift bridge from nearby driftwood. Beyond the creek, you can head due west to the breakers or turn north and head for the westernmost of the Ossagon Rocks. If you are heading north, be sure the rising tide does not cut off your return.

Leave ample time before sunset to return to the trailhead.

14

BROWN CREEK
RHODODENDRON
SOUTH FORK LOOP
PRIMEVAL FOREST ON A BABBLING BROOK

The Brown Creek Trail provides a rewarding break for travelers to stretch their legs before continuing north or south. The trail, built in 1951, is just long enough to stimulate your tight muscles. Its dramatic pristine beauty will stretch your eyes, mind and imagination as well. One of the park's most beautiful hikes at any time of the year, it will reward you in spring with a dazzling array of rhododendrons and other wildflowers.

You can stroll up Brown Creek and return by the same trail for an easy 2½-mile (or less) round trip. Or you can follow the loop exactly as described for a steeper 3⅜-mile loop. If you want a longer hike, continue south on the Rhododendron Trail beyond the South Fork Trail. If you have a driver to pick you up where the trail crosses Cal Barrel Road, the hike is about 3¾ miles. If you continue to the end of the Rhododendron Trail and loop back on the Foothill Trail or the Prairie Creek Trail (across the Parkway), the distance is 8 or 8½ miles. Whichever option you take, your entire hike will be in primeval redwood forest.

Start out on the South Fork Trail, heading east from Elk Prairie Parkway into a forest of immense virgin trees. The path meanders above the south bank of Brown Creek, crossing the Foothill Trail around ⅛ mile.

Your South Fork Trail soon follows the tiny South Fork of Brown Creek. Cross it on a small bridge before ¼ mile, then turn left on the Brown Creek Trail. You head northwest, traversing the base of the ridge separating the two forks of the creek.

The trail turns north past craggy giants beside Brown Creek. Cross the creek on a sturdy new bridge before ½ mile, then climb gradually north through primeval forest alongside the creek. Your path soon tunnels under immense fallen logs.

The forest consists of redwoods of varying shapes and sizes. Its understory is jammed with deer and sword ferns, redwood sorrel and salal. In March and April, trilliums abound, and you may see delicate calypso orchid. In May or June, the shocking pink blooms of rhododendrons splash the forest with color.

Your trail winds through the forest, but you never lose the sound of the murmuring stream. Descend briefly before climbing along the creek again. Iris and huckleberry are prolific here.

BROWN CREEK/RHODODENDRON
SOUTH FORK LOOP:

DISTANCE: 3⅜-mile loop with options for an 8- or 8½-mile loop.

TIME: Two to 4 hours.

TERRAIN: Ascends a canyon of primeval redwood forest, climbs to a ridge, then descends the ridge to complete loop.

ELEVATION GAIN/LOSS: 675 feet+/675 feet-.

BEST TIME: Spring for wildflowers, late afternoon for best lighting.

DIRECTIONS TO TRAILHEAD: On east side of Elk Prairie Parkway at M.129.0, 2 miles north of main park entrance. Parking on either side of highway. (Exit Highway 101 at M.137.45 from north, M.125.9 from south)

FURTHER INFO: Prairie Creek Redwoods State Park (707) 488-2171.

OTHER SUGGESTIONS: You can drive CAL BARREL ROAD to the upper portion of the RHODODENDRON TRAIL. Turn east off Elk Prairie Parkway at M.127.5. At 1.8 miles you cross the Rhododendron Trail. You can hike south 2¼ miles to the Cathedral Trees Trail, or north for 4 miles to its end at the CREA Trail. You can also bike Cal Barrel Road.

Your path climbs along the base of the canyon wall.

Beyond ¾ mile you come to a spur trail. It crosses Brown Creek and enters the Trees of the Great Grove, dedicated to Carl Schenck, founder of America's first school of forestry. To this forester is attributed a wonderful quote: "Forestry is a great thing but love is better." It took much love and energy (not to mention money) to save the virgin forests of Prairie Creek.

Your trail stays near the creek, climbing gradually to another grove of immense redwood giants. This one is dedicated to Frederick Olmstead, co-founder of the Save-the-Redwoods League and designer of New York's Central Park.

Continue up the canyon. Beyond one mile your trail climbs above the creek to cross two boardwalks. A steep downhill crosses a tributary and brings you back beside the creek at 1⅛ miles. Ascend to the junction with the Rhododendron Trail.

Now you must make your decision. For the shortest hike, retrace your steps to the road (2½ miles round trip). Either direction you take on the Rhododendron Trail climbs steeply out of Brown Creek Canyon, gaining 300 to 350 feet in elevation in ½ mile. Our described route heads south on the Rhododendron Trail.

Your trail crosses a bridge over Brown Creek, then climbs moderately. At 1⅜ miles the path wraps around an immense redwood with a huge fire scar on its back side. You climb southeast, with views back into the canyon. The ascent steepens around 1⅝ miles. Beyond 1⅞ miles your trail levels briefly, providing a break from the steep climb.

The trail narrows through a brushy area where Douglas firs and hemlocks mingle with the sempervirens. You come to another grove of giant redwoods at 2 miles. Large sword ferns cover every inch of available ground. The distant roar of surf drifts through the silent forest.

Just before 2⅛ miles, you duck under a fallen tree. The mostly level trail winds along the side of a steep hill. Many rhododendrons grow here, as well as an abundance of huckleberries. Descend to cross two small streams around 2¼ miles, then climb by several short, steep switchbacks to a junction atop a ridge at 2⅜ miles.

For a 3⅜-mile loop, turn right and descend the South Fork Trail. Those wanting a longer hike can continue south along the Rhododendron Trail. It climbs 120 feet to its 960-foot summit in ½ mile. Then it descends to cross Cal Barrel Road (1¼ miles from here) and drops steeply to Boyes Creek, connecting with the Cathedral Trees, Elk Prairie and Foothill Trails.

The South Fork Trail descends along a ridge. Redwoods, rhododendrons, tanoaks, redwood sorrel, trilliums and huckleberries thrive here. Your trail leaves the ridge for its steep, lush north face around 2⅝ miles. Descend steeply by numerous short, tight switchbacks.

The trail finally levels at 3⅛ miles, meeting the Brown Creek Trail. Turn left and cross the small bridge, then retrace your steps on the South Fork Trail, returning to the trailhead at 3⅜ miles.

15.

WEST RIDGE TO BUTLER CREEK CAMP

SOLITUDE, FOREST AND SURF

The West Ridge Trail traverses the backbone of Prairie Creek Redwoods State Park. You can use it for a moderately short but varied day hike by looping back on the Zig Zag Trail #1 (6 miles), a longer loop day hike with the Zig Zag #2 (9 miles), or an overnight backpack (14⅜ miles or more). All these choices offer the solitude and silence of virgin forest. If you choose the overnight option, be sure to register at the entrance kiosk. Then leave your car securely parked near the kiosk and spend a weekend or a week exploring the backcountry.

Butler Creek Backpack Camp nestles in the heart of the park's roadless area. The wilderness beach, a herd of elk, steep-walled canyons, virgin forests, the site of a Yurok village, and more lie within a mile of camp. Here you can feel far removed from civilization, though you are about two miles from busy Highway 101 as the crow flies.

Your trail starts at the Visitor Center, where you can inquire about current trail conditions. Follow the Nature Trail for just over ⅛ mile, then go right on the Irvine Trail, which heads north. Just beyond ¼ mile, you meet the West Ridge Trail on your right. Take this trail heading east-northeast.

Climb steadily by many short switchbacks to gain the ridge before ⅝ mile. The virgin forest stretches in all directions, with large redwoods, trilliums and evergreen violets crowding the trail. Continue climbing, with occasional switchbacks. Your trail levels briefly at ¾ mile, then begins a more gradual climb. Douglas firs mingle with the redwoods in this drier habitat. Climb steeply again, then descend briefly to one mile. The roar of traffic from the nearby road is softened by the forest.

From 1⅛ miles your trail follows the ridgetop which rolls up and down through the forest. Leather ferns grow on a redwood to the left. You climb intermittently to 1½ miles where the top of the ridge becomes broad and level. Redwoods grow to 16 feet in diameter here.

The ridge soon narrows. Your trail climbs again, reaching an 800-foot peak on the ridge at 2 miles, the highest point in the first 5 miles. Descend briefly, then contour, winding along the ridgetop. You pass a grove with a rest bench carved from a fallen giant.

Climb by short switchbacks around 2¼ miles, then descend to a low notch in the ridge. At 2½ miles you meet Zig Zag Trail #1, which descends east to the Prairie Creek Trail. You can turn right and return to your starting point for a 6-mile loop.

West Ridge Trail heads northwest, quickly coming to the comfortable rest bench of Forever Grove. Look for iris and false solomon's seal in spring. Descend slightly, then climb with intermittent level stretches, heading northwest. Pass a stand of western hemlock and Douglas fir, then make a short, easy descent to 3 miles. The sound of the surf drifts in from the west.

Contour along the top of the ridge to 3½ miles, with steep slopes to the left and right. Two switchbacks drop you to a low saddle by 3⅝ miles. Climb to 3⅞ miles then descend briefly to the junction with Zig Zag Trail #2. Day hikers can turn east here, descending to the Prairie Creek Trail in ½ mile and following it south to the trailhead for a 9-mile loop.

WEST RIDGE TO BUTLER CREEK CAMP:

DISTANCE: 7⅜ miles one way, with options for loops of 6, 9, 14⅜, 14¾ or 16¼ miles.

TIME: Full or half day for shorter loops, overnight for longer loops.

TERRAIN: Climbs along ridge in virgin redwood forest, then descends along ridge and canyon to backcountry camp on Coastal Trail.

ELEVATION GAIN/LOSS: One way to Zig Zag #1: 700 feet+/100 feet-; to Zig Zag #2: 920 feet+/340 feet-; to Friendship Ridge: 1560 feet +/820 feet-: to camp: 1560 feet +/1660 feet-.

BEST TIME: Spring.

WARNINGS: No camping in backcountry, except in designated camps.

DIRECTIONS TO TRAILHEAD: Turn west off Elk Prairie Parkway (exit Highway 101 at M.137.45 from north, M.125.9 from south) at M.127.3, the main entrance to Prairie Creek Redwoods State Park. Trail starts from Visitor Center.

FEES: Day use/parking: $5/vehicle ($4 for seniors). Backcountry camping: $3/person/night.

FURTHER INFO: Prairie Creek Redwoods State Park (707) 488-2171.

After the junction, the West Ridge Trail turns sharply left and heads west, then northwest along the ridge. The trail is mostly level to 4¼ miles. The next section of trail has a series of short, steep ups and downs along the ridgetop. At 4¾ miles you climb to a high point that has been marred by a fire.

In 1987 a hiker camped here illegally, then lit a fire inside the goose pen of the scorched redwood on the right. The fire roared to ignite the top of the tree and spread to the surrounding forest. This foolish act cost $100,000 and could have resulted in the tragic devastation of Prairie Creek's virgin forest. But fast-acting firefighters were able to extinguish the blaze without major damage. The charred giants stand as a dramatic reminder to be careful with fire.

Your trail contours north, passing gnarled old redwoods in a forest mixed with Douglas fir and hemlock. After a short uphill stretch at 4⅞ miles, the trail hugs the ridgetop where it is dense with brush, mostly salal and huckleberry. Then comes an area of dense conifer regeneration with big rotting stumps. Backpackers may need to unsling their packs to duck under an immense fallen log. Descend through a tunnel of young growth to meet a broad old road that you follow north.

At 5⅛ miles a sign indicates that you are ½ mile from the Boat Creek Trail. You head north along a shady lane, passing a spur trail to Brown Grove on the left. Climb gradually, then steeply through regenerating forest where you may see thimble-, salmon-, elder- and huckleberry plus wild ginger.

At 5⅝ miles the trail forks. The old trail/road on the right no longer goes to Butler Camp. Go left for all points. The trail descends west along a wooded ridge. Climb briefly at 5¾ miles to meet the new Friendship Ridge Trail on the left, one of several options for your return hike (see Trail #19). You can descend Friendship Ridge, then return to the trailhead by the Irvine Trail for a 12⅞-mile loop. The left fork also meets the old Boat Creek Trail, which no longer goes through to the coast.

Backpackers contour northwest on the West Ridge Trail, soon returning to virgin forest. Checker lily, false lily of the valley and clintonia brighten the understory in spring. The ridgetop trail descends gradually around 6 miles. Pass a redwood bench before climbing to one last knob on the ridgetop.

Your trail turns north to descend steadily as the roar of the surf rises through the forest. Many spruce, hemlock and alder trees grow along this ocean-facing ridge. Around 6¼ miles your trail contours through a majestic grove of redwoods. You soon resume a gradual descent, then descend steeply by two switchbacks around 6½ miles.

The path soon leaves the ridge to drop along its west face, passing spruces to eight feet in diamter. Descend steeply again at 6¾ miles. You soon cross a bridge over a tributary of Butler Creek, lush with verdant growth. Descend this canyon to meet the old Butler Creek Trail, then cross Butler Creek on a bridge around 7 miles. Follow the canyon downstream through spruce forest. You descend steep steps and come to Butler Creek Camp at the mouth of the canyon, 7⅜ miles from the trailhead.

Butler Creek Camp's three sites offer tables, fire rings and a pit toilet. Be sure to purify water from the stream. Please pack out all refuse. Fine day hikes can be taken north or south along the beach (see Trails #12, 13 and 19), or you can just lie around camp and soak up the silence.

There are four great options for your return hike to park headquarters. You can take the Coastal Trail south to Fern Canyon, then follow the James Irvine Trail southeast for a 7-mile return. You can return the way you came, hiking the length of the West Ridge Trail (7⅜ miles). You can follow West Ridge to Friendship Ridge Trail, then return along the Irvine Trail (8⅞ miles) Or you can follow the West Ridge Trail to the Zig Zag Trail #2 and complete your return via the latter and the beautiful Prairie Creek Trail, a 7⅜-mile return.

16

ELK PRAIRIE LOOP
STALKING THE MIGHTY ELK

*About 200 Roosevelt elk (Cervus elaphus rooseveltii) live around
Prairie Creek Redwoods. The elk is the second largest member of
the deer family, smaller than the moose. Males grow up to 1100
pounds, stand four to five feet at the shoulder, and grow antlers
five feet long, with a four- to six-foot spread at the tips.*

*Elk once inhabited much of Northern California. They were
hunted nearly to extinction for their meat, hides and canine
teeth (believed to bring good luck). Now protected from hunting
in California, they range north to British Columbia and east to
the Rockies.*

*Each March the bulls shed their antlers, growing up to 40
pounds of new antlers by August. As the mating season approaches
in September, solitary bulls join the herd. Mature bulls compete
for a harem of up to 40 cows. If you visit during mating season,
you may hear the bugle-like call of the bull, followed by the clash
of antlers as two bulls try to knock each other to their haunches.
Consider yourself lucky if you get to see such a mating joust. Next
May or June, some of the cows bear single calves weighing 25 to
40 pounds at birth that will grow to three-quarters of their adult
size by fall.*

*Though the elk are primarily peaceful, grazing animals, they
should never be approached on foot. Bulls especially may give
chase if they feel threatened or cornered, charging at up to 35
miles per hour. They may look tame, but they are wild animals.*

This description starts at the southwest corner of the campground, near campsite 67, one good place to start this loop. It
circles Boyes Prairie, home to one of the park's three herds of
elk, letting you view elk habitat first hand. Carry binoculars to
observe the elk without getting too close.

Your trail heads south into a forest of alder and Sitka spruce.
About ¼ mile you cross a small creek, then leave the forest for
the open prairie, joining a spur trail from the hike/bike campsites. You follow an old road, soon paralleling a redwood split-
rail fence.

At a break in the fence, the trail turns left and crosses the
south end of Boyes Prairie. As you head toward the parkway,
watch for elk on the trail. If you find them, be sure to make a wide
detour around them.

After a small bridge, you come to Elk Prairie Parkway at ½
mile. Use extreme caution crossing the busy road. Pick up the
trail on the other side at another bridge and head into a forest

```
┌─────────────────────────────────────────────────┐
│              ELK PRAIRIE LOOP:                  │
├─────────────────────────────────────────────────┤
│ DISTANCE: 2¼-mile loop.                         │
│ TIME: One or 2 hours.                           │
│ TERRAIN: Contours across prairie, then slight ups and downs
│    through the forest.                          │
│ ELEVATION GAIN/LOSS: 100 feet+/100 feet-.       │
│ BEST TIME: Spring for wildflowers. Anytime for elk.
│ WARNINGS: Elk are wild animals. Never approach them on
│    foot. Use caution crossing road. Trail may be muddy in
│    winter.                                      │
│ DIRECTIONS TO TRAILHEAD: Turn west off Elk Prairie
│    Parkway (exit Highway 101 at M.137.45 from north, M.125.9
│    from south) at M.127.3, main entrance to Prairie Creek
│    Redwoods State Park. Go south through campground to
│    campsite #67, the starting point for this description. (You
│    can also start from the Visitor Center.)     │
│ FEES: Day use/parking: $5/vehicle ($4 for seniors). Car
│    camping: $12-14/night.                       │
│ FURTHER INFO: Prairie Creek Redwoods State Park
│    (707) 488-2171.                              │
│ OTHER SUGGESTION: REVELATION TRAIL starts south of
│    the Visitor Center, circling through a redwood grove for ⅓
│    mile. Wood and rope guide rails, tape recorders and signs
│    allow the blind or otherwise disabled visitor to explore the
│    forest independently.                        │
└─────────────────────────────────────────────────┘
```

of hemlock, redwood and spruce. After climbing a short hill, your trail turns left and parallels the road above the prairie.

Walking through the forest you will see many signs of elk: trees with bark rubbed off by bulls scraping their antlers; droppings and hoofprints along the trail; elk wallows, the depressions dug in the ground by hooves and antlers; munched deer ferns and branches stripped of their bark.

Your trail meanders gently up and down through the forest. At ⅝ mile the forest thins for a view of the prairie and perhaps a herd of elk. You pass large redwoods, including one with a base 16 feet in diameter. Large bigleaf maples compete for sunlight at the border of the forest and prairie. California bay laurel, wild ginger, huckleberries and sword ferns grow along the trail.

At one mile you come to the first of several dilapidated bridges that have been trampled by the elk. Watch your step on the slippery, broken boards. You quickly come to a grove of large redwoods. At 1⅛ miles you pass a big redwood root ball, then parallel the fallen length of the tree for 300 feet.

At 1¼ miles, cross another small bridge, then an old service road behind some park residences. You pass several redwoods that were cut around 1900 to build the Boyes' houses and barn. At 1½ miles your trail passes through a dense berry thicket that towers overhead. After crossing a larger bridge, you come to a junction. The right fork leads to the Rhododendron and Cathedral Trees trails.

The Elk Prairie Trail turns left and soon meets an arm of the prairie. You follow its border with the redwood forest. A rest bench looks over the beautiful grasslands. About 1⅝ miles you meet the start of the Foothill Trail, which goes north. Your trail turns left, crossing a bridge over Boyes Creek, then passing through a marsh.

At 1¾ miles you pass under the parkway. Then follow the main park road past the entrance kiosk and Visitor Center, returning to your starting point at campsite 67.

17.

JAMES IRVINE MINERS RIDGE LOOP

ROUTE OF 1851 GOLD SEEKERS

In spring 1850, five frustrated prospectors left the Klamath mines and headed for the coast. At the mouth of the Klamath River they turned south. Though always keeping their eyes open for gold they perhaps were more enticed by stories of new settlements at Trinidad and Humboldt Bays south on the coast, places where one could find such rare amenities as hot baths, beds, women and fresh food. But after trekking another ten rugged miles through virgin forests and steep terrain, their dreams of comfort were postponed. Near the mouth of Home Creek, Hermann Ehrenberg found fine gold dust mixed with coarse, dark sand on the beach. The prospectors hastily gathered samples, marked their claim, then continued their journey south.

After another 25 miles of hard travel, they reached the boomtown of Trinidad. That same year they organized the Pacific Mining Company and began to develop their claim at what came to be called Gold Bluffs and Gold Bluff Beach.

The gold was abundant when first found, though in the form of the tiniest gold flakes imaginable. The principals of the Pacific Mining Company, optimistic after their initial excavations,

JAMES IRVINE/MINERS RIDGE LOOP:

DISTANCE: James Irvine Trail: 4¼ miles, one way. Miners Ridge Trail: 3⅞ miles, one way. Clintonia Trail: one mile, one way. Combined loop as described: 9¼ miles.

TIME: Minimum 4 hours. Best as full day with lunch.

TERRAIN: Climbs gently through virgin forest to a low summit, descends along Home Creek to mouth of Fern Canyon. Return trail climbs through more virgin forest to and along Miners Ridge, then descends to starting point.

ELEVATION GAIN/LOSS: Full loop: 1350 feet+/1350 feet-. James Irvine Trail east to west: 350 feet+/490 feet-. Round trip: 840 feet+/840 feet-.

BEST TIME: Spring for wildflowers. June to September for footbridges in Fern Canyon. Still recommended: March through October.

WARNINGS: May be wet and muddy November to February after big storms.

DIRECTIONS TO TRAILHEAD: Turn west off Elk Prairie Parkway (exit Highway 101 at M.137.45 from north, M.125.9 from south) at the Main entrance to Prairie Creek Redwoods at M.127.3. Trail starts near Visitor Center.

FEES: Day use/parking: $5/vehicle ($4 for seniors). Car camping: $12-14/night.

FURTHER INFO: Prairie Creek Redwoods State Park (707) 488-2171.

OTHER SUGGESTION: A DIFFERENT LOOP can be made by walking the Irvine Trail to its west end, then following the beach south one mile to the western Miners Ridge Trailhead and returning the full length of that trail. The first portion of the latter follows an old corduroy logging road. Distance: 10¼ miles.

predicted a return of 43 million dollars for each member of the Company.

Word quickly spread among the settlers at Trinidad and Humboldt Bay. Only the arrival of harsh winter storms kept them from setting out immediately. But in the spring of 1851, thousands headed north to the Gold Bluffs. They left the recently established trail to the Klamath mines at Madison Prairie and

headed west on a narrow track, known today as the James Irvine Trail. Arriving at Gold Bluffs, they rapidly built a tent city in a clearing above the beach.

The boom was short-lived, however. Retrieving the gold required labor- and machine-intensive methods only a few were patient and resourceful enough to pursue. Although thousands of dollars in gold were eventually recovered, the boom tent city quickly dwindled to a small company mining camp. Still the Irvine Trail remained the main route to the gold fields, being used extensively during the Civil War when gold was at a premium, and again in the 1870s, as two other companies tried to succeed. In the end Gold Bluffs mining may have produced more debts than gold.

Today the explorers come for different reasons: to see the magnificent virgin forest, to revel in nature's quiet, and to explore the non-negotiable treasure of Fern Canyon.

To walk the James Irvine Trail west to Fern Canyon and Gold Bluffs, take the Nature Trail from the Visitor Center. You cross a sturdy bridge over Prairie Creek and pass the start of the Prairie Creek Trail, just 500 feet from your starting point. Your trail meanders toward the creek until the James Irvine Trail branches right, ⅛ mile from the trailhead. The Irvine Trail heads north, climbing gradually to the West Ridge Trail junction at ¼ mile.

The Irvine Trail runs northwest, following the gentle drainage of Godwood Creek, named for an early homesteader. Ancient redwoods stand along the trail. Some reach diameters of 18 feet. The virgin forest is a mix of redwood, Sitka spruce, Douglas fir, western hemlock and occasional hardwoods like tanoak, alder and maple. At ½ mile you are alongside Godwood Creek.

The well-beaten trail continues mostly level through the primeval forest. Watch out for roots that disrupt the surface of the trail. Also watch your footing on the corduroy bridges; they are slippery when wet. At ¾ mile you cross a sturdy bridge, then walk a recently-built boardwalk spanning a marshy area. Sword and deer ferns, salal, saxifrage and skunk cabbage thrive here.

After two more corduroy bridges, you pass the one-mile point. Cross many more corduroy bridges as you climb gradually toward the summit. At 1¼ miles you cross Godwood Creek on a sturdy bridge, putting you on its west side. At 1⅝ miles you cross the creek twice more, finally leaving it as its headwaters swing northeast.

At 1¾ miles you pass through a blowdown area. Many fallen trees lie along and across the trail here, prey to ferocious winds. At 2 miles you come to a rest bench carved from a fallen log, beyond which another fallen log spans the trail at head height. Don't forget to duck! At 2⅛ miles you cross a dilapidated boardwalk.

The trail winds around an immense redwood with a swollen base of 16 feet. It marks the halfway point to the beach. You cross a small gully, then climb to the summit of the Irvine Trail, at the elevation of 300 feet.

You descend slightly to the Clintonia Trail at 2⅜ miles. It leads to the Miners Ridge Trail, described in the return portion of this hike.

The Irvine Trail descends gradually, then more rapidly by rough steps. At 2¾ miles you cross a bridge over the headwaters of Home Creek. The trail then levels before passing under two fallen logs, after which a series of short ups and downs brings you to a bridge over a side canyon at 3 miles. Beyond the bridge, a side trail leads to a grove on this quiet side stream.

The vegetation becomes more dense as you approach the coast. Deer ferns, red and evergreen huckleberries and delicate redwood violets thrive here. Follow the sound of a waterfall down to another bridge, this one over a 50-foot-deep canyon lush with ferns. After the bridge is another grove spur trail.

From 3⅛ miles you meander up and down the slope above Home Creek, crossing more corduroy bridges. At 3½ miles a very large Sitka spruce sits on the left, on the edge of upper Fern Canyon. The trail contours before descending to cross a beautiful canyon at 3⅝ miles. Baldwin Bridge has a lovely bench overlooking the gorge.

You soon pass the junction with the new Friendship Ridge Trail (see Trail #19). After crossing a small bridge at 3¾ miles you again approach Fern Canyon. But you must hike another ½ mile before meeting the trail into the canyon. On this fairly level stretch, notice a Sitka spruce on your left growing atop a fallen redwood.

About 4¼ miles from the trailhead, you meet the upper end of the Fern Canyon Trail. You may descend into the canyon here, or walk the Irvine Trail to the beach and return by way of Fern Canyon. Our description follows the Irvine Trail to its end. The trail descends steps through alder forest. On your left is the Alexander Lincoln Prairie, the site of the Gold Bluffs tent city of the 1850s, now with no hint of its strange history. Descend more steps, follow a 100-foot boardwalk, and drop to the beach, just north of the mouth of Fern Canyon.

For a total loop of 10¼ miles, you can walk south one mile on beach or road, then return the full length of the Miners Ridge Trail.

Our described loop follows Trail #18 through marvelous Fern Canyon to its junction with the Irvine Trail. Then retrace your steps east to the junction with the Clintonia Trail (1⅝ miles from the beach). If you want the shortest route back, continue to retrace your steps on the Irvine Trail.

If you are still game for new country, follow the Clintonia/Miners Ridge Loop described below. It requires only an extra ⅝ mile and an extra 500 feet in elevation gain and loss. Most of the extra climbing comes in the first ¼ mile. You start out steeply uphill, following a spur ridge up to Miners Ridge. You are rewarded with views on all sides down upon the virgin forest.

After a short level but winding stretch, you climb steeply again. In spring, watch for the bright red flowers of the clintonia on long stalks. In summer they bear dark-blue, inedible berries. Your trail levels, then descends a bit as you enter dense, young-growth forest. Where a spur trail forks right, you veer left into a dark tunnel of young growth.

At ½ mile you return to open virgin forest. Your trail remains mostly level, then descends to meet the Miners Ridge Trail where it climbs steeply from Squashan Creek. Right beside the junction, the Miners Cabin Loop heads south.

Our route turns left to follow Miners Ridge back to the Visitor Center. Climb steeply until your trail levels along the ridge, passing huge fire-scarred redwoods. You climb to 1¼ miles. Continue up, down and level along the ridge, with grand views of the virgin forest.

At 1⅞ miles from Irvine Trail, notice the lack of big trees to the south. It is only ¼ mile to the park boundary. Though now national parkland beyond, it was clearcut in the 1960s. At 2 miles you start to descend, gradually at first, and still with a few uphill stretches. To the north the Irvine Trail is less than ⅛ mile away, but far below. At 2⅝ miles you descend steeply and continuously.

You come to the junction with the Nature Trail at the 3-mile point, alongside Prairie Creek. Alders and bigleaf maples grow in the canyon. In fall these deciduous trees provide brilliant splashes of gold and red in the otherwise verdant forest.

Go left at the junction. It is just ¼ mile to the Visitor Center and hike's end.

18.

FERN CANYON LOOP
FIFTY-FOOT WALLS OF FERNS

Known as the jewel of Prairie Creek Redwoods State Park, Fern Canyon nestles in the heart of Gold Bluffs Beach. Though its name is common along the fog-enshrouded North Coast, this one stands alone for its geology, history and singular beauty.

About four million years ago, the Klamath River emptied into the sea here. The river deposited gravels from the Klamath Mountains 40 miles to the east. Rough ocean waves washed and eroded these gravels for thousands of years until they were laid out in flat, uniform deposits. In more recent geologic times, Home Creek carved its way through these layers of gravel to create the canyon you see today. Its nearly level floor differs from the steep slopes of most North Coast streams.

The ancestral Klamath River also deposited the fine particles of gold that brought prospectors to the area from 1850 to the 1920s. The gold was so fine that much of it could not be separated from the tons of dark sand and gravel mixed with it. Mining activities peaked in the 1880s, when 300 people lived near Fern Canyon to work the gold deposits. Most of them lived on the Lincoln Prairie, a grassy clearing north of Fern Canyon. Today the signs of past mining and logging have vanished.

Coastal fog and an annual rainfall of 80 inches help to create the verdant, fern-filled habitat of Fern Canyon. The most common fern here is the five-finger fern, a relative of the maidenhair. The Yuroks gathered these ferns for the black stems with which they wove designs into their beautiful baskets. Other ferns grow in the canyon in less abundance: sword, lady, deer, woodwardia, California wood and leather. Less common but found occasionally are bladder, bracken and licorice ferns, nine species in all. Other moisture-loving plants grow here: saxifrage, common and tooth-leaved monkeyflower, coastal manroot, fairy lantern and twisted stalk. One of the most lethal plants in North America grows here, California water hemlock. As little as one centimeter of the plant can be fatal. The oenanthe is another poisonous plant commonly found in the canyon. Edible plants include salmonberry and thimbleberry.

Many water-loving animals call Fern Canyon home. The Pacific giant salamander lives in the still pools of Home Creek, feeding on banana slugs, bugs and mice. It is one of the largest North American salamanders, up to 10 inches long. Other amphibians include the rare tailed frog, the Olympic salamander and the more abundant western red-legged frog. The American dipper or water ouzel is a bird that hunts insects in the stream. It actually flies underwater to catch its prey. Winter wrens are the only other birds living in the canyon, though others may visit, like the majestic great blue heron. Mink, river otter, coastal cutthroat and steelhead trout round out the community.

The loop trail through Fern Canyon is less than ¾ mile long. It has temporary bridges from June through September. If you visit during other times of the year, you may get your feet wet but you will not have to contend with the crowds of summer. Fern Canyon provides a rewarding short walk during any season.

Your trail begins at the Fern Canyon picnic area at the end of Davison Road. You head north across Home Creek, then take the trail that forks right, quickly entering the mouth of the steep-walled canyon. You cross Home Creek twice more in the first ⅛ mile. Take your time and observe the lush riparian community of plants thriving here.

FERN CANYON LOOP:

DISTANCE: ¾-mile loop.

TIME: Thirty minutes, but it is worth taking more time or planning a picnic.

TERRAIN: Follows nearly level canyon floor upstream beneath fifty-foot-high, fern-covered walls, then climbing out of the canyon into virgin forest and descending to its mouth.

ELEVATION GAIN/LOSS: 180 feet+/180 feet-.

BEST TIME: Bridges to keep your feet dry June to September. Otherwise, any time the creek is not flooding.

WARNINGS: Wet stream crossings in winter and spring.

DIRECTIONS TO TRAILHEAD: Turn west off Highway 101 at M.123.9 onto unpaved, steep and winding Davison Road (no trailers). Go 8 miles to the Fern Canyon parking area at road's end.

FEES: Day use/parking: $5/vehicle ($4 for seniors). Car camping: $12-14/night. Hike/bike camp: $3/person/night. Environmental Camp: $7-9/night.

FURTHER INFO: Prairie Creek Redwoods State Park (707) 488-2171.

OTHER SUGGESTION: THREE GREAT CAMPING OPTIONS are near the trailhead. Gold Bluffs Beach offers car camping. A hike/bike camp across the road offers seclusion in a pretty spot. Environmental Camps nestle in a wooded canyon east of Espa Lagoon to the south.

Beyond ⅛ mile the steep canyon walls get higher. The north wall rises vertically for over 60 feet at one point. Five-finger ferns grow nearly everywhere on the sheer walls. The trail passes under a large fallen log, also covered with ferns, moss and lichens. Saxifrage grows along the canyon floor. The canyon winds as you cross the stream several more times.

The canyon broadens at ¼ mile. A side trail branches right, climbing a narrow side canyon to its boxed end where a small waterfall tumbles down in winter and spring.

The main trail continues up Fern Canyon for 250 feet beyond the side trail. There a sign proclaims the end of Fern Canyon. The loop trail climbs the canyon's north wall. You ascend by uneven steps, switchbacking out of the canyon and into Sitka spruce forest. Meet the James Irvine Trail at ⅜ mile. Go left to return to the end of the Beach Road. You cross a small bridge and head northwest above the edge of the Alexander Lincoln Prairie, the site of the mining town of Gold Bluffs.

Cross a long boardwalk, then descend many steps through alder forest to return to the mouth of Fern Canyon. Energetic hikers will find many other trails in the area. See Trails #17 and 19.

19.

FRIENDSHIP RIDGE COASTAL LOOP

THROUGH VIRGIN FOREST TO WILDERNESS BEACH

Many changes have been made in this corner of the park since our first edition in 1988. This new loop replaces the closed Boat Creek/Butler Creek Loop. The new route provides a marvelously varied day hike. In less than 8 miles you encounter steep-walled canyons, virgin forests, high ridges, and an expansive wilderness beach where a herd of wild elk roam at the base of waterfall-draped cliffs.

The Coastal Trail (formerly called Beach Trail) heads north from the trailhead at road's end. In the first 100 feet, you ford Home Creek at the mouth of Fern Canyon, then come to a trail that forks right. Turn right for Friendship Ridge Trail (also for Fern Canyon and James Irvine trails). After you head east for 150 feet, fork left on the Irvine Trail, leaving the mouth of Fern Canyon to climb by rough steps. You ascend into Sitka spruce forest for ¼ mile, then contour past the Lincoln Prairie on your right, meeting the top end of the Fern Canyon Trail before ⅜ mile. Continue on James Irvine Trail, climbing to cross a bridge over a small stream at ½ mile. In 150 feet you turn left on the Friendship Ridge Trail.

The new trail climbs north, then west through a lush understory with many deer ferns beneath spruce forest. Redwoods dominate the forest by ⅝ mile as you ascend northwest. A switchbacking climb brings you to Friendship Ridge around ¾ mile. Ascend along the ridgetop through virgin forest with plentiful salal, huckleberry, evergreen violet, sword fern and trillium in the understory.

Your trail ascends sporadically along the ridgetop, with views into pristine forest in every direction. Redwoods and firs grow to six feet in diameter, with Oregon grape joining the under-

FRIENDSHIP RIDGE/COASTAL LOOP:

DISTANCE: 7¼-mile loop.

TIME: Four hours or more.

TERRAIN: Climbs up and along one ridge, then down another, descends canyon to beach, contours along the beach below coastal bluffs.

ELEVATION GAIN/LOSS: 860 feet+/860 feet-.

BEST TIME: Spring for wildflowers. Fall also nice.

WARNINGS: Do not approach the elk. Give them plenty of room.

DIRECTIONS TO TRAILHEAD: Turn west off Highway 101 at M.123.9 onto unpaved, steep and winding Davison Road (no trailers). Go 8 miles to Fern Canyon parking area at end of road.

FEES: Day use/parking: $5/vehicle ($4 for seniors). Car camping: $12-14/night.

FURTHER INFO: Prairie Creek Redwoods State Park (707) 488-2171.

story. Descend briefly around 1½ miles, then contour just west of the ridgetop as hemlock joins the forest.

The path makes a gradual winding descent to 1¾ miles, where you cross a small seasonal creek. Contour north, winding through several more side canyons, tributaries of Boat Creek to your west. Pass redwoods to ten feet in diameter. Beyond 2 miles your mostly level path makes several brief ascents. Cross a large side canyon jammed with fallen logs at 2⅜ miles.

Resume a winding, gradual climb to cross a seasonal creek at 2½ miles. Your trail almost regains the ridgetop around 2¾ miles, but continues its winding ascent along the ridge's west face, passing redwoods of diverse sizes.

Ascend to a junction at 3 miles. The dead-end trail on the left descends west, then southwest into rugged Boat Creek Canyon for 1¾ miles. Lady fern and red huckleberry grow at the junction. Friendship Ridge Trail climbs moderately northwest past Wheeler Grove. Ascend by several short switchbacks to meet the West Ridge Trail on the ridgetop at 3¼ miles.

Turn left on West Ridge Trail and follow the undulating ridgetop northwest, then north (see Trail #15 for more about West Ridge Trail). From 4 miles the trail descends steeply, leaving the ridgetop to drop along its lush west face. You cross a bridge over Butler Creek around 4½ miles, then descend along the creek to the mouth of the canyon at 4⅞ miles.

Butler Creek Camp sits beneath alders at the mouth of the

canyon, where West Ridge Trail ends at the Coastal Trail. To camp here you must preregister at the Visitor Center and leave your car there. Water from the creek must be purified before drinking. The Coastal Trail continues north ½ mile to the Ossagon Creek Trail, 2 miles to Carruthers Cove (see Trails #12 and 13).

Our described loop turns left to head south on the Coastal Trail, paralleling the cliffs known as Gold Bluffs on your left and the shore on your right. Watch for the elk that live here; you may have to detour to stay out of their way. In summer and fall you can follow the level, easy track that leaves the alder forest and heads south through grasslands near the base of the bluffs. During a wet winter or spring, this section of trail may be flooded, impassable in anything but shin-high rubber boots. (The author got swamped here in late April 1993.) When the trail is flooded, detour west about ¼ mile to walk the dunes or beach south for ⅞ mile, then turn east to return to the trail.

Presuming the trail is not flooded, your path follows the base of the bluffs south, passing a large spruce snag around 5⅛ miles, then climbing over a small rise. Pass a gravelly slide and veer right around some alders around 5⅜ miles, where you have a view north to Ossagon Rocks. Your trail skirts the edge of spruce forest along the base of the wooded bluffs. The roar of the surf echoes loudly from the cliff face above you.

Before 5⅞ miles a spur trail forks left into spruce/alder forest to the base of an 80-foot waterfall. In 300 feet another short spur on the left leads to a rest bench below Gold Dust Falls, where a small stream plunges 100 feet to disappear in the sandy soil beneath the spruce forest. A third waterfall in alder forest beyond 6 miles flows in the wet season.

Your trail skirts alder/spruce forest at the base of the steep bluffs. Lupine thrives in the grasslands. At 6⅜ miles you round a point to look south to the alder thicket marking the mouth of Boat Creek. Follow dry, gravelly tread past a stand of dead trees. Around 6⅝ miles sandstone rocks on both sides of the trail are crowned with beach strawberry. Wind through the alders to ford Boat Creek where it emerges from its heavily wooded canyon at 6⅞ miles. Continue south through grasslands, then into alder forest. You meet the Irvine Trail at 7¼ miles to complete the loop. Ford Home Creek and return to the trailhead.

20.

LOST MAN CREEK
OLD ROAD THROUGH VIRGIN FOREST TO VIEWS

One of the least used trails in Redwood National Park, Lost Man Creek Trail lies one mile east of Highway 101 on a gravel road. It provides easy access to a beautiful redwood grove beside the pristine pools and rapids of the creek. Photographers love its combination of forest, clearings and creek. People in wheelchairs can reach the picnic area, restrooms and first portion of trail.

In 1982 a special dedication ceremony took place here. Redwood National Park was designated a World Heritage Site by UNESCO, the United Nations Educational, Scientific and Cultural Organization. About 250 international sites have been chosen as World Heritage Sites because of natural and cultural properties of outstanding universal value to the human race.

The short, easy trail becomes arduous if you continue beyond the third bridge. The trail steepens and soon enters lands that were logged.

Lost Man Creek Trail offers mountain bikers a rugged but thrilling 21 ¾-mile loop: 11 ½ miles of motor-vehicle-free riding on Lost Man Creek and Holter Ridge Road, followed by a 6-mile descent on paved Bald Hills Road, then returning on Highway 101 and Lost Man Creek's gravel access road.

The parking area is a clearing beside Lost Man Creek. Pass through a stile (broad enough for wheelchairs) and immediately come to several picnic tables beneath immense redwoods in a pleasantly shady spot above the creek. Head southeast on the graveled Geneva Road, climbing gradually through the forest. At ¼ mile you cross a bridge over Lost Man Creek. From the bridge you have fine views of the rocky pools upstream.

Your climb steepens after the bridge. The trail recrosses the creek in 200 feet and continues climbing moderately, the creek again on your right. After a level stretch around ½ mile, the path

LOST MAN CREEK:

DISTANCE: 2 miles, round trip; 11½ miles, one way to Bald Hills Road; 21¾-mile mountain bike loop.

TIME: One hour or all day.

TERRAIN: Climbs gradually through picturesque virgin forest alongside creek, then steeply through logged area up and along a high ridge; bikers can descend on paved road to complete loop.

ELEVATION GAIN/LOSS: First mile: 160 feet+/-, round trip. To Holter Ridge: 1600 feet+/1600 feet-, round trip. To Bald Hills Road: 3740 feet+/1100 feet-. Bike Loop: 4040 feet+/4040 feet-.

BEST TIME: Spring for wildflowers, but nice anytime.

WARNINGS: Very steep after the first 1½ miles. Bikers use caution returning on roads with traffic.

DIRECTIONS TO TRAILHEAD: Turn east off Highway 101 at M.124.4 and follow gravel road 0.9 miles to picnic area at its end.

FURTHER INFO: Redwood National Park (707) 464-6101.

climbs gently, offering views of the creek tumbling around boulders below. Young hemlock and Sitka spruce struggle for light beneath towering redwoods. The understory includes sword, lady, five-finger and deer ferns, iris, salal, redwood sorrel, wild ginger and inside-out flower. In spring trilliums grow beneath salmon-, thimble- and huckleberry.

At ¾ mile your trail levels again, drawing alongside the creek. Then climb gradually again as the path angles away from the stream. Pass a logged area on the left at one mile. You cross a creek (your third bridge) that enters Lost Man Creek from the north.

Then the old road begins to climb a long, steep hill, with views of the cascading creek on your right. You re-enter virgin forest as you begin to climb high above the creek. Those preferring an easy hike should turn back before climbing far up the hill. By 1½ miles you are 100 feet above Lost Man Creek. Below to the south the creek splits. The main fork flows down from far to the south. Geneva Road climbs steeply up a side drainage coming from the east.

The road steepens at 1½ miles. Beyond 1¾ miles the forest

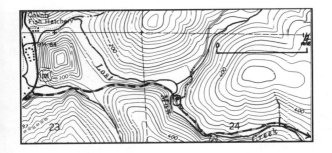

starts to thin as the habitat becomes drier. Your path turns
briefly north before 2 miles, where the road almost levels,
providing relief from the steady climb. The climb steepens
again as you turn east, then northeast. Beyond 2¼ miles the
forest has been logged. You have occasional views down to the
virgin forest of Lost Man Creek.

By 2½ miles you have climbed 1000 feet from the trailhead.
The road continues to climb without relief until you level at 3¾
miles and come to a fork in the road. You are on the eastern park
boundary at a 1500-foot elevation. To continue, turn right onto
Holter Ridge Road. It generally follows the ridge and the park
boundary south to meet Bald Hills Road in about 6 more miles,
climbing to an elevation of 2300 feet. You meet Bald Hills Road
in its sixth mile, about a mile north of C-Line Road.

While hikers do best to return on the designated trail they
ascended, mountain bikers can complete the 21¾-mile loop on
paved Bald Hills Road, Highway 101 and the gravel Lost Man
Creek access road (watch for traffic!).

21.

SKUNK CABBAGE CREEK
SPECTACULAR APPROACH TO COAST

*A beautiful new 1½-mile segment of Skunk Cabbage Creek Trail,
which traces the coastal ridge north from the headwaters of
Skunk Cabbage Creek, is detailed in this revised description. The
trail is now described from south to north, the most dramatic
approach to the wilderness beach. You may also hike it from the
north end, starting at the Gold Bluffs Beach entrance kiosk.*

*This trail was built in 1987 as a segment of the Coastal Trail.
The Coastal Trail has now been rerouted to follow the beach
south to the mouth of Redwood Creek, where it continues south
along the shore. The Coastal Trail is still not marked where it
leaves Davison Road. You must climb over driftwood before*

heading south on the beach. A low tide is required to scramble around Mussel Point.

Your trail starts at a new parking area about ½ mile west of the old southern trailhead. The trail heads west beneath young alders, descending briefly to cross Johnson Creek. Climb past several ancient redwoods, remnants of the the virgin forest that once covered most of these canyons. The understory has plentiful salmonberry, lady, deer and sword ferns, Siberian miners lettuce, giant skunk cabbage and tiny club moss. Contour north past huckleberry and evergreen violet.

By ¼ mile you climb gradually northwest, leaving the redwoods for a dense second-growth forest of young alder and Sitka spruce with scattered Port Orford cedar, western redcedar and hemlock. Descend to a bridge over a tiny side stream where red elderberry thrives. Your path then descends through lush growth, crossing a boardwalk over another stream.

At ½ mile you pass through Sitka spruce forest with a luxuriant understory of skunk cabbage, fairy bells, twisted stalk and false lily of the valley. Mushrooms and other fungi thrive in this damp environment. Contour along an old road, crossing several boardwalks over tiny creeks and seeps. You soon pass spruce two feet in diameter growing in the road bed. The broad bed of Skunk Cabbage Creek on your right supports an abundance of its namesake plant beneath spruce forest. The boggy

DISTANCE: 7⅜-mile loop or 6-mile round trip to beach. One
   way to Davison Road: 5⅜ miles.

TIME: Three to 5 hours.

TERRAIN: Climbs gently along wooded canyon, then up to and
   along coastal ridge before descending to beach.

ELEVATION GAIN/LOSS: Loop: 960 feet+/960 feet-. One way to
   beach: 600 feet+/640 feet-.

BEST TIME: Spring or summer, but nice anytime.

WARNINGS: Watch for rogue waves at the beach.

DIRECTIONS TO TRAILHEAD: SOUTH END: Turn west off
   Highway 101 at M.122.7 onto side road. Where road bends
   left at .1 mile, a gravel road goes right. Go .65 mile to
   trailhead parking.

   NORTH END: Turn west off Highway 101 at M.123.9 onto
   unpaved, steep Davison Road (no trailers). Go 5 miles and
   park opposite entrance kiosk.

FEES: Day use/parking at Gold Bluffs Beach: $5/vehicle
   ($4 for seniors).

FURTHER INFO: Redwood National Park (707) 464-6101.

soil there is too wet for redwoods.

Your easy path crosses a feeder creek at ¾ mile, then two
more around ⅞ mile, where a few large redwoods mix with the
spruce forest. Continue contouring to 1⅛ miles, beyond which
only a few redwoods grow. Your trail climbs gradually, winding
to cross a small creek.

Around 1¼ miles the path turns northeast to cross a bridge
over Skunk Cabbage Creek. The creek splits into two forks just
above the crossing. Ascend past healthy young spruce and
redwoods with bleeding heart in the understory. As your trail
turns northwest you can hear the surf roaring to the west.

At 1½ miles you climb past young redwoods with their bark
scraped off by elk. An immense snag is nearby. Standing dead
trees provide habitat for birds and other animals of the forest.
Ascend along the North Fork of Skunk Cabbage Creek, soon
crossing it twice by bridges. Red huckleberry mingles with its
evergreen kin. Salal, yerba de selva and bedstraw join the
understory.

Beyond 1¾ miles you descend briefly to level ground beside
the creek. Sitka spruce and alder dominate the forest, punctuated
by the rotting remnants of immense redwood stumps. Your trail
contours, then climbs along the creek.

You soon cross one more bridge over the headwaters of Skunk Cabbage Creek. Look for saxifrage and watercress at the crossing. The trail ascends along the west bank of the south-flowing creek. Switchback twice at 2 miles to climb above the creek, then ascend a switchback with steps, heading away from the creek.

After one more switchback, your trail contours around 2¼ miles. Then climb to a gap at the very head of the creek before 2½ miles. The trail splits in two here. The left fork drops ⅜ mile to the beach, while the newly constructed right fork follows the coastal ridge north. Whichever path you choose, be sure to walk 50 feet west from the junction for a grand view through alder forest to the wild beach below.

Our described route takes the right fork, climbing east, then southeast on the new trail as cow parsnip, foxglove and wild cucumber thrive beneath alders. You soon begin a steep, switchbacking ascent through redwood forest on the east side

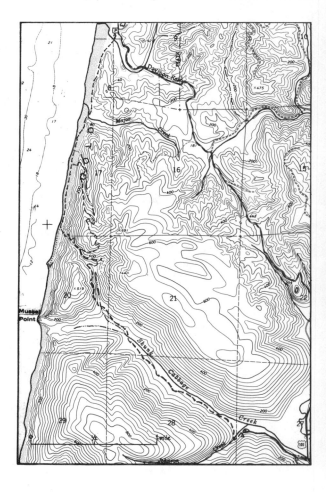

of the ridge.

Beyond 2⅝ miles you pick up an old road grade to climb northwest and north to coastal views. Your trail veers left around 2¾ miles to make a winding descent north along the ridgetop. Pass an immense, blackened redwood stump around 3 miles, then continue a gradual descent along the ridgetop, with glimpses of the Pacific to the west.

At 3¼ miles you cross a small boardwalk over a wet gully, then continue on a winding descent. Views of the breakers alternate with glimpses east into a fern-choked canyon. By 3¾ miles the trail steepens for a switchbacking descent to the mouth of an unnamed creek. At 3⅞ miles California polypody grows on an alder leaning over the trail. Descend along a magical stretch of creek, where osprey nests decorate twisted Sitka spruces.

Pass lupines in a dense thicket of coastal scrub and break through to a view of the beach. On a clear day you can see all the way north to Midway Point on the Del Norte coast. Five miles offshore sits Redding Rock, a breeding ground for seabirds. Your trail drops to the beach, coming to the high tide line at 4 miles, just south of the mouth of the seasonal creek along which you descended. (It is almost 1⅜ miles north along the beach, the designated Coastal Trail, to Davison Road and the Gold Bluffs entrance kiosk.)

Our described hike heads south along the beach, which is broad at first, then narrows. At 4½ miles a big slide on the bluff above the beach is your sign to start looking for the trail to Skunk Cabbage Creek. The trail lies about 400 feet beyond the big slide, after an outcrop of black rock laced with white veins where beach strawberry is abundant. The trail is now marked by a bright orange triangle that is difficult to miss. The path climbs to a steep, grassy slope. (If you continue south along the beach on the Coastal Trail, you come to the prominent rock outcrop called Mussel Point in ¾ mile. The beach disappears there. It is possible to scramble over rocks and around the point only at low tide. From there you can continue on the beach for about 2 miles to the mouth of Redwood Creek.)

Your return trail zigzags by six switchbacks up the grassy slope scattered with lupines, poppies and other wildflowers. Around 4¾ miles you enter a dwarf forest of alder and spruce. Climb through this forest by more switchbacks, with views of the beach and Redding Rock to the west. At 5 miles you switchback left and climb steeply to a wooded saddle. A level spot at the saddle provides fine views. In 50 feet your trail completes the loop, returning to the junction. Retrace your steps down the canyon of Skunk Cabbage Creek to reach the trailhead at 7½ miles.

22

LADY BIRD JOHNSON GROVE LOOP

LUSH HIGHLAND VIRGIN FOREST

When she was First Lady, Lady Bird Johnson spoke out for the creation of Redwood National Park. Her stand helped break a deadlock in Congress over establishment of the controversial park and the acquisition funds were allocated. Appropriately, she came to dedicate the park in 1968. The ceremony occurred in what is today called Lady Bird Johnson Grove.

A short easy loop trail, 1 ⅜ miles in length, explores the virgin grove, located on a high ridge. People in wheelchairs can follow the trail with little or no assistance.

The master plan for trail development in Redwood National Park includes plans for a trail to connect the coast with the east side of the Redwood Creek basin. One segment of the trail would head south from the LBJ Grove parking area. Another section, 3 ¼ miles in length, would descend from the north end of the Grove Loop to meet Bald Hills Road near Highway 101. The trails will not be finished before the late 1990s.

The trail leaves the parking area and crosses Bald Hills Road on a pedestrian bridge. In 300 feet a dispenser provides pamphlets for the self-guiding nature trail. The trail heads northwest through virgin forest of redwood, Douglas fir, grand fir and hemlock. This high-elevation forest differs from the coastal forests of redwood and Sitka spruce and the drier forests farther inland.

The trail climbs gently along the north end of Bald Hills Ridge. Numerous rest benches provide stopping places. The lush understory growth is dominated by salal, sword fern, red and evergreen huckleberry, salmonberry and red-flowering currant. Other understory plants include tanoak, wild rose, redwood sorrel, coltsfoot, redwood violet, rhododendron, Oregon grape and blue flag iris.

At ¼ mile a rest bench sits at the spot where the return trail enters on the right. The trail climbs gradually, then starts a gentle descent. Salmonberries grow to ten feet tall here, with hairy honeysuckle vines twining through the understory.

The easy descent continues to ½ mile, where a plaque on the right marks the spot of the 1968 dedication of Redwood National Park by Lady Bird Johnson. The redwoods here have broad, thick-barked trunks but do not grow as tall as the trees sheltered in the deep, protected canyons. The maximum heights are generally less than 250 feet.

LADY BIRD JOHNSON GROVE LOOP:

DISTANCE: 1⅜-mile loop.
TIME: Thirty to 60 minutes.
TERRAIN: Gentle loop along high ridge through virgin forest.
ELEVATION GAIN/LOSS: 150 feet+/150 feet-.
BEST TIME: Spring for wildflowers.
WARNINGS: Steep winding road to trailhead not advisable for trailers.
DIRECTIONS TO TRAILHEAD: Turn east off Highway 101 at M.122.3 onto Bald Hills Road. Go 2.6 miles to the Lady Bird Johnson parking area on the right.
FURTHER INFO: Redwood National Park (707) 464-6101.

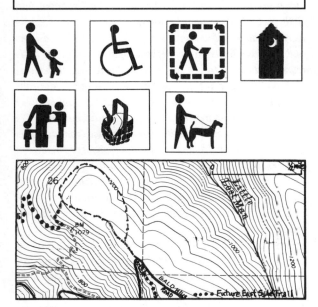

Soon the Pacific Ocean peeks through the trees as you near the edge of a clearcut. Most of the land between here and the coast is now protected in state and national parks. The trail bends right at the edge of the clearcut, then starts a gentle climb.

About ¾ mile from the trailhead, your trail bends right again and heads southeast. On your left the forest drops steeply toward Little Lost Man Creek, ½ mile away and 700 feet below. Your trail levels before ⅞ mile. Giant rhododendrons grow on the left with trunks four inches in diameter.

The level path continues through a forest of big trees with a lush understory. In spring trilliums and redwood sorrel present white and purple flowers. Tiny calypso and coral root orchids may also grow along the trail. Licorice ferns grow on the bark of trees. Native Americans mixed them with the tobacco they grew to sweeten the smoke.

At one mile a rest bench sits beside the edge of the steep drop into Little Lost Man Creek. The trail climbs a short hill, then descends gradually to meet the return trail at 1⅛ miles. Turn left and descend ¼ mile to the parking area.

23.

REDWOOD CREEK
EASY BACKPACK TO TALL TREES

Two trails reach the Tall Trees Grove of Redwood National Park. Both routes have seasonal limitations; hikers must heed the warnings about off-season travel on both the Redwood Creek and Tall Trees Trails. To ignore them could mean disaster at the worst, or a ruined trip or cold night in the woods, at the least. Redwood Creek Trail is the longer route into Tall Trees Grove. This easy trek avoids the steep terrain surrounding Redwood Creek by following the creek's gradual canyon upstream. The problem for off-season travelers lies in the two crossings of the creek. In summer (generally May to September; inquire at Redwood Information Center) temporary bridges are installed at the crossings. In late spring and early fall when the bridges have been removed you can usually ford the creek (inquire!) to find solitude at Tall Trees Grove. But as waters rise with the rains, you cannot get beyond the first ford.

Redwood Creek was the domain of the Chilula people, an Athapascan group related to and allied with the Hupa to the east. The Chilula had about 20 small villages, mostly on sunny south slopes east of Redwood Creek, from McArthur Creek upstream to Minor Creek, near where Highway 299 is today. In summer they would leave their creekside homes to camp in the Bald Hills to the east, where they were consummate at snaring game and also gathered abundant seeds and bulbs. Fish from Redwood Creek provided the balance of their sustenance. They had virtually no contact with European immigrants until the Trinidad Trail to the Klamath and Trinity mines came through their territory in the 1850s. This led to twelve years of hostilities, after which the few Chilula survivors were removed to the Hupa Reservation.

From the parking area, the Redwood Creek Trail heads southeast. The level trail passes through a streamside forest of alders, bay laurels and willows. You pass your first redwood after ⅛ mile. The young tree on the right is dwarfed by a huge old redwood stump with spring board cuts on the left. These notches indicate that this area was logged long ago, before the

REDWOOD CREEK:

DISTANCE: 8½ miles one way. 17 miles round trip.

TIME: Four to 5 hours, one way.

TERRAIN: Follows meandering, nearly level canyon of Redwood Creek.

ELEVATION GAIN/LOSS: One way: 420 feet+/390 feet-. Round trip: 810 feet+/810 feet-.

BEST TIME: Late spring or fall for solitude. May 15 to September 15 for bridges.

WARNINGS: Creek fords are usually treacherous to impassable during rainy season (October-April); inquire before you go. Watch for poison oak.

DIRECTIONS TO TRAILHEAD: Turn east off Highway 101 at M.122.3 onto Bald Hills Road. Go .4 mile to turnoff on right, then .5 mile to trailhead parking.

FURTHER INFO: Redwood National Park (707) 464-6101.

OTHER SUGGESTIONS: A NETWORK OF HORSE TRAILS starts at the Orick Rodeo grounds east of town. About 34 miles of trail, with two free camps, loop through clearcut areas and some old growth forest west of Redwood Creek. For guided horse trips in Redwood National Park, contact Rollin' R Ranch, 7355 Elphick Road, Sebastopol, CA 95472, or call (707) 829-7829. CROSS COUNTRY HIKING: In summer the most rewarding backcountry experience comes to the hiker who walks the gravel bars of Redwood Creek. The creek repeatedly swings across the route, forcing the hiker to ford knee-deep water. You can go about 14 miles before the steep, narrow gorge of Rocky Gap bars progress. You can camp anywhere on the gravel bars, except within ¼ mile of the Tall Trees crossing.

advent of chain saws.

Your trail soon comes to the bank of Redwood Creek. From here you have your most expansive view up the creek, with big redwoods along both sides. In 100 feet you come to a station where you can write your own backcountry camping and fire permit.

Continue southeast beyond ¼ mile, where you cross a bridge over a side stream, then turn south. At ½ mile you come to a big meadow between the trail and Redwood Creek. Blackberries thrive in the sunny clearing.

You come to a second meadow at ⅝ mile. Your trail bends right and brings you alongside the creek again at ¾ mile. An osprey nest sits atop a tall tree about 200 feet east of the meadow. Continue across two small bridges into an area of lush

97

riparian vegetation. Sitka spruce, alder, salmonberry, water hemlock and saxifrage grow here.

Pass through a third meadow at 1⅛ miles, right beside the gravel bed of the creek. A riot of wildflowers grows here in the spring. After the meadow comes an immense berry patch, then an area where stinging nettles crowd the trail in late spring and summer. The next meadow stretches along the trail for ¼ mile. At its end you pass through a tunnel of vegetation, then drop onto the gravel bar of the creek bed at 1½ miles.

In summer you cross the creek on a temporary bridge. But in the off-season you must ford the creek. The gravel crossing 200 feet upstream from where the trail meets the creek usually provides the best ford. To find the trail south, look for the two red diamonds on the opposite bank, south-southwest from where you meet the creek. When the author hiked here in October, two mergansers floated downstream, perturbed by my intrusion.

On the west bank duck under a fallen maple and enter more riparian forest. On your right a giant maple stands against a fern-covered cliff. The path drops to a crossing of McArthur Creek beyond 1¾ miles. Your trail then runs along the base of the steep canyon wall until you descend onto the gravel bed of Redwood Creek at 2 miles. On the canyon wall grow five-finger and sword ferns and many saxifrage plants. Bracken and deer ferns grow a bit farther along the trail. At 2¼ miles pass a large redwood on your left, then climb a short, steep hill. This is followed by three short up and down stretches.

You drop to a bridge over Elam Creek at 2⅝ miles. The canyon becomes very broad here. Cross a small seasonal creek and head due east at 2⅞ miles, passing under large maples draped with lichen.

Your level trail stays near Redwood Creek, making a big, slow bend to the right. Drop back beside the creek at 3½ miles, heading south. Pass some big redwoods before the trail veers onto the gravel bar of Redwood Creek at 3⅝ miles.

You are soon back under the alders. At 3¾ miles the steep slope of the canyon is right beside the trail. The trail passes under a huge, still-growing fallen redwood. After crossing a small stream, you come to a broad spot in the trail at 4 miles, a pleasant rest spot with dry ground and a good view of Redwood Creek Canyon.

The trail contours upstream following the creek. Beyond 4¼ miles you enter a logged area. Only a few small- to medium-sized redwoods remain. Make a gradual climb to 4½ miles, then cross a bridge high over an unnamed creek. Cross two more bridges over nameless creeks in the next ¼ mile, then descend alongside Redwood Creek again at 5 miles.

After large redwood stumps at 5¼ miles, you start another

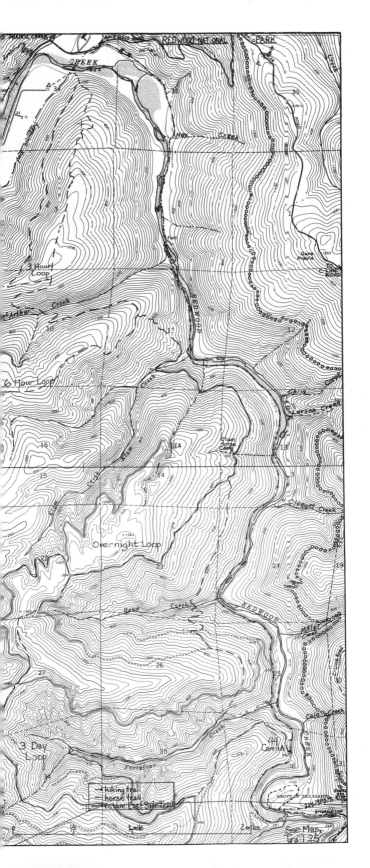

gradual climb. By 5½ miles you are about 100 feet above big pools in Redwood Creek. You drop quickly to a bridge over Bond Creek, then angle left at 5¾ miles and climb gradually, heading southeast. This is the biggest climb on your way to Tall Trees Grove; you gain 200 feet in the next ¾ mile. You pass a stand of virgin redwoods but most of the remainder of the trail passes through an area clearcut before this became a national park. A young alder forest has grown quickly to cover the scars and provide shade along most of your route. The shade of alders also helps the light-sensitive young redwoods get established.

A wooden post marks the 6-mile point of your hike. You continue to climb, passing another stand of virgin redwoods below the trail. You come to a sunny rest bench at the top of the hill. Then you descend gradually to cross a rustic bridge over cascading Fortyfour Creek.

Begin another gradual ascent, gaining 100 feet in a mile to reach the highest elevation on the trail, 290 feet above sea level, at 7⅜ miles. Your broad trail follows what was once a major logging road. Ruffed grouse nest along this section of the trail. One might spook with a noisy flurry of wings.

The road narrows and levels as you come to a sign marking the 7½-mile point. You arrive at the top of a large slide stretching 180 feet down to Redwood Creek. Next to a wooden guardrail you have a fine view of Tall Trees Grove to your southeast and Redwood Creek snaking through the canyon below. This is one of the best places in the redwood country to see the immense size these ancient trees can attain. The creek looks so far below you, yet the tops of the gargantuan redwoods rise far above you. Can you tell which one is the world's tallest tree? (Hint: it has one live top and one dead top.)

For the next ⅝ mile your trail descends, circling the Tall Trees Grove. You can see the grove through breaks in the alder forest as you descend along a cool north slope. Young redwoods grow on the right of the trail.

You reach the bottom of the hill and a trail register at 8⅛ miles. Sign in here, like fellow visitors from around the world. A sign indicates that camping is not allowed within .3 mile of the Tall Trees crossing. Pause here once more to appreciate the heights of the trees across the creek. Once you are in the grove you will be too close to get any sense of their height.

It is 500 feet across the creek and into the grove. A temporary footbridge crosses the creek from May to September. In other months you will have to get your feet wet. When you reach the grove, the tallest tree is on your left. A ¾-mile loop trail circles through the Tall Trees Grove. It passes under immense bigleaf maples, then leads to the third and sixth tallest trees. It also passes a brine vat used by an early settler to salt the fish he

caught in the creek.

If you are camping on Redwood Creek, put on your old tennis shoes and shorts and hike upstream along the gravel bars. As the creek wanders from one side of the canyon to the other, you must ford the azure stream many times. But you are rewarded with solitude, as well as a chance to sight herons, ducks, hawks, perhaps even a golden eagle, black bear, mountain lion or fox. Or perhaps you can spot their tracks in sand along the creek.

It is 1½ miles upstream to the Emerald Ridge Trail (see Trail #24). You can continue about two more miles before you encounter Rocky Gap, a narrow, steep-walled jumble of huge boulders that blocks further progress. Only hikers with rock climbing experience and a minimum party size of three should attempt to get beyond Rocky Gap.

If you camp on the gravel bars of Redwood Creek, treat your drinking water, hang food beyond the reach of bears, bury body waste at least 150 feet from the water, do not wash or let even biodegradable soap get into the streams, and use only dead, downed wood for fires. Of course hikers should carry out all their trash at all times.

24

TALL TREES
EMERALD RIDGE LOOP

EASY WALK TO WORLD'S TALLEST TREE,
STEEP WALK OUT

You can now get a permit to drive your private vehicle (motor homes and RV's prohibited) to the Tall Trees Trailhead. The free permits are issued daily between 8 a.m. and 2 p.m. at Redwood Information Center, one mile south of Orick on Highway 101. Come early, especially in summer, since permits are limited to 35 cars per day. Please note that all day hikers must be outside the locked gate at Bald Hills Road by 7 p.m.

From late May until the end of summer a shuttle bus runs from the Redwood Information Center south of Orick to the Tall Trees Trailhead. The bus leaves once or twice a day, stopping at the Redwood Creek Trailhead along the way. When the bus is running, it provides an easy, relaxing way for day hikers to reach the Tall Trees Grove. You may also bring a backpack on the shuttle, camp along Redwood Creek, then hike out on the Redwood Creek Trail (see Trail #23) for the full tour. From Tall Trees Grove in winter you will not be able to cross swift-flowing Redwood Creek when you get there, requiring that you return the way you went in.

After passing through the clearcuts along graveled C-Line Road for six miles, you come to the Tall Trees Trailhead. The trail descends south, quickly passing two shady picnic spots with tables. The ridge to the west of the trail was saved from logging, making this a pleasantly shaded hike. A forest of redwoods and Douglas firs to four feet in diameter provides shade for you and the lush understory plants: rhododendron, evergreen violet, huckleberry, ceanothus, salal, yerba de selva, chinquapin and tanoak. These are soon joined by western hemlocks, lichen-draped maples and occasional Port Orford cedars.

At ⅛ mile you come to a junction; the Emerald Ridge Trail on the left heads southeast, while the main trail turns west. Descending toward the grove, the habitat grows more moist and the trees are larger. Rest benches sit along the trail.

You turn northwest around ¼ mile and draw closer to the ridge. The trail zigzags, descending across a small stream cascading down the steep hillside. Cross another small creek at ⅝ mile, where deer and sword ferns thrive. Continue your descent, passing more rest benches.

Your trail levels at an alluvial flat deposited by Redwood Creek

TALL TREES/EMERALD RIDGE LOOP:

DISTANCE: 1¼ miles, one way; 2½ miles, round trip (plus ¾-mile Tall Trees Loop); or 4-mile loop.

TIME: To Tall Trees: 30 minutes.
Return to bus stop: 45 minutes to an hour.
Emerald Loop: 2 to 3 hours.

TERRAIN: Descends steeply to the world's tallest trees in a big bend of Redwood Creek. Loop follows creek upstream, then climbs ridge to trailhead.

ELEVATION GAIN/LOSS: Round trip to Grove: 680 feet-/680 feet+. With Emerald Loop: 720 feet-/720 feet+.

BEST TIME: Shuttle bus runs May to September. Off season visit offers solitude and serenity; get permit at Redwood Information Center first.

WARNINGS: Redwood Creek cannot be forded in winter, early spring. Steep trail on return hike. Watch for poison oak.

DIRECTIONS TO TRAILHEAD: Get permit first. Turn east off Highway 101 onto Bald Hills Road at M.122.3. Go 7.1 miles to Tall Trees Road on right, open and close gate, then drive 6 miles on winding, gravel road. Or take the shuttle bus from Redwood Information Center.

FEES: Shuttle bus: $7 donation requested.

FURTHER INFO: Redwood National Park (707) 464-6101.

eons ago, before it had cut as deep a canyon as it follows today. The gold-rush-era Trinidad Trail came through here on its way to the Trinity mines.

Descend once again, coming to a restroom at 1⅛ miles. Then you drop quickly to the floor of Tall Trees Grove, passing a redwood with a goose pen on the right. You meet the Redwood Creek Trail (see Trail #23) at 1¼ miles. Go right for 250 feet to meet the world's tallest tree. The twin trunks of the 600-year-old Tall Tree rise 367.8 feet, the trunk on the right being the tallest. Also in this grove are the third tallest (364.3 feet), fifth and sixth tallest trees.

Be sure to take time to walk the ¾-mile loop trail that winds through the grove. If you want a longer hike but do not want to hike 8.2 miles on the Redwood Creek Trail, you can make the Emerald Ridge Loop described below.

You can only hike upstream along Redwood Creek during the time of low water, generally from May until October. Even then you must make several knee-deep crossings of the creek. Head upstream from the Redwood Creek Trail crossing, just south of Tall

Trees Grove. You head east for ½ mile. Then the creek and canyon make a big bend right. You turn south about ¾ mile, then head south-southeast as the creek bed broadens to wide gravel bars. An old road meets the west side of Redwood Creek just after one mile. The creek bends left until you are heading southeast. About 1¼ miles, creek and canyon again bend to the left.

Soon a stream with a small waterfall enters Redwood Creek on your right, beside some lichen-covered rocks. A pleasant swimming hole is here in summer. The Emerald Ridge Trail is about 200 feet beyond. It heads north from the southernmost bend in this section of Redwood Creek. If you miss the trail, you will come to Emerald Creek on your left within ¼ mile. IF YOU COME TO EMERALD CREEK YOU HAVE PASSED THE TRAIL. (You can follow Redwood Creek for 2 more miles to Rocky Gap, where you can go no farther.)

The Emerald Ridge Trail climbs away from Redwood Creek, passing a huge circle of redwoods on the right. Climb through moss-draped forest with eight-foot diameter redwoods and Douglas firs, with glimpses of Emerald Creek canyon below. You pass the lower end of Dolason Prairie Trail (see Trail #25) around 1⅞ miles. If you want to extend your hike, consider a side trip along this new trail. It is ⅜ mile round trip to the pretty crossing of Emerald Creek.

Emerald Ridge Trail soon climbs away from the creek into drier habitat, heading generally northwest. Descend briefly just before 2¼ miles. A redwood root ball of fine geometric shape lies on the left. Climb gradually again before leveling amidst many large rhododendrons. Then resume your climb, winding around a shattered and scarred redwood giant.

You gain the crest of Emerald Ridge at 2½ miles and wind along it, climbing steeply, then more gradually. Climb northeast with several switchbacks through a forest of fire-scarred redwoods, scattered hemlocks and Douglas firs. The trail climbs and winds through the forest, leaving the ridge and heading north after 2⅝ miles. Then you turn west and climb more steeply. After two more turns you meet the Tall Trees Trail ⅛ mile from the shuttle bus stop. Turn right and climb back to the trailhead. The entire loop is 4 miles, 4¾ miles with the loop through Tall Trees Grove.

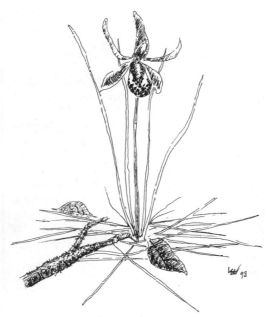

25.

DOLASON PRAIRIE
STEEP PRAIRIES AND VIRGIN FORESTS

*The newest trail in Redwood National Park explores the "balds"
or prairies, large grassland clearings in the forest, then drops into
virgin forests upstream from Tall Trees Grove. Dropping through
steep terrain, the trail requires a moderately strenuous 9⅜-mile
round-trip effort with a steep climb out. During peak season
(mid-May to mid-September), you can reduce the effort required
to explore this trail by arranging to meet the shuttle bus at the
Tall Trees Trailhead at the bottom end, reducing the hike from
the 9⅜ miles round trip to a 5¾-mile one-way shuttle. Or you
can limit your hike to the easy 2⅜ miles round trip to the Dolason
Barn for the grand views of Redwood Creek basin.*

The large prairies of this area were so important to the Chilula
people native to the area that their name originates from the
Yurok term meaning "people of the Bald Hills." The Chilula
dwelt in the upper reaches of these prairies during the summer,
gathering abundant seeds and bulbs and snaring game. In the
1850s they came into conflict with the gold-seekers who crossed
the area while journeying from the coast to the Trinity and
Klamath mining districts.

In the 1860s the Lyons family started a cattle ranch in the area,
switching to sheep in the 1870s. Lyons Ranch won a prize for
their wool at a Paris exhibition, bringing them international
acclaim. Redwood National Park inherited three barns from

DOLASON PRAIRIE:

DISTANCE: 9⅜ miles round trip; 2⅜ miles round trip to barn.

TIME: Full day.

TERRAIN: Descends moderately through forest to prairie, then steeply down a ridge to cross Emerald Creek, then climbs to meet Emerald Ridge Trail.

ELEVATION GAIN/LOSS: One way to Dolason Barn: 540 feet-; to Emerald Ridge: 2280 feet-/240 feet+. Round trip to Redwood Creek: 2800 feet-/2800 feet+.

BEST TIME: Late spring, early fall. Can be hot in summer.

WARNINGS: Steep trail, recommended for fit hikers. Watch for poison oak and rattlesnakes. No overnight parking at trailhead. No bikes or horses.

DIRECTIONS TO TRAILHEAD: Turn east off Highway 101 (M.122.3) onto Bald Hills Road. Go 11.5 miles to trailhead on right.

FURTHER INFO: Redwood National Park (707) 464-6101.

their spread, one of which is along this trail.

The trail descends south from the trailhead and picnic area on Bald Hills Road. You quickly turn southeast, descending through grasslands at the edge of Douglas fir forest. These grasslands have been invaded by Scotch broom and foxglove, non-native plants. By ⅛ mile your trail descends steadily through second-growth forest. You soon switchback to the right and descend west on an old road.

You veer right to descend a narrow path through the forest, then return to grasslands. At ⅜ mile you meet a broad gravel road. Turn right and follow it for ¼ mile, then veer left to descend a trail into the forest. Your path makes a moderate, winding descent, passing bay laurel, Indian plum and red-flowering currant. Switchback left to descend steadily south on another old road, then wind right and descend across two seasonal streams where gooseberry grows. Beyond the second drainage you get a glimpse of the barn ahead.

Your descending path passes the barn beyond 1⅛ miles. The nineteenth century barn has an intriguing steep-roofed design. Enjoy the sweeping views up Redwood Creek to the high peaks at the headwaters, snow-covered in winter and early spring.

The trail continues, descending across the large expanse of Dolason Prairie, brightly sprinkled with poppies, lupines and other wildflowers in April and May. Your descent steepens by

1½ miles, where you drop along a ridge, ducking in and out of Douglas fir forest. Wild strawberry and iris thrive in the grasslands, while the forest understory has evergreen and red huckleberry, Oregon grape, clintonia, trail plant, trillium and evergreen violet. You will likely see the scat of some of the many wild animals that inhabit the area: elk, coyote, bobcat, perhaps bear or mountain lion.

Your route continues winding down the crest of the ridge, passing Douglas firs to eight feet in diameter. At 1⅞ miles you leave the forest and the old ranch, entering a logged area on the north side of the ridge where you see the first redwoods along the trail. In spring the modest blue-violet flowers of snow queen

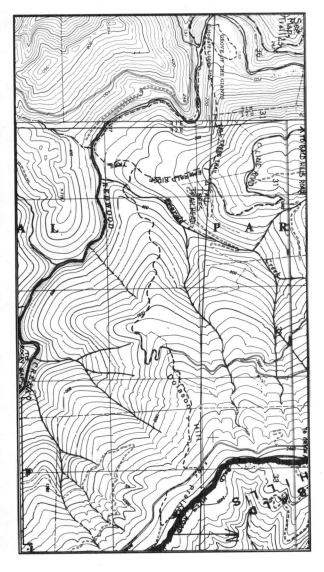

bloom here, as do showy calypso orchids. Look northwest for a view of the tall virgin forest near Tall Trees Trailhead.

Continue your descent into the deep canyon below. The trail winds through long switchbacks, offering views up the canyon of Redwood Creek. By 2¼ miles you again descend through forest along the ridge. Look for slink pod, vanilla leaf, redwood sorrel and wood rose. Large redwoods soon dominate the forest, with scattered Douglas fir, hemlock, grand fir, madrone, tanoak and bay.

Your switchbacking trail drops along the north face of the ridge. At 2⅞ miles a big redwood with a deep fire scar in its swollen base stands on the left. The path soon levels beside a rock outcrop. You can hear Emerald Creek murmuring to the north. Climb briefly past false solomon's seal and rhododendron.

From 3 miles you descend west along a ridge for ¼ mile. Then descend by two long switchbacks, returning to the ridge briefly at 3½ miles. Descend along a steep northwest-facing slope, dropping gently to 3¾ miles, then moderately as you pass redwoods and Douglas firs to ten feet in diameter, with chinquapin in the understory.

At 4 miles your trail turns north to ascend briefly, then resumes its winding descent. Descend north again at 4¼ miles, where a redwood on your right has a 17-foot diameter base and leans like the Tower of Pisa. Wind down to a beautiful redwood suspension bridge spanning the deep canyon of Emerald Creek at 4½ miles, a pleasant spot for a break. The creek's beryl waters tumble from pool to pool below.

Your trail winds steeply up the far bank to 4⅝ miles, then gradually up to its junction with the Emerald Ridge Trail (see Trail #24). If you turn right, the trail ascends ⅞ mile to Tall Trees Trail, one mile to Tall Trees Trailhead and the shuttle-bus stop. If you turn left on Emerald Ridge Trail you descend to Redwood Creek in just over ½ mile.

Unless you have arranged for the shuttle bus to pick you up at Tall Trees Trailhead, be sure to leave enough time and energy for the steep climb back to Dolason Trailhead.

26.

DRY LAGOON TO BIG LAGOON BEACH

BARRIER BEACH ALONG LAGOON SHORE

In 1931 the Department of Parks and Recreation acquired the Gillis Ranch and made it a state park. Today Humboldt Lagoons State Park encompasses 1924 acres. The hike along the barrier beach of Big Lagoon has a wilderness feeling. In winter or at extreme high tides, it may be impassable as high water breaches the barrier. When the author hiked here in spring 1993, the beach was impassable at a tide of +1.0 foot or more. But this figure varies from one season to another. If you arrive at high tide, you can picnic at the tables surrounding the parking area while you wait for the tide to recede.

A pleasant walk-in or bike-in campground lies south and east of the trailhead and picnic area. Six beautiful sites are located in a spruce forest, some with views of the ocean or Dry Lagoon. The camps have tables, fire pits, food cabinets and pit toilets, but you must bring your own water. They cost $7-9 per night.

The second most populous Yurok village on the coast was Opyuweg or Oketo (meaning lake), located at the southwest corner of Big Lagoon. Four smaller villages were on the eastern shore. The Yuroks would take their redwood dugout canoes out onto the 1470-acre lagoon to fish.

Prospectors came through here after the 1849 gold strikes on the Klamath and Trinity Rivers. Following the Gold Bluffs excitement, some prospectors worked Big Lagoon's barrier beach in the 1850s, but with little success. Ranchers settled the area in the 1870s. Timber firms acquired the forests to the east about the same time, although no logging occurred here until after World War II.

In 1994 the Coastal Trail will lead north from here to Stone Lagoon. It will wind east to a walk-in camp on the west shore of Stone Lagoon, then follow the shore to the Stone Lagoon Picnic Area.

To get to the barrier beach of Big Lagoon, go left from the parking area and follow the beach, which runs south-southwest from here. The high, wooded bluff on your left is the site of the Dry Lagoon Environmental Camps.

Walking the beach of salt-and-pepper pebbly sand, you come to the first of several large rocks at tide line after ⅛ mile. Around ¼ mile a landslide on the bluff has made the beach very narrow at high tide. Consult your tide table before proceeding. If the tide is higher than +1.0 feet for your hike, you may not be able to pass this point on your return. While the bluff has slide activity for the next ⅜ mile, the narrowest point was at the ¼-mile point as of this writing.

More rocks are scattered along the tide line, including a very large one before ⅜ mile. If the surf is large on the day of your hike, watch out for waves that surge through the gaps in the shoreline rocks. At ⅜ mile the beach broadens. Beyond the landslide at ⅝ mile, you can see Big Lagoon ahead.

You reach the north end of the lagoon at ¾ mile. At the flood channel here, Big Lagoon may drain into the Pacific after breaching. At extreme high tides, waves may dump their salt water into the lagoon here as well. If you can cross the flood channel, climb to the high barrier beach beyond. At ⅞ mile a driftwood log rests atop the barrier beach, providing a bench overlooking lagoon and channel. Big Lagoon stretches south for more than 3 miles.

Walk the crest of the barrier beach, heading toward Patrick's Point. At one mile you encounter scattered pockets of coastal strand vegetation; yellow-flowered northern dune tansy and sand verbena dominate.

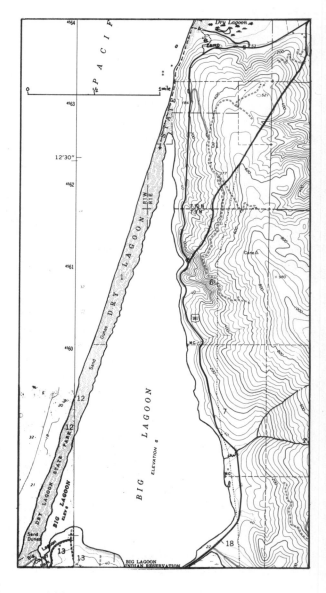

DRY LAGOON TO BIG LAGOON BEACH:

DISTANCE: Round trip as described: 6 miles (can go 8½ miles or more).

TIME: Two to 4 hours.

TERRAIN: Narrow beach at base of steep bluffs, then broad barrier beach between ocean and Big Lagoon.

BEST TIME: Medium to low tide.

WARNINGS: Beach may be impassable at tide of +1.0 foot or more. Do not get cut off by the rising tide. In winter, the lagoon breaches its barrier and the beach walk may be impassable. Watch for rogue waves as you walk on the beach.

DIRECTIONS TO TRAILHEAD: NORTH END: Turn west off Highway 101 at M.114.4. Go 1 mile to end of road and beach parking area.

SOUTH END: Turn west off Highway 101 at M.108.4 onto Roundhouse Creek Road. Go .3 mile, then turn right on Big Lagoon Park Road. Go .5 mile to day use parking area.

FEES: NORTH END: None for day use; Environmental Camps: $7-9/night. SOUTH END: Day use/parking: $2/vehicle.

FURTHER INFO: Information and reservations for Environmental Camps: (707) 488-2171. Big Lagoon County Park: (707) 445-7652.

OTHER SUGGESTIONS: At STONE LAGOON (M.117.4), a similar hike starts at the southwest corner of the picnic area, following the barrier beach (2 miles round trip, may be impassable November to April). From there A NEW SEGMENT OF COASTAL TRAIL heads southeast to a walk-in camp; by 1994 it will continue over Sharp Point to Dry Lagoon (4 miles total). At DRY LAGOON, a one-mile loop trail leads through the Environmental Camps and follows a portion of old highway. From Dry Lagoon Beach parking area, you can also walk the BEACH NORTH to Sharp Point, less than one mile. From June to September, HUMBOLDT LAGOONS VISITOR CENTER (M.115.) offers interpretive exhibits. SOUTH END: You can also walk Big Lagoon's barrier beach north from Big Lagoon County Park. See DIRECTIONS TO TRAILHEAD.

The barrier beach broadens at 1⅛ miles and stays very broad for ½ mile. Low dunes provide shelter for salt-tolerant plants. Sea rocket and sea fig join the dune tansy and sand verbena. Denser vegetation grows along the lagoon's shore. Big Lagoon is an important stop on the Pacific Flyway. Thousands of birds rest and feed here in winter. Year-round residents include members of the heron family, egrets and various shore birds.

Beyond 1⅝ miles the barrier beach gradually narrows as Big Lagoon increases in width. Dense patches of dune and cord grass grow near the lagoon's shore, providing nesting cover for shore birds. At 2⅛ miles, you come to one of several low spots in the beach. At extremely high tides, the breakers carry over the top of the sand spit, adding seawater to the brackish waters of the lagoon. About 30 species of fish inhabit the lagoon, as well as Dungeness crab, soft-shelled clams and bay mussels.

Continuing along the crest of the barrier beach, you encounter beach strawberry and seaside daisy growing with the other coastal-strand plants. Two more high-tide breaches lie around 2½ miles. The sand along the crest gets softer and looser here. You might want to veer west to the hard-packed sand near tide line. If you do, watch out for the large, churning waves that break quickly and run up the beach. An extremely violent undertow lies offshore as well. You can also veer east to the lagoon's shore.

At 2⅞ miles a log atop the beach crest is posted "State Park Property." At 3 miles Big Lagoon is over a mile across. Highway 101 runs along the east shore. A dense forest of windblown redwood, Sitka spruce and grand fir grows there. On the barrier beach, large driftwood logs provide seating and some shelter for a picnic and/or bird watching.

It is 1¼ miles farther to Big Lagoon County Park on the south shore. Beach-walk fanatics can continue another 2 miles along Agate Beach to Patrick's Point State Park.

Most hikers will want to turn back by the 3-mile point, for a 6-mile round trip. Before you do, notice the spectacular view of the rugged coastline of Agate Beach and Patrick's Point. You may want to walk closer to the lagoon's shore on your return, watching for birds as you go. But try to stay above the dense patches of grass along the shore so as not to disturb the birds and other small native creatures living there. Plan 1½ hours for your return.

PATRICK'S POINT STATE PARK

This 645-acre state park sits upon a level promontory surrounded on three sides by the rugged Pacific Ocean. Long ago the level headland was beneath the Pacific before sea level receded. Ceremonial Rock and Lookout Rock now stand high above the headland. When the headland was flooded they were sea stacks, like the ones offshore today.

The park was named for Patrick Beegan who homesteaded the area in 1851. Patrick's Point became a state park in 1929. The Yurok had a seasonal village called Sumeg at Patrick's Point. It has recently been reconstructed so that you can get an idea of the setting of ancient Yurok life (see OTHER SUGGESTION, Trail #28).

The annual rainfall averages 65 inches, most of it falling between October and April. Coastal fog can shroud the headland almost year round. It occasionally lingers for days at a time, especially in summer. But spring and fall often bring crystal-clear days, making those seasons the best time to visit. On the clearest days you can stand atop Ceremonial Rock and see the mouth of the Klamath River 30 miles north. From the top of Wedding Rock you may be able to see Cape Mendocino, 50 miles south.

27.

AGATE BEACH
CLIFFS ABOVE THE CRESCENT SHORE

From the northeast corner of the parking lot, your trail heads northeast, then east, descending 15 steps to the best view of Agate Beach, 160 feet below. Beyond the beach lie Big Lagoon and Sharp Point. Descend through Sitka spruce forest where understory plants include dense salal up to five feet deep, coltsfoot, azalea, salmonberry, fairy bells and yellow skunk cabbage.

At ⅛ mile a picnic table on the right has a fine view of Agate Beach. Your trail descends north along a narrow ridge, then into a ravine where the forest gives way to dense coastal scrub of salal, bush lupine, coastal manroot, yarrow, elderberry, blackberry and red-flowering currant.

As you descend toward the beach, you have an excellent view of the evenly tilted sandstone strata in the cliff above the beach. Your trail bends to the left and descends steeply to the beach at ¼ mile.

The beach ends at a cliff 300 feet west of the trail. It extends northeast, then north for 7 miles. It is 2 miles to the south end of

AGATE BEACH:

DISTANCE: ½ mile round trip to beach, up to 4½ miles round trip.

TIME: Thirty minutes or more.

TERRAIN: Short, steep descent to beach backed by high cliffs. Don't forget the steep climb back to trailhead.

ELEVATION GAIN/LOSS: 180 feet+/180 feet-.

BEST TIME: Spring for wildflowers. Low tide for greatest beach access. After winter storms for agate and jade collecting.

WARNINGS: Dangerous undertow here. It is unsafe to wade or swim.

DIRECTIONS TO TRAILHEAD: Exit Highway 101 onto Patrick's Point Drive (M.106.6 from north, M.105.9 from south). Go .5 mile to park entrance, where you turn right. Go past entrance station and follow signs to Agate Beach. The parking area is one mile from the park entrance.

FEES: Day use/parking: $5/vehicle. Car camping: $12-14/vehicle. Hike/bike camping: $3/person/night.

FURTHER INFO: Patrick's Point State Park (707) 677-3570.

OTHER SUGGESTIONS: OCTOPUS TREES NATURE TRAIL leaves .1 mile beyond Agate Beach Trailhead, looping through a grove of Sitka spruce. The ⅛-mile trail features the park's plant life. CEREMONIAL ROCK is reached by several trails of about ¼ mile in length. You climb 94 steps to the top of the 287-foot-high ancient sea stack. It was used for ceremonies by the Yurok people.

Big Lagoon. The broad beach then continues north to Sharp Point.

From the stairway, walk northeast for 75 feet to cross a small creek. The mouth of the creek has layers of dark graywacke sandstone, backed by towering cliffs of light yellow sandstone (unfortunately defaced by carvings of names and initials). Continuing along the beach, at ⅜ mile you are beyond the steepest portion of the sandstone cliff. The beach curves north in a gentle crescent.

At ½ mile lupine covers the face of the cliff, providing a spectacular display of color at the peak of bloom from April to June. At ¾ mile a steep gully cuts through the cliff. Just beyond the gully, the magnificent cliffs reach their highest point, rising almost vertically for 400 feet.

By now you may have seen people scurrying along the beach with collecting bags. Rockhounds frequent Agate Beach to collect small pieces of agate and black jade polished by the waves and cast upon the beach.

Continue along the beach as long as you wish, leaving time to return to the trailhead before sunset. Beyond the one-mile point, you will have improving views back to the spectacular, rocky coastline of Patrick's Point.

After your return walk along the beach, you end your hike by climbing steeply to the trailhead.

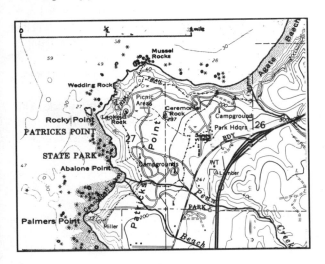

28.

RIM LOOP

STAIRS, SEA STACKS AND BEACHES

The Rim Trail follows an old Yurok path along the edge of the park headlands. This easy, mostly level trail provides access to six steep spur trails that lead to promontories with breathtaking views. You can approach most of these spur trails by car but the Rim Trail provides an intimate look at the wild side of Patrick's Point.

The described trail begins at Agate Beach Trailhead and parking area, then circles the shore in a counter-clockwise direction. It circles back through the center of the park to your starting point. The trail is 3⅛ miles long without any of the spur trails, 4½ miles long if you take them all.

Head west from the parking area, descending along an obtrusive chain link fence. (The fence prevents foolish people from risking life and limb on the steep 200-foot bluff that drops to the ocean.) In 450 feet a wide spot provides an excellent view of Agate Beach. Sitka spruce rise above a dense understory of salal, blackberry, twinberry, ferns, angelica and azalea.

At ⅛ mile a spur trail meets the main trail. On your right is another fine view, with Mussel Rocks visible to the northwest and Agate Beach to the northeast. Red alders and shore pines join the forest as you dip through a small gully. Tall salmon-, elder- and thimbleberries shade the path where old apple trees also grow.

Enter dense forest again at ¼ mile. Tiny Beaver Creek gurgles on your left. Soon you turn right toward the edge of the bluff and another overlook. The trail bends left, crossing a bridge above a waterfall at ⅜ mile. Pass through a dense tunnel of foliage and descend some steps to meet the Mussel Rocks trail on your right before ½ mile.

If you turn right, the path descends steeply to the rocks, with a fantastic view of Agate Beach stretching north to Big Lagoon. It is ⅛ mile to the end of the spur, where you can fish or look. Climb 146 steps to return to the Rim Trail.

The Rim Trail climbs steps to level, then turn south. Pass between two big rocks, then descend stone steps to a convenient picnic spot.

Your trail heads west to another view of the coast. At ⅝ mile you pass another picnic spot (with a water spigot). As you approach the Wedding Rock parking area, take the first right fork to avoid the congestion at the popular day-use area. You soon meet the Wedding Rock spur trail.

The Wedding Rock spur descends rough steps, then climbs to the top of Wedding Rock at ⅛ mile. From the top of the 120-foot-high ancient sea stack, you have a spectacular view of the coast to the south. This is also a great spot for whale watching and storm watching.

Returning to the Rim Trail, head south. You climb steps to join a paved, wheelchair-accessible path, then meet the Patrick's Point spur trail at ¾ mile.

The Patrick's Point trail branches right. The paved path descends to a picture-postcard view of Wedding Rock and the surrounding coast. The detour to Patrick's Point and back totals ¼ mile.

The Rim Trail wraps around the base of Lookout Rock on your left to meet the Lookout Rock spur in just 150 feet. (It is ⅛ mile to the top of the ancient sea stack and back.)

Then the Rim Trail descends gradually through Sitka spruce forest. Descend steps to cross tiny Ickie Ughie Creek, then climb to the Rocky Point side trail. (Turn right to walk down to

RIM LOOP:

DISTANCE: 3⅛- to 4½-mile loop.

TIME: Two to 3 hours.

TERRAIN: Follows a convoluted shore through dense vegetation, with access to rocky points and beaches. Loops back through the center of the park.

ELEVATION GAIN/LOSS: Rim Loop: 180 feet+/180 feet-. To Mussel Rock, Wedding Rock and Abalone Point: add 320 feet+/320 feet-.

BEST TIME: Spring and fall.

WARNINGS: Stay back from edge of steep cliffs. Watch for poison oak. On the shore, never turn your back on the ocean; watch for rogue waves.

DIRECTIONS TO TRAILHEAD: Exit Highway 101 onto Patrick's Point Drive at M.106.6 (north) or M.105.9 (south). Go .5 mile to park entrance and turn right. Follow signs to Agate Beach parking area, about one mile.

FEES: Day use/parking: $5/vehicle. Car camping: $12-14/vehicle.

FURTHER INFO: Patrick's Point State Park (707) 677-3570.

OTHER SUGGESTIONS: A WHEELCHAIR ACCESSIBLE PATH explores PATRICK'S POINT, about ⅜ mile round trip. A short trail explores the newly reconstructed YUROK VILLAGE OF SUMEG, where there are now seven traditional Yurok buildings and a picnic area; park at the lot by the entrance kiosk for a ¼-mile round trip, or at park headquarters for a ⅛-mile round trip.

Rocky Point, a ⅛ mile round trip.)

Beyond the Rocky Point spur, the Rim Trail climbs a hill to meet a trail to the hike/bike camps then heads south through alder forest. The relatively open forest provides glimpses of the rugged coast. At one mile from the trailhead, a large cypress stands between the trail and the sea. You continue through forest and coastal scrub along the western edge of Abalone Campground. At 1⅛ miles you meet the side trail to Abalone Point, where the Yurok tribe once had a seasonal village. (The steep spur descends to oceanside fishing and diving access—⅛ mile round trip.)

The Rim Trail turns southeast. Follow the wooded bluff, soon crossing a small bridge. At 1⅜ miles you meet a paved trail from Abalone Campground. Turn right onto the paved trail and cross a bridge over Penn Creek, coming to the junction of three trails. On your left is the return path to the trailhead. The middle trail continues to the Campfire Center. Unless your time or energy is running short, take the right fork to one last magnificent viewpoint: Palmer's Point.

You follow Penn Creek to a bench and overlook, then veer left. Turn right at a junction. At 1½ miles you cross a bridge over Beach Creek and head northwest. The trail passes through dense forest of Sitka spruce, shore pine and Bishop pine. The trail bed ends before 1¾ miles at the paved road to Palmer's Point. Walk the road shoulder for ⅛ mile to its end where a picnic area has a wonderful view up and down the coast. One spur trail leads west to the end of Palmer's Point. Another forks north to descend to rocky Cannonball Beach, a popular tidepooling spot.

Now retrace your steps back to the Penn Creek bridge. Do not cross the bridge, but instead take the trail that leads east, heading upstream with the creek on your left. Soon you cross a paved road. At 2⅜ miles you cross Penn Creek and come to a fork. Bear left to return to the trailhead.

The trail climbs gradually through dense spruce forest, turning north as it crosses six small bridges. You meet the park entrance road just east of the entrance station. Walk northwest on the road shoulder for 250 feet. Turn northeast before the entrance kiosk, passing the bookstore at 2⅝ miles and taking the paved trail beyond the parking lot. In 150 feet veer left on a gravel path (the paved trail continues to the reconstructed Yurok village—see OTHER SUGGESTION).

Descend north to cross a tiny creek and meet another fork at 2⅞ miles. You can take the right fork to Park Headquarters, then walk the road back to your trailhead. I prefer to take the left fork. Veer left again on the trail to Ceremonial Rock. Take another left at an unmarked junction and walk 30 feet to a marked intersection at 2⅞ miles. The left fork climbs to the top of Ceremonial Rock, a ⅜ mile round trip. To return to the trailhead, take the right fork, marked Agate Beach Campground.

You come to coastal prairie, then cross a road. Descend to a bridge over Beaver Creek and ascend to a restroom in Agate Beach Campground. Go northeast on the campground road to return to the parking area at the trailhead.

TRINIDAD STATE BEACH

The town of Trinidad is the oldest in Humboldt County and with a population of 350 one of the smallest incorporated cities in the state. The history of habitation here goes back much farther. The Yurok village of Tsurai, their largest coastal village, was located on the north shore of Trinidad Bay. Archaeological evidence shows it was inhabited continuously for over 1000 years, perhaps much longer. This southernmost village of the Yuroks was occupied until 1916.

Spanish explorers entered the bay on Trinity Sunday in 1775 naming it and claiming it for Spain. Russian fur trappers visited several years later. The Josiah Gregg party stopped here on December 7, 1849, carving the latitude and date into a tree. They named it Gregg's Point, unaware of the previous Spanish discovery. As the gold fever grew in California, ships left San Francisco searching for the protected harbor described by Gregg's party. Three schooners finally succeeded in March, 1850. A month later streets were laid out, temporary buildings erected and 140 people voted in the first election. By July Trinidad boasted 300 residents and opened a trail to the Klamath and Trinity mines. A sawmill opened in 1852. But as Eureka and Arcata grew, Trinidad's star faded. Still, a lighthouse was established in 1871 and the town boomed briefly again as a whaling port in the 1920s. Today the sleepy little city on a marine terrace caters mostly to tourists and fishermen, not miners and whalers. The charm of Trinidad State Beach lies in its wildness. Although its 159 acres are within and adjacent to town, the short easy trails transport you to a rugged and wild shoreline with spectacular views.

29

ELK HEAD/COLLEGE COVE

WILD GARDEN AND SHORE

The Elk Head Trail leaves from the north end of the unpaved north parking area. The trail heads northwest through coastal scrub and grasslands, quickly turning west onto the broad promontory of Elk Head. The tall shrub cotoneaster grows here with its attractive red berries, as do Sitka spruce, red alder, wood rose, red-flowering currant, wild ginger and the endangered Eureka lily. The Columbia lily and black crowberry reach their southern limit here. Your trail descends gradually, approaching the southern shore of the headland. At ⅛ mile a side trail on the left descends by many steps to the north end of the beach at College Cove. The Elk Head Trail continues west on the flat-topped promontory. This is a marine terrace, ancient ocean floor uplifted by the geological forces which continue to shape this coast. Dense clumps of salmon-, elder- and thimbleberry grow along the trail.

At ¼ mile bear left as the trail forks. The coastal scrub opens up on your left. Take a few steps to the edge of the bluff for a spectacular view of College Cove, Pewetole Island and Trinidad Head. After your trail turns southwest, you leave the scrub for grasslands with scattered pockets of scrub.

Your trail leads to bluff's edge before ⅜ mile. Below you is jagged Omenoku Point. A brushy fisherman's trail leads down to the point. Your trail bends right, heading northwest past many western dog violets to scrub-covered Elk Head and Megwil Point.

Just before ½ mile, the trail makes a big right bend. Here,

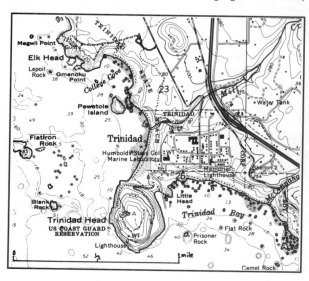

ELK HEAD/COLLEGE COVE:

DISTANCE: ⅞ mile or 1½ mile semi-loop.

TIME: One hour.

TERRAIN: Level headland to grass- and scrub-covered promontory. Possible tidepooling and walk on beach.

ELEVATION GAIN/LOSS: Less than 100 feet to Elk Head. To College Cove: 100 feet-/100 feet+.

BEST TIME: Spring, early summer. Medium to low tide for beach.

WARNINGS: Watch for poison oak. Stay back from edge of cliffs.

DIRECTIONS TO TRAILHEAD: Exit Highway 101 at Trinidad, M.100.9 from north, M.100.1 from south. Go west on Main Street, then right on Trinity Street (which becomes Stagecoach Road) for .7 mile and turn left into unpaved parking lot. Trail leaves from north end.

FURTHER INFO: Trinidad Chamber of Commerce (707) 677-3448.

OTHER SUGGESTION: A HORSE TRAIL leaves from west end of parking area and winds south to Mill Creek and Trinidad Beach. WHEELCHAIR ACCESS follows Elk Head Trail to Megwil Point.

near the tip of Elk Head, another side trail on your left heads west, then north for ⅛ mile to the tip of Megwil Point (last section too steep for wheelchairs), where you can see the coast to the north. Offshore sits Green Rock, with one of the state's largest colonies of common murres, 16-inch tall, black and white seabirds of the auk family. The population of Green Rock is estimated at 55,000 murres! To the southwest is Flatiron Rock, home to 24,000 more murres and five other bird species, as well as seals and sea lions. At low tide you can descend to excellent tidepools at Megwil and Omenoku Points. Be careful!

The main trail turns east, making a short loop. Pass shore pine, Sitka spruce and cypress, then scattered pockets of heather. At ⅝ mile you rejoin the main trail. Continue east ¼ mile to your car.

You may prolong your hike with a walk on College Cove Beach. To do this, take the side trail ⅛ mile from the trailhead.

It descends by 100 rough steps to the north end of the beach. You can walk southeast on the beach for ¼ mile, although at high tide you must scramble over a pile of boulders. South of the rockpile, the sandy beach continues. A beautiful, large specimen of coast silktassel grows just above the beach. A small waterfall lies just beyond. Return by the same route to your trailhead.

30.
MILL CREEK TO BEACH
TO THE FOOT OF PEWETOLE ISLAND

The paved southern parking area lies within the city limits of Trinidad. A pleasant picnic area with restrooms and piped water is on a lawn-covered hillside. The Mill Creek Trail to Trinidad Beach starts here.

The trail heads north, passing to the right of the restrooms. Descend by switchbacks into forest of Sitka spruce, grand fir and red alder. You descend above the creek, crossing a boardwalk before coming to a rest bench with a pleasant view of Mill Creek Canyon. The lush understory includes sword, deer and lady ferns, redwood sorrel, mitrewort, bleeding heart, fairy bells

---

MILL CREEK TO BEACH:

DISTANCE: ½ mile, round trip to beach. Full hike: 1⅜ miles, round trip.
TIME: One hour.
TERRAIN: Descends along Mill Creek to Trinidad Beach. Beach walking to south, tidepooling to north.
ELEVATION GAIN/LOSS: 160 feet-/160 feet+, round trip.
BEST TIME: Low tide. Spring.
WARNINGS: Do not get trapped by the rising tide. Watch for rogue waves on beach.
DIRECTIONS TO TRAILHEAD: Exit Highway 101 at Trinidad, M.100.9 from the north, M.100.1 from the south. Go west on Main Street, then right on Trinity Street, where first left leads to the paved parking area.
FURTHER INFO: Trinidad Chamber of Commerce (707) 677-3448.

---

and skunk cabbage.

At ⅛ mile a giant evergreen huckleberry towers over the trail. Continue a gradual descent, paralleling the creek. The forest soon gives way to coastal scrub with blackberry, bush lupine, twinberry and coltsfoot. You come to an expansive view of the beach and wooded Pewetole Island just offshore.

The trail turns right and descends steps to a junction with a horse trail. (If you turn right, it is ¾ mile to the northern parking area. See Trail #29.) Go left at the junction and drop to the beach at the mouth of Mill Creek, ¼ mile from the trailhead. You can walk the broad beach south for ⅜ mile to the base of Trinidad Head, where you can turn east and walk city streets back into town if you wish. Or you can return the way you came.

The beach north of the creek's mouth is best at low tide. At a tide of -1.0 foot or better, you can walk west about 400 feet, then walk northwest to the base of Pewetole Island. This steep rock island has a heavily forested top. Black oystercatchers nest there. This 17-inch-high black bird has a long red bill for prying shellfish from the rocks.

If you are here at low tide, be careful that the rising tide does not block your return.

MORE TRINIDAD TRAILS

The Trinidad area is a paradise for the hiker who likes short and scenic seaside trails. In addition to the trails of Patrick's Point State Park and Trinidad State Beach, the trails described below provide access to the spectacularly rugged coast and beaches.

31.

TSURAI LOOP
ON TRINIDAD HEAD
CLIMB HIGH ABOVE THE PACIFIC

Park your car at the beach parking lot at the west end of Edwards Street. Walk 200 feet south, where a sign marks the start of the Trinidad Head trails (day use—no vehicles except Coast Guard beyond that point). The trail starts as a narrow path that climbs steeply for 150 feet. Then climb west on a narrow paved road, entering the Coast Guard Reservation.

After the gate, the road climbs through dense coastal scrub as

the hill steepens. At ¼ mile, as you come to a big bend left, a dirt trail leaves the road heading west. Benches at the start of the path provide views north to Trinidad Beach, Pewetole Island and Elk Head. Take the dirt trail, descending 4 steps, then climbing to more benches with grand views. Just beyond those benches, a side trail forks right. It descends in 500 feet to more view benches at the base of a rock outcrop.

Beyond the fork the main trail climbs southeast. You pass many berry vines that flower in March and April and bear fruit from June through September. The moderately steep trail switchbacks left, then to the right before ⅜ mile. You level and come to more benches; this is a good whale-watching spot when gray whales are migrating, December through April. Look beyond the buoy for their spouts.

Your trail climbs again, heading south. Ahead you see your destination, a high rocky point. Climb through a thicket of silktassel to another rest bench at ½ mile. Unless it is very windy or foggy, take the side trail on the right. The short spur climbs steps to the top of the rock outcrop on the western edge of Trinidad Head. You are 300 feet above the Pacific, with views in every direction. Although you are about 60 feet below the summit of Trinidad Head, the view from here is more expansive than the view from the top. Pilot Rock, due south of here, was used by early explorers to locate and navigate the entrance to Trinidad Bay.

When you get enough of the view, descend to the main trail and head south through a pocket of lush vegetation where cow parsnip abounds. Soon, another short spur on the right leads to a view down the steep southwest face. The main trail switches left and climbs again, switching right in 150 feet. You pass through tall coastal scrub dominated by wax myrtle. Another view bench looks south at ⅝ mile. On a clear day you can see Cape Mendocino.

DISTANCE: 1½-mile loop.

TIME: One hour.

TERRAIN: Climbs from sea level through coastal scrub on the promontory of Trinidad Head to a rock outcrop 300 feet above the Pacific, then loops back to starting point.

ELEVATION GAIN/LOSS: 300 feet+/300 feet-.

BEST TIME: Spring. Any clear day.

WARNINGS: Watch for traffic on paved road. Watch for poison oak on trail.

DIRECTIONS TO TRAILHEAD: Exit Highway 101 at Trinidad, M.100.9 from north, M.100.1 from south. Go west on Main Street, then left on Trinity Street to its end. Go right on Edwards and descend to beach parking area. Signed trail starts to the south.

FURTHER INFO: Trinidad Chamber of Commerce (707) 677-3448.

Your trail contours past a mountain beaver den, then through more tall scrub. You quickly come to a large granite cross marking where the Spanish explorers placed a wooden cross during their visit in 1775. Two benches overlook the coast and a grove of large Sitka spruce growing on the south face below.

Now head north toward the microwave station at the summit. At ¾ mile you come to a gravel road. Turn right on the road and descend toward town. You can see boats anchored in Trinidad Bay below. To the east lie Houda Point and Little River Rock.

At ⅞ mile you pass another bench and switchback right. You wind back to the left at one mile and meet the paved road. Go left on the pavement, making a gradual descent past several rest benches with fine views of Prisoner Rock just offshore, Trinidad Harbor, Little Head and Indian Beach.

At 1¼ miles your descent steepens. The road bends right, completing your loop as you pass the dirt trail on the left. Descend to your car, a total hike of 1½ miles.

32

INDIAN BEACH

EASY TO REACH SECLUDED BEACH

Walk east on Wagner Street past the first house on the right. The trail heads south toward Trinidad Bay across a paved driveway. In 100 feet you come to a plaque inscribed "Indian Beach Trails—Humboldt North Coast Land Trust and the Citizens of Trinidad." The trail turns left at the plaque. Follow the grassy trail 500 feet to where it turns south toward the beach, passing between alders and Sitka spruce. You descend a total of 92 steps, then cross a gravel driveway and drop to the beach before ¼ mile.

You can walk west for ¼ mile along the sand to a pile of boulders at the end of the beach. Fishing and pleasure boats lie at anchor in Trinidad Bay on your left, as you walk west toward Trinidad Head. On your right a thicket of alders and willows gives the beach a secluded feeling, even though you are right next to town. The bluff above you was the site of the Yurok village of Tsurai, an important settlement that saw 1000 years of continuous use until 1916. As you return to the east, you have excellent views of the rugged, rocky shoreline to the east and south.

Going east from the trail, you can walk almost ⅜ mile. In 300 feet is a beached sea stack with a grassy top. A rough trail climbs to its top. At ⅛ mile east of the trail, Indian Beach ends. Unless

---

INDIAN BEACH:

DISTANCE: Round trip to beach: ½ mile. Total hike: 1⅜ miles.
TIME: One hour.
TERRAIN: Descends to secluded beach right below town. Beach walking and tidepooling.
ELEVATION GAIN/LOSS: 160 feet-/160 feet+, round trip.
BEST TIME: Medium to low tide.
WARNINGS: Do not trespass on adjacent private property.
DIRECTIONS TO TRAILHEAD: Exit Highway 101 at Trinidad, M.100.9 from north, M.100.1 from south. Go west on Main Street, then left on Trinity Street to its end. Go left on Edwards Street for one block. Where it turns left and becomes Ocean Street, park at the corner of Wagner Street.
FURTHER INFO: Trinidad Chamber of Commerce (707) 677-3448.

---

it is high tide, you can easily scramble over the rocks, where Pacific silverweed grows. On the far side of the rocks is a rocky tidepool area to explore at low tide.

Stretching to the east is a pebbly beach called He'Woli-Wroi Cove. You can walk this beach to the cliff at its east end, which blocks further progress. As you walk the beach, the many offshore rocks and sea stacks provide spectacularly changing vistas of the rugged coast.

Return to the trail and climb the 92 steps to your car. If you walked to both ends of the beach and back, you hiked 1⅜ miles.

33.

OTHER TRINIDAD TRAILS
SHORT HIKES TO RUGGED COAST

The other Trinidad area trails leave from Scenic Drive, the scenic old portion of Highway 101 which follows the coast south from the main Trinidad exit. They are listed from north to south.

The BAKER BEACH TRAIL leaves the road about .2 mile south of Baker Beach Road. The trail leaves from the north end of the parking area, descending steeply through alder and spruce forest to reach the beach in 350 feet. The beach stretches north for ⅜ mile. After you come to a rocky point, good rocky tidepools lie offshore from the pebbly beach.

The LUFFENHOLTZ BEACH TRAIL leaves from the north end of the large paved parking area for Luffenholtz County Park. It descends steeply west to reach the sandy beach in 300 feet. Another trail from the southwest portion of the parking area leads out onto narrow, scrub-covered Tepona Point, ending in ⅛ mile.

The HOUDA POINT TRAIL leaves from a cypress grove, descending stone steps. In 150 feet the trail forks. The left fork leads to Houda Point; the right fork descends in another 300 feet to a popular surfing beach beside Little River Rock. The flat beach is broad at low tide, narrow to submerged at high tide.

MOONSTONE COUNTY PARK is reached by a side road on the right, descending to a parking area at the beach. There is no developed trail here, just access to the beach. You can walk south along the beach for miles, though you must ford Little River to do it (easy ford in summer and fall, may be deep in winter and spring).

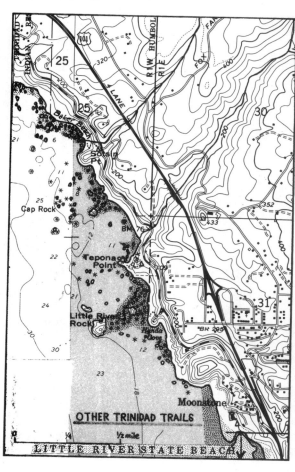

OTHER TRINIDAD TRAILS

LITTLE RIVER STATE BEACH

DISTANCE: ⅛ mile to 1 mile round trip each. At Moonstone you can walk as far as you want.

TIME: Less than one hour.

TERRAIN: Steep trails to small pocket beaches.

ELEVATION GAIN/LOSS: 100 feet-/100 feet+, each.

BEST TIME: Medium to low tide.

WARNINGS: Watch for oversize waves on beach. Do not trespass on adjacent private property. Watch for poison oak along trails to beach.

DIRECTIONS TO TRAILHEAD: Exit Highway 101 at Trinidad, M.100.9 from north, M.100.1 from south. At four-way stop, go south on Scenic Drive. It is 1.5 miles to Baker Beach Trail, 2 miles to Luffenholtz, 2.3 miles to Houda Point, 3 miles to Moonstone Road, where you go right.

FURTHER INFO: Trinidad Chamber of Commerce (707) 677-3448.

34.

MAD RIVER BEACH AND DUNES

NINETEEN MILES OF UNBROKEN BEACH

The steep and rocky shores running from Del Norte County to Trinidad change abruptly at the mouth of Little River. From there a continuous beach stretches south-southwest for 19 miles to the mouth of Humboldt Bay. Most of it is backed by high and low sand dunes that provide a wild and varied habitat for the adventurous hiker, not to mention shelter for the coastal-strand community of plants.

An ambitious hiker could start south from Moonstone County Park, ford Little River and hike the entire beach. The major obstacle is the crossing of Mad River. This major stream can be easy to ford in late summer or early fall. During the rest of the year, however, one must head east to the Hammond Bicycle Trail, cross the river on Hammond Bridge and return to the beach at Mad River Beach County Park. No obstacles lie from there to the jetty at the mouth of Humboldt Bay.

The hike described here explores the beach and dunes around

Mad River Beach County Park. The park includes 150 acres south of the river mouth. It provides access to river and ocean fishing, clamming, hiking, horseback riding and (unfortunately) four-wheeling. No developed trail is here, just acres of beach and dunes to explore; you can keep walking along the beach for as long as time and motivation will permit.

From the parking area follow a jeep trail west-northwest through low dunes. You come to the tide line in about ⅛ mile. Head south along the firm sand just beyond the reach of the waves. By ½ mile the beach becomes broader, and the dunes east of the beach are taller. From the one-mile point, much large driftwood lies along the beach. Sandpipers, sanderlings and curlews feed along the water line.

At 1½ miles a pole stands atop the dune nearest the beach; you can use it as a landmark. You can walk south along the

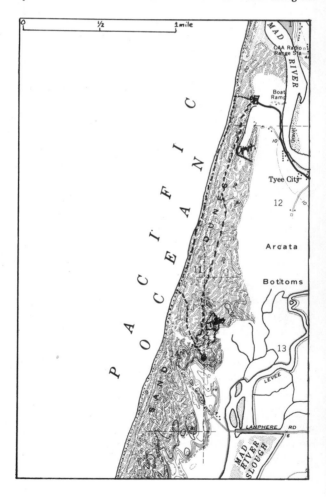

MAD RIVER BEACH AND DUNES:

DISTANCE: 4-mile loop or open-ended beach walk.

TIME: At least 2 hours.

TERRAIN: Long, unbroken beach backed by high dunes.

ELEVATION GAIN/LOSS: 125 feet+/125 feet-.

BEST TIME: Spring for wildflowers, any day that is not foggy for views.

WARNINGS: Watch for killer waves on beach. You may share the beach and dunes with motorized vehicles. Be aware of them. Poison oak may be found in the dune vegetation.

DIRECTIONS TO TRAILHEAD: Exit Highway 101 onto Janes Road at M.89.05 from north, M.88.6 from south. Go west on Janes Road, then right on Heindon Road for .4 mile. Go left on Miller Lane for .7 mile. Then go right on Mad River Road, coming to Hammond Bridge in 1.7 miles. The road turns west to reach the parking area and trailhead in 1.1 miles (4 miles from Highway 101).

OTHER ACCESS TO 19 MILE BEACH: Moonstone County Park: Exit Highway 101 at M.98.5.

Little River State Beach: Exit Highway 101 at M.97.4.

Clam County Beach: Exit Highway 101 at M.95.8 from north, M.95.5 from south.

Also off Highway 255 near Manila and Samoa.

FURTHER INFO: County Parks (707) 445-7652.

OTHER SUGGESTION: MOUTH OF MAD RIVER is 2 miles north. The estuary is used by hundreds of migratory waterfowl and shorebirds. Snowy plovers nest south of the river mouth. You may also see bald eagles, prairie falcons and Aleutian Canada geese. THE HAMMOND TRAIL is being developed from Clam Beach to Arcata. Particularly for bikers and equestrians, it crosses the Mad River on the Hammond Bridge, one mile east of Mad River Park. It winds through the beautiful farmlands of the Arcata Bottoms. Call Adventure's Edge (707) 822-4673.

beach for another 11 miles, but the described hike follows the beach for ⅛ mile beyond the pole. Where two large driftwood stumps lie at tide line, a double track heads east into the dunes. Follow this to the top of the first dune. From there you can see a high dune to your east with a top covered with Sitka spruce.

Look southeast for the tallest dune in that direction. Your route heads cross-country through the dunes for the top of that 75-foot-tall sand hill. As you walk through an area lush with coastal-strand plants, please try not to trample them. Along with

dune grass grow yellow bush lupine, sea rocket, beach strawberry and yarrow.

At 2 miles you are heading up the last incline to the top of the
high dune. You reach the top before 2⅛ miles. It provides fine
views (unless you are fogbound). An old ranch sits in a lush
green valley to the south. Beyond it is the Nature Conservancy's
Lanphere-Christensen Dune Preserve. East of that is Mad River
Slough, the ancient mouth of Mad River when it emptied into
Humboldt Bay. Beyond the slough lies the north arm of Humboldt Bay. The town of Arcata spreads along its shore. To the east
lie the farmlands of the Arcata Bottoms, the Trinity Mountains
rising beyond. When it is very clear you can see Trinidad Head
to the north.

Your return route goes cross-country through the dunes,
heading generally north. Before you leave the high dune, study
your route: stay west of the tree-covered dune to the north and
head generally toward the left side of a distant stand of trees
near the mouth of Mad River.

Descending the high dune, aim for the west side of the
spruce-covered dune, which you reach at 2½ miles. Then head
for the trees near the river mouth (15 degrees NNE if you have
a compass). At 3 miles is a hollow where bush lupine and beach
strawberry thrive. Continuing toward the far stand of trees, you
encounter dense vegetation. You might want to detour left to
find bare sand for easier walking.

At 3¾ miles a big barn lies to your east. Steer wide of it,
because it is surrounded by an electric fence. Continue past the
left side of the trees and come to the parking lot at 4 miles.

35.
ARCATA'S REDWOOD PARK
WITH MODEL COMMUNITY FOREST

*Few city parks have enough trails to be included in hiking guides,
but this is no ordinary city park. Redwood Park and Community
Forest include 600 acres on the north slope of Fickle Hill, prime
redwood-growing land. The City of Arcata acquired the land
through several purchases, starting in 1905. In 1955 it was
dedicated—the first municipally owned forest in the state of
California.*

*Today Redwood Park and Community Forest include 10 miles
of trails, many of which are available to equestrians and mountain
bikers (see map). Trails are open except when logging occurs in
a particular area. In that case the closure is posted. The trails are*

ARCATA'S REDWOOD PARK:

DISTANCE: 6⅛ mile loop.

TIME: Two to 4 hours.

TERRAIN: Up and down steep canyons of a north-slope redwood forest.

ELEVATION GAIN/LOSS: 1200 feet+/1200 feet-.

BEST TIME: Anytime.

WARNINGS: Bikes and horses restricted (see map).

DIRECTIONS TO TRAILHEAD: Exit Highway 101 at Arcata on north at Sunset Avenue (M.87.2), on south at Samoa exit (M.85.5). Go east on 11th Street (hikers) or 14th Street (bikers: Meadow Trailhead), following signs to Redwood Park. Main parking area is at end of road.

FURTHER INFO: City of Arcata (707) 822-5953 or 822-3619.

OTHER SUGGESTION: AZALEA STATE RESERVE provides a mile of trails through dense stands of fragrant azalea in spring. Exit McKinleyville South at M.89.8 from south, M.90.1 from north, and go east on North Bank Road.

well used by the residents of Arcata, being no more than a ten-minute walk from downtown or Humboldt State University.

The city is striving to create a model forest. All logging is done to strict environmental standards. Low-impact, balloon-tired vehicles are used. Sustained-yield timber harvesting is the law here. The enhancement of wildlife, watershed and aesthetic values of the forest is a primary goal. Proceeds from logging support recreational facilities in the city.

The loop described below samples the best of the trail system in the park. Since bikers and equestrians are not allowed on the first ¾ mile of trail, they should use the Meadow Trailhead, where 14th Street enters the park.

The parking area is at the end of 13th Street, where a grassy field has picnic tables and other facilities. Look across the field to a sign, "Redwood Park Trails." Climb the steps by the sign and enter a forest of redwood and Sitka spruce. Your trail climbs through the forest. At ⅛ mile you encounter the first of many

133

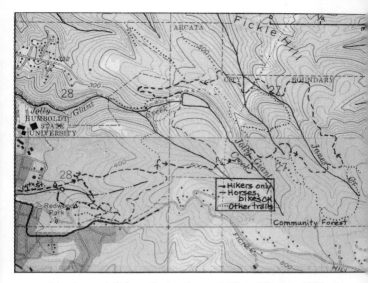

big stumps left from the logging activities of the late 1800s. In 200 feet, a canyon lies on the left. The trail climbs along its edge.

In 300 feet the Short Trail forks right. You return by it at the end of the described hike. Now go left on the Nature Trail. Descend across two small bridges. Go left on a bridge over tiny Campbell Creek, climbing steps on the other side.

You soon descend again, passing a huge stump at ⅜ mile. Go down the steps and recross the creek. The trail descends along Campbell Creek. Cross a bridge over a side canyon and come to a boardwalk at ½ mile. You cross a second boardwalk and come to a junction.

The end of the Nature Trail is on the left, but our described trail goes right on the Sitka Trail. It descends over boardwalks and bridges to recross Campbell Creek. You can see the old skid, or corduroy, road in the creek bed. Imagine a dozen oxen pulling a giant log down the creek. The trail climbs gradually to some rest benches at ⅝ mile. Descend to meet the Meadow Trail before ¾ mile. A picnic table sits by the junction. People on horses or bikes should come up the hill to meet the trail here, just ⅛ mile from 14th Street.

From the junction, climb the steep hill to the ¾-mile point, where you go right and continue a moderate climb. You are heading east along the north boundary of Redwood Park. The trail steepens at ⅞ mile, then continues its steady climb beyond one mile. The trail levels briefly in a clearing where redwood violets and other wildflowers grow. You climb gradually to the next junction.

Beyond 1⅛ miles you meet two dirt roads. The second one is Fickle Hill Grade. (You can turn right for a shorter hike of 2 miles.) Go left and head north, passing the Big Rock Trail at 1¼ miles. Follow Fickle Hill Grade as it veers right and heads east, descending slightly. Red-flowering currant, trillium, coltsfoot and iris grow along the trail. Berries include elder-, salmon- and thimbleberries. You climb gradually again from 1⅜ miles.

At 1½ miles you cross a fork of Jolly Giant Creek, then climb steeply to a junction. Fickle Hill Grade ends here, but you continue on the same road surface, now called Community Forest Loop Road. You pass under the power line and climb through an area planted with young trees. Descend to cross Jolly Giant Creek at 1¾ miles.

After the creek you climb north. The trail levels at a junction with the Ridge Road. (You can go left on Community Forest Loop for a shorter hike of 4½ miles.) Our described route goes right on Ridge Road and climbs, passing a spur on the right, then one on the left. After a steep hill, you meet the Upper Janes Creek Trail on the left, which you follow. (You can go right for a loop one mile longer.)

The Upper Janes Creek Trail climbs for 250 feet, then levels. Cross a boardwalk and descend through a swampy area where skunk cabbage thrive. After a brief climb, you descend toward Janes Creek. You come to another swampy area at 2¼ miles and promptly cross tiny Janes Creek. The trail switches left and climbs above the creek. Wild ginger and deer fern thrive in the moist habitat. At 2⅜ miles you switchback right and climb steeply through healthy second-growth forest.

Meet Janes Creek Road at 2½ miles. Turn left and climb through an area recently planted with redwood and Douglas fir seedlings. In 250 feet you reach the summit of your hike, 900 feet in elevation. If you are tired, it might please you to know that most of the return hike is downhill. Descend generally north. Violets, irises and trilliums brighten the path in spring.

You pass several small clearcut areas. Beyond 3⅛ miles your trail descends generally west, with views of the coast north of Arcata. The sunny clearings along the road provide an ample harvest of berries in summer: red and black huckleberries, blackberries, thimbleberries, salmonberries, salal berries, currants and Oregon grapes.

At 3⅜ miles you meet the power line cut and descend a steep hill. After you cross Janes Creek, the Lower Janes Creek Trail branches left. Your trail leaves the clearing, crosses a feeder creek, bends right and climbs for ⅛ mile. The trail levels and meets the Vista Road at 3¾ miles. Go left on Janes Creek Road and descend a steep hill. The road then climbs briefly to end at the junction with the Community Forest Loop Road.

You head straight (west). After passing a large water tank, the road descends past the California Trail at 4 miles. Continue a gradual descent, with private houses on the right. On your left is the canyon of Jolly Giant Creek. Your track bends left at 4¼ miles and descends into the canyon. At an unmarked junction you veer left and head east. (The right fork leads to the HSU campus.)

The trail climbs along Jolly Giant Creek for ⅛ mile, then crosses the earth-fill dam of an old reservoir. Ascend through the forest to the Big Rock Cutoff Trail at 4½ miles (hikers can go right for a shorter but steeper route). The Community Forest Loop Road climbs for over ¼ mile before it tops a hill and descends to Fickle Hill Grade at 4⅞ miles.

Turn right and retrace your steps of the early part of the hike, descending to the Meadow Trail at 5¼ miles. Bikers and equestrians should descend the Meadow Trail to the starting point. Hikers stay on Fickle Hill Grade, climbing for 150 feet before descending in a big loop around the lush headwaters of Campbell Creek.

The descent steepens at 5⅜ miles. At 5½ miles you descend gradually around a big bend left, where grand fir mixes with the redwoods. At 5⅝ miles you climb briefly, coming to a water tank, then to Fickle Hill Road. Immediately veer right onto the Short Trail and descend through the forest.

You join the Nature Trail Loop at 5⅞ miles. Go left, returning to the parking area at 6⅛ miles.

36.

ARCATA MARSH AND WILDLIFE SANCTUARY
RESTORED WETLANDS PROVIDE FINE BIRDING

In 1979 the City of Arcata created its Marsh and Wildlife Sanctuary, reclaiming the area along South I Street that had become an industrial wasteland left over from the post-World War II logging boom. The Sanctuary, considered a model wetlands restoration project, serves as an integral part of Arcata's waste water treatment system.

The city built three freshwater marshes and a lake at the site. They planted the marshes with sedge, sago pondweed and ditch grass, and stocked the lake with rainbow trout. Today the 154 acres of wetlands are a haven for some 200 bird species. Amateur birders will find the Saturday morning walks led by local Audubon Society members a wonderful introduction to the birds of the Sanctuary. Salmon and trout raised in the wetlands are used to stock local creeks.

Each year over 100,000 visitors enjoy the many aspects of nature in the Arcata Marsh and Wildlife Sanctuary by

136

birdwatching, walking, jogging, fishing, boating and picnicking—all within seven blocks of downtown Arcata.

The trail starts beneath pines at the south end of the parking area at the end of I Street. You can see the rotting pilings of the Arcata Wharf, built in 1855, which extended 1½ miles into Humboldt Bay. The trail passes the restroom, heading southeast. The shore of Klopp Lake is on the left, the mudflats of Humboldt Bay on your right. At high tide the mudflats are submerged, but at low tide they are busy with feeding dowitchers, curlews, godwits, willets, egrets, herons, sanderlings and sandpipers. On the lake float surf scoters, cormorants, coots and various gulls (seven or more species) and ducks. Pass benches on your left facing the lake.

At ¼ mile your path bends left. The mouth of Butcher Slough lies on your right, with the sewage treatment plant in the background. The first fork is at ⅜ mile. The path on the left leads to an observation hill overlooking the lake. You continue on the main path, which comes to a "T" intersection at ½ mile. A tree in the salt marsh before you is a common place to spot black-shouldered kites. Marsh wrens also live in the marsh.

Turn left and head west, with the salt-water marsh on your right. You soon come to a fork, where you go straight. (The trail on the left heads onto the rise with scattered Monterey pines and bird blinds.) The main trail comes to a dike at ⅝ mile, which separates the salt-water marsh you have been walking along from the freshwater Allen Marsh ahead.

Your trail gradually bends right and heads northwest, drawing nearer to the freshwater marsh, a great place to spot ducks. Seen here in one day were mallard, pintail, cinnamon teal, shoveler and bufflehead. A bird blind sits facing the freshwater marsh at ¾ mile. In the willow trees along the marsh's western edge usually rest at least two dozen black-crowned night her-

137

ARCATA MARSH AND WILDLIFE SANCTUARY:

DISTANCE: 2-mile loop.

TIME: At least one hour. It is easy to spend hours here when the birdwatching is good.

TERRAIN: Mostly level around fresh- and salt-water marshlands.

BEST TIME: Audubon-led walks every Saturday at 8:30 a.m. Low tides in spring and fall best for birding.

WARNINGS: Open sunrise to sunset. Be quiet along the trail, or you may be the target of a bird watcher's wrath. Quiet dogs on leash only please.

DIRECTIONS TO TRAILHEAD: Exit Highway 101 at M.86.2 from north, M.85.5 from south onto Highway 255 going west. Turn left on I Street. Go one mile to parking area at end of road.

FURTHER INFO: Audubon Society (707) 822-6918. City of Arcata: (707) 822-5951.

OTHER SUGGESTION: The new ARCATA MARSH INTERPRETIVE CENTER (.4 mile south of Samoa Blvd. on G Street, wheelchair accessible, open afternoons daily) provides detailed educational displays about the environments of the marshes and the systems at work there. Open: ARCATA ARCHITECTURAL TOUR: A morning of birding might well be followed by an afternoon of touring fine old Victorian buildings. Maps of the self-guided tour are available at the Chamber of Commerce, 1062 G Street, (707) 822-3619.

ons. You come to a parking area on the paved road. If you take the footpath on the left, it returns to the main parking area for a one-mile loop.

For a longer walk, go right, paralleling the paved road. From this path you can see the freshwater Gearheart Marsh on the left and Allen Marsh on the right. Along the edges of these marshes you may see black phoebes and song and savannah sparrows. Overhead you may spot a belted kingfisher, osprey, harrier (marsh hawk), or, with luck, a peregrine falcon searching for dinner.

You come to the end of the freshwater marshes and cross the railroad tracks, one mile from the trailhead. In 300 feet go right on the Jolly Giant/Butcher Slough Swamp Trail. It crosses a bridge over Butcher Slough, the tidal portion of Jolly Giant

Creek (which you crossed if you hiked in the Community Forest). Go right at the fork, along the dike between Butcher Slough on your right and the recently restored swamp habitat on your left. On the elevated dike you have an overview of the entire Arcata Marsh and Wildlife Sanctuary. As you proceed south on the dike, the swamp turns to marsh, then to deeper open water. The changes provide varied habitat for the young salmon and trout raised in the city's aquaculture program.

The path veers left at the end of the pond, crosses a bridge, and goes right, paralleling G Street. At 1½ miles you come to the parking area for the trail to the marsh pilot project and oxidation ponds. Although this loop is not included in the described trail, you can cross the tracks and go left to add about 2½ miles and more opportunities for birding (100 species of birds have been spotted on the ponds or their marshy edges).

Our described trail crosses the tracks and veers right, crossing a bridge over Butcher Slough and joining the first loop at the ½-mile point. You then head west and northwest before taking the path that veers left and heads south near the shore of freshwater Hauser Marsh. You return to the parking lot beside Klopp Lake at 2 miles.

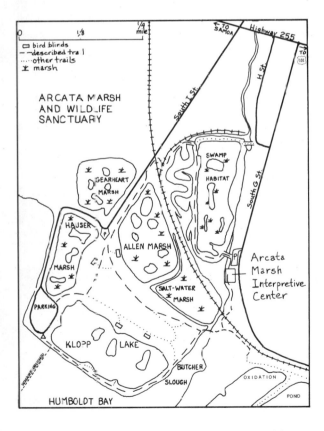

37

ELK RIVER
WILDLIFE REFUGE

BIRDS AND WILDFLOWERS WITHIN CITY LIMITS

Elk River is Humboldt Bay's largest tributary. In 1984, after years of farming and industrial development, the City of Eureka restored 100 acres of riparian and marsh habitat near its waste-water treatment plant on the east side of the estuary. Like the Arcata Marsh (see Trail #36), the restored area is open to hiking and bird-watching. It provides a natural habitat amidst the industrial development of Eureka.

The trail heads south from the parking area, following an old railroad grade. On your right is the Elk River estuary, with a large sand spit on its west side. On the left is the Eureka Wastewater Treatment Plant. The trail crosses open grasslands sprinkled with wildflowers in spring and summer.

At ⅛ mile your trail veers left and runs along the fence of the treatment plant. You pass through a stand of willow, wax myrtle and alder, the only tall shrubs in the area. By ¼ mile a marsh lies on the left of the trail. Ducks often take flight as you approach the marsh. Beach strawberry, buttercup, poppy, owl's clover, low-growing ceanothus and Pacific silverweed grow along the trail. Side trails on your left lead to the marsh.

The main trail passes through a thicket of coastal scrub, then

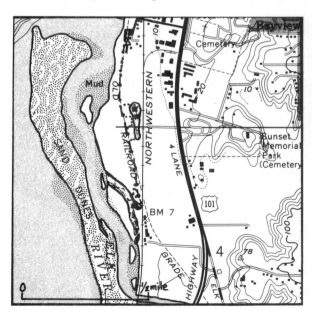

DISTANCE: 1¼ miles round trip.

TIME: At least one hour.

TERRAIN: Level ground surrounded by marsh and estuary.

BEST TIME: Spring and early summer for wildflowers. Anytime is good.

WARNINGS: Do not trespass on adjacent private lands. No firearms, vehicles or camping. Pets on leash only.

DIRECTIONS TO TRAILHEAD: Turn west off Highway 101 onto Hilfiker Lane (south end of Eureka at M.75.4). Go .5 mile to parking area to right of entrance to Wastewater Treatment Plant.

FURTHER INFO: City of Eureka (707) 445-3037.

OTHER SUGGESTION: PALCO MARSH (turn west off Highway 101 onto Del Norte Street at M.76.8 and go .4 mile to parking on left) provides more trails at the city's edge. A ¼-mile loop explores the bay shore; a longer trail just east of the railroad tracks explores the edge of a freshwater marsh. FORT HUMBOLDT STATE HISTORIC PARK is ¼ mile north of Hilfiker Lane on the east side of Highway 101. The fort was established in 1853 to control raids by local Indians. Today there is a small museum, picnic area and wheelchair-accessible restrooms. Call (707) 445-6567.

returns to grasslands, where an old-fashioned rose grows on the right. Look west as you leave the scrub to see the Coast Guard headquarters near the mouth of Humboldt Bay. Beyond ⅜ mile more spurs fork left to the marsh which supports an abundance of cattails.

Just before ½ mile, a final side trail leads to the marsh in 200 feet. Your trail draws beside the river estuary beyond ½ mile, where lupine and yellow and white johnny tuck grow in spring. Much bird life can be seen here, including ducks, egrets and herons in the estuary. Osprey, kites, hawks and northern harriers often hunt overhead.

Your trail veers left as the vegetation is dominated by salt-tolerant plants like cordgrass, pickleweed, hairgrass and northern dune tansy. Two big driftwood logs here make pleasant picnic spots. The trail ends at the railroad tracks at ⅝ mile. Return by the same trail to the parking area.

38

TABLE BLUFF COUNTY PARK
BEACH/DUNE WALK TO MOUTH OF EEL RIVER

The Wiyot tribe inhabited the coastal lowlands from Mad River on the north to the tidelands of Eel River on the south. The tribe came from the Algonkian family, the dominant linguistic group of eastern and central North American native peoples. But their customs followed the Yurok pattern in houses, baskets, canoes and the use of dentalium money.

The Wiyots had two settlements at Table Bluff on the south end of Humboldt Bay—Yachwanawach and Legetku. Legetku was located near the trailhead of this hike. In these villages salt-water fishing and clam digging provided the main food sources. Hunting was of little consequence. Today an Indian rancheria is located on Table Bluff.

In the 1850s settlers, attracted by the rich soil of the bluff, established a small agricultural community, and farming continues today. A lighthouse built on Table Bluff in 1892 served ships entering Humboldt Bay until 1972. From atop Table Bluff on a clear day, one has fine vistas north to Humboldt Bay and south to the Eel River delta. The persistent winds make the 170-foot cliff at Table Bluff a popular spot for hang gliding.

There is no trail for this hike, just a 4 ¼-mile-long sand spit between the ocean and the tidal marshlands of the Eel River. The easiest walking is generally on the hard damp sand near the tide line. But the most interesting part of the area lies in the low dunes east of the beach, near McNulty Slough and North Bay. This is the Eel River Wildlife Area. The described hike follows the beach south and returns through the dunes. You can vary the hike as you prefer.

From the base of Table Bluff, jeep trails lead south through the dunes. Follow the main jeep track for ⅛ mile to the westernmost point of the bluff. Then veer toward the beach on a narrower track that drops to the beach at ¼ mile. The best walking is on the hard sand near the tide line.

Follow the dark sand beach south for at least 2 miles to get to the bays, sloughs and estuaries, the best features here. Beyond 2 miles large stacks of driftwood are along the high tide line. It is just over 4 miles to the mouth of the Eel River. A colony of harbor seals lives on the beach at the river's mouth. The Eel is a reasonable destination for a full-day hike. But keep in mind that walking in soft sand is tiring and that your return hike will probably be against the wind.

Whether you go 2, 3 or 4 miles on the sand spit, head east to explore the low dunes and the shore of North Bay. The dunes shelter beach strawberry, yellow sand verbena, northern dune tansy, sea rocket, bush lupine, purple seaside daisy, silky beach pea and beach morning glory.

Hike back just east of the ridge of the tallest dune where you can find some protection from the wind. Even without a trail, the route provides good walking on mostly hard-packed sand. A four-wheel-drive track winds through the dunes to your east. Its generally loose sand makes poor walking.

One mile north of the river, the mouth of Mosley Slough lies to the east. In another mile you reach the north end of North Bay. It breaks into McNulty and Hawk Sloughs, which swing to the northeast and east, respectively. As you walk through the dunes, you may scare out a black-tailed jack rabbit, the most abundant mammal in Eel River Wildlife Area.

In the 2 miles before Table Bluff, the route along the sand ridge becomes vague. Take your choice of dune, beach or four-

wheel track. As long as you head for the left side of Table Bluff, you cannot go wrong.

CENTERVILLE BEACH

Five miles west of Ferndale is four-acre Centerville Beach County Park, providing access to 9 miles of ocean beach. You can walk north to the mouth of the Eel River or south toward False Cape. Dairy farms back the wild beach in the north, steep cliffs in the south. The original stagecoach road from Ferndale to Petrolia, completed in 1871, went through Centerville, followed the beach south before climbing steeply along Oil Creek Ridge, then descended to Capetown.

Today Centerville Beach is open to four-wheel-drive vehicles, so you may have to share the beach and dunes with the whine of gas-powered engines, especially on weekends. But the wild beach can absorb many people and machines before feeling crowded.

39.
CENTERVILLE BEACH NORTH
MORE DUNES AND ESTUARIES BY THE EEL

For walking north along the broad beach from the county park, the best path lies along the firm, moist sand near the tide line. East of the steep wave slope, a flat expanse of sand is riddled with 4-wheel-drive tracks. Low dunes lie east of the tracks.

As you walk north, you pass several driftwood sculptures around ¾ mile. At one mile the beach broadens. From 1½ to 1¾ miles, the lower part of the beach is so steep you cannot see the dunes for the sand bank.

Beyond 2 miles a more gradual slope lies between tide line and dunes. Sandpipers scurry along the water's edge. Cormorants, seagulls and pelicans glide above the surf. Harbor seals may peer curiously from the breakers. On a clear day you can see the abrupt rise of Table Bluff to the north.

The beach cuts in to the east at 3 miles, then cuts in even farther at 3¾ miles, where the westernmost dune is only 200 feet from the surf. The dunes stretch north to Table Bluff. A vast wild area of grasslands and marshes lies to the east. To the northeast is the Eel River, with farms along its shore.

The dunes east of the beach are lower after 4 miles. At 4⅝ miles the last high dune lies to the east. At 5½ miles you come

CENTERVILLE BEACH—NORTH AND SOUTH:

DISTANCE: North: up to 11¼ miles round trip.
    South: up to 6¾ miles round trip, depending on tide.
TIME: North: full day. South: 3 to 4 hours.
TERRAIN: Mostly level beach and dune walking.
BEST TIME: Low to medium tide. Spring for wildflowers.
WARNINGS: Heed tide warnings on south hike; do not get
    trapped by the rising tide. Watch for rogue waves as you walk
    the beach. Watch for off-road vehicle traffic.
DIRECTIONS TO TRAILHEAD: Leave Highway 101 at Ferndale
    exit M.64.5 on north, M.62.9 on south. Cross Fernbridge and
    go west 5 miles through town. At south end of Main Street
    turn right and go 5 miles to Centerville Beach parking lot.
FURTHER INFO: County Parks (707) 445-7652.

Centerville Beach North:

Centerville Beach South:

to the mouth of the Eel River. Fresh water surges into the ocean here. At high tide, the flow may be reversed. A colony of harbor seals living on the sand bank at the mouth are in prime position to feed on the salmon and steelhead that enter the Eel to spawn.

For the return hike, follow the shore of the Eel River to its confluence with the Salt River in ¼ mile. Then follow the Salt River south, passing the high dune at ⅞ mile. As you walk upriver, the extent and variety of vegetation increases. Beach morning glory and dune grass dominate.

At one mile from the mouth of the Eel, you come to two redwood stumps on the shore of the Salt River, the larger stump being about eight feet in diameter. Imagine virgin redwood forest extending this close to the mouth of the Eel. In fact, when the first settlers came to Ferndale in 1852, redwood forest covered much of the delta. Some trees were said to be over 400 feet tall. Most of the trees were cut by the 1870s. Barnacles growing on the base of the redwood stump indicate that this land is too wet and brackish to grow redwoods today, suggesting that either this land has sunk since the trees were alive or the river level has risen.

At 1⅛ miles the Salt River estuary splits. Follow the right fork

(Cutoff Slough) for ⅛ mile until it splits. Then follow a jeep track along the dry (except at high tide and after heavy rains) channel veering right. At 1½ miles the road splits; take the right fork. It gets sandy, then veers left through loose sand to join a broader track at 1⅝ miles. This heads southwest, then veers back toward Centerville Bluff at 1¾ miles. Dune tansy, beach morning glory, yellow sand verbena and other flowers line your route.

At 2 miles a sign to your east marks a gun club. Egrets and great blue herons congregate beyond the sign. In winter many tundra swans live in these wetlands. From 2¼ miles your route follows an arm of Cutoff Slough. Before 2½ miles your path splits; stay left unless you want to return to the beach. At 2⅝ miles you come to a level, grassy area, then climb onto a levee near a high dune. Head west from here through the dunes to avoid private property surrounding the barn ahead.

After you pass the barn, 3 miles from the Eel River mouth, you can continue on the beach or return to the east edge of the dunes, staying west of private property signs. Pacific silverweed, with bright yellow flowers, and lupine grow along the base of the dunes. You approach another barn at 4 miles. Stay west of the barn and fence at 4⅜ miles.

At 4½ miles your path veers right. Trudge through loose sand near the top of the first dune. You may want to return to the beach here because the last mile through the dunes leads through loose sand and an impromptu dune buggy park ¾ mile from the parking area. Come to the parking lot at the county park 5¾ miles from the mouth of the Eel.

40

CENTERVILLE BEACH SOUTH
TOWARD FALSE CAPE

You can walk the beach south from Centerville Beach County Park as well as north. This hike is recommended at a low tide of -1.0 foot or lower.

Head south along a beach of pebbly salt-and-pepper sand. From ¼ mile, sandstone cliffs rise to the high bluffs. A stone cross at ⅜ mile memorializes the wreck of the steam schooner *Northerner*. In 1869, en route to the Columbia River, it hit an uncharted rock off Cape Mendocino. Attempting to reach Humboldt Bay, it started sinking off Centerville Beach. Though hundreds of local people came to Centerville to help in the rescue efforts, 38 of the 108 passengers were lost in the stormy seas.

At ½ mile the cliffs rise 240 feet above the beach. At ⅝ mile wire cables descend to the beach from the Naval Oceanography Station on the bluff. Just 250 feet beyond, layers of gray and orange sandstone protrude to the surf. You must have a minus tide in order to continue.

There are two more narrow spots on the beach at the base of soft cliffs of gray sandstone between ¾ and ⅞ mile. Come to the mouth of Fleener Creek at 1⅛ miles. Cattle graze on the grass above the beach.

Walking south, you follow the base of more sculpted gray cliffs. At 1½ miles they reach their highest point, towering nearly 500 feet above the beach. A small waterfall drops 20 feet to the beach at 1¾ miles. Then the beach broadens at the base of a slide area.

Before 2¼ miles you come to a protruding high point, where progress south is blocked at tides higher than -1.0 foot. Do not pass this point unless the tide is low enough and is still ebbing, or else you will not be able to get back around it on your return trip. You may get wet feet even if you wait for a break in the waves. The high cliffs taper to 2⅜ miles where you come to Guthrie Creek.

The mouth of the creek is jammed with driftwood. You can find a sheltered spot for a picnic among the logs. A small lagoon lies between the cliffs at the mouth of the creek. Upstream Guthrie Creek is mostly wooded, unlike the pastures of Fleener Creek.

Just ¼ mile beyond Guthrie Creek, another shelf of gray sandstone protrudes to the surf. You must climb over slippery rocks to proceed. At a tide of -1.0 foot you are able to walk ¾ mile beyond Guthrie Creek. Even that involves scrambling over several areas of slippery rock.

The route south beyond 3⅜ miles is safely passable only at the lowest tides of the year: -1.5 feet or lower. An immense slide of mucky mud that now blocks the route north of Oil Creek may be impassable. Oil Creek is 4⅜ miles from the trailhead. Beyond it, the steep promontory of False Cape rises 600 feet. Offshore lie False Cape Rocks, a rookery for several thousand common murres, pigeon guillemots, Brandt's cormorants and western gulls.

On your return hike, be sure to leave time to get around the protruding rocks 2¼ miles from the county park before the tide comes in.

41.

RUSS PARK

VERDANT WILDERNESS IN A CITY PARK

Ferndale (founded 1852, population 1402) has remained largely unchanged since the 1890s. Dozens of well-preserved Victorian buildings can be found around town. This haven for artists has many galleries and craft shops along Main Street.

Russ Park lies within the city limits. The 105-acre primitive park has over 50 species of plants and 65 species of birds during various times of the year. The park's 2 ½ miles of trails lead through dense vegetation on the steep terrain. It feels more like a wildlife and plant sanctuary than a typical city park.

Zipporah Patrick Russ, an early settler, donated Russ Park to the city in 1920 "as a park. . .and a refuge and breeding place for birds."

From the parking area, the Lytel Ridge Trail climbs south into the forest. At 200 feet you come to a wooden trail map. The park's lone picnic table sits on the right. Continue steeply uphill through dense vegetation, passing large Sitka spruce and bigleaf maples. Salmonberry and red elderberry tower overhead. Ascend gradually as your trail bends left.

By ¼ mile you climb steadily south again. Then your climb eases, passing through dense thimbleberry thickets. As the path levels briefly, go left at a fork. Your trail winds, climbing again at ⅜ mile. In 200 feet go left at another fork. (Take the right fork for a shorter hike to Zipporah's Pond.)

You climb to ½ mile, where the trail tops a ridge and forks into three paths. The two paths on the right are rather overgrown.

DISTANCE: 2⅛-mile double loop.

TIME: At least 2 hours.

TERRAIN: Climbs a steep, lush coastal ridge from bottom to top, then returns.

ELEVATION GAIN/LOSS: Full double loop: 700 ft+/700 ft-. Lytel Ridge/Bluff Loop only: 460 feet+/460 feet-.

BEST TIME: Spring is heavenly. Summer and fall good too.

WARNINGS: No motor vehicles or bikes allowed. Open 6 a.m. to dusk. Watch for poison oak and nettles. Trails are slippery and muddy after rain. Steep terrain; take it easy.

DIRECTIONS TO TRAILHEAD: Exit Highway 101 at Ferndale (M.64.5 from north, 62.9 from south). Cross Fernbridge and go west 5 miles through town. At south end of Main Street go left on Ocean Street. It is .75 mile to Russ Park. Dirt parking on right.)

FURTHER INFO: City of Ferndale (707) 786-4224.

OTHER SUGGESTION: FERNDALE WALKING ARCHITECTURAL TOUR is a self-guided tour of the city's fine Queen Anne, Eastlake, Gothic Revival and Italianate style buildings. Maps are available at the Ferndale Museum, 515 Shaw Ave. (707) 786-4466.

The right fork leads to Zipporah's Pond and the Bluff Creek Trail. You can follow it now if you prefer a shorter loop of 1⅜ miles. The described trail takes the left fork to make the ¾-mile Francis Creek Loop, which will return to this point by the center path.

The left fork contours southeast along a ridge. On your right is a steep, wooded canyon. The left side of the trail is covered with false lily of the valley and Douglas iris. As your trail bends to the right, you climb steeply. At ⅝ mile you veer right again and the climb eases.

The trail forks in 300 feet. The left fork climbs to the highest point in the park, a grassy knob in its southeast corner (elevation 660 feet) with views across the flood plain of the Eel River. The main trail is the right fork. It contours to the ridge in 200 feet. Follow the ridge, descending gradually to ¾ mile, then more steeply.

The trail switches north, then returns to the ridge briefly as you descend by several more switchbacks. Beyond ⅞ mile you leave the ridge for good, descending north, then northeast. Watch out for uneven footing on this section.

At one mile you are descending into a shady canyon. You pass a grand fir eight feet in diameter. Then switchback left on a fern-shrouded section of trail. As you turn left again, the path heads down the center of the canyon. In just 100 feet you come to a fork. Straight ahead, the trail to Francis Creek quickly comes to private property. Take the right fork, climbing gradually northwest. Watch for poison oak here.

The trail switchbacks to the right before 1⅛ miles, climbing through sword ferns by several more switchbacks. At one of these bends grows a western redcedar two feet in diameter. This represents the southern reach of its range. In Washington, where it is a major forest tree, it reaches heights of 200 feet. Climb more switchbacks to complete the Francis Creek Loop at 1¼ miles.

Now take the fork on your left. The overgrown trail climbs to overlook green Zipporah's Pond. The trail bends right and

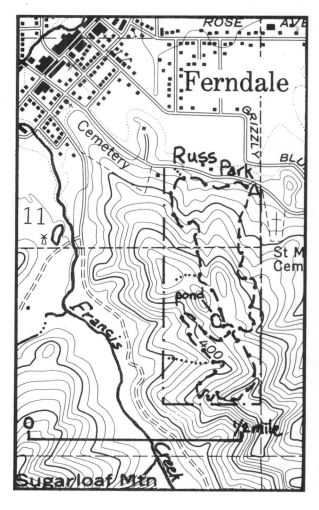

descends to the shore in 100 feet. You may smell the giant skunk cabbage at the pond before you see them.

The pond nestles in a hollow in the Sitka spruce forest. Skunk cabbage grows in the shallows. The entire surface of the pond is covered with duckweed. This is a special spot, very tranquil, with only the chirp and buzz of birds and insects. Sedge, ferns, coastal manroot, morning glory and alder line the shore. Berries include evergreen and red huckleberry, thimbleberry, salmonberry and red elderberry.

Take the trail heading north along the shore of the pond. On the north shore is William Crane Grove. The grand fir Sitka spruce and alder are native; the redwoods were planted as seedlings and watered by hand for years. The grove makes a wonderful picnic spot. Please keep it clean!

The trail continues north, climbing a hill and passing scotch broom 15 feet tall. At a fork, the path on the left leads to a point where the village of Ferndale lies 500 feet below like a storybook town. Continuing on the main trail, you soon descend steeply. Watch for rough spots in the trail. At 1½ miles the descent eases briefly. Star solomon seal and holly grow along the trail. You soon come to a fence on your right. Behind it is a steep drop into Bluff Creek Canyon.

The trail descends moderately steeply, winding through dense salal and sword ferns. It levels briefly, then makes a side hill descent into the canyon. Watch out for stinging nettles growing tall along this section of trail. Watch your step, too; the dense vegetation may obscure the uneven tread on this steep descent. Descend through dense vegetation at 1¾ miles. Native hazel bushes arch gracefully overhead. Elderberry, thimbleberry and nettle also tower above you in season. Ripe salmonberries may be found as early as April, as late as August.

The trail switchbacks left, then right, as it becomes steep and slippery. At 1⅞ miles you enter a fragrant eucalyptus grove. In 100 feet a trail on the left leads to the road but not to the parking area. (You can exit the park here if you walked from town.) The main trail veers right, climbs through a moist area and back into spruce forest at 2 miles. Descend through another salmonberry patch, then level in spruce forest again. Descend by rough steps, then descend steeply without steps. As you head uphill again, watch for poison oak. You descend steeply into a dense brush thicket and break out into the parking area at 2⅛ miles.

42

CAPE MENDOCINO

DRIVE AND BEACH WALK

Cape Mendocino rises dramatically from the Pacific to its 1200-foot summit in less than a mile. The sparsely settled, windblown cape is the westernmost point of land in California. (A widely believed untruth says it is the westernmost point in the continental U.S., but Cape Flattery in Washington extends ten miles farther west.) The prominent cape and its hazardous, rock-strewn coast were first charted in 1543 by the crew of the Manila galleons of Cabrillo's expedition, returning from the Philippines to Mexico with silk and other oriental treasures. Appropriately, they dubbed it Cabo de Fortunas—Stormy Cape or Cape of Perils. It was given its present name in the 1580s in honor of the viceroy of New Spain, Lorenzo Suarez de Mendoza.

The rugged cape has been a major landmark for coastal navigators ever since. The wind-whipped waters off the cape are among the most dangerous in the Pacific Ocean, with rocks, reefs and shoals often shrouded in dense fog. Although a lighthouse was established on Cape Mendocino in 1868, more than 200 shipwrecks off its shore took dozens of lives from 1850 to 1950. The Japanese Navy torpedoed an American steamship off the cape in 1941, claiming five lives.

Nearly all the steep, rolling grasslands of Cape Mendocino are privately owned, but a paved public road leaves from Ferndale on the north (or Honeydew on the south) to explore the remote ridges, valleys and coastline. The 28 miles from Ferndale to Petrolia lack towns, lodgings or gas stations; they provide some of the most lovely pastoral scenes in California. You have the bonus of access to a wild 4 miles of beach south of Cape Mendocino.

DISTANCE: Drive: 66 miles Ferndale to Petrolia to South Fork.
Beach hike: 8 miles or more round trip.

TIME: Drive: Plan 4 hours minimum. Beach hike: up to 5
hours.

TERRAIN: Steep winding drive with access to a wild, wind-
swept beach.

BEST TIME: Spring; fall is next best.

WARNINGS: Drive slowly and enjoy the scenery. Walking on
the beach, watch for oversized waves and do not get cut off
by the rising tide. Do not trespass on adjacent private
property.

DIRECTIONS TO TRAILHEAD: Take Ferndale Exit from Highway 101 (M.64.5 from north, M.62.9 from south). Follow
signs across Fernbridge and go 5 miles to south end of Main
Street. Go right on Ocean Street, then left on Mattole Road.
Description starts there.

*Just south of the hamlet of Petrolia, this route provides hiking
access to the north end of 25 miles of wilderness beach, the Lost
Coast of King Range National Conservation Area (see Trail #27).*

The Mattole Road heads south from the charming Victorian
village of Ferndale. It climbs steeply above the flat Eel River
delta. In 6 miles you come to "Malfunction Junction," where
Bear River Ridge Road forks left. You have climbed to 1800 feet.
Mattole Road winds along the ridge, passing ranches and barns.
A clearing at 7 miles affords views north to Humboldt Bay and
Trinidad Head.

After 13 miles of winding through forest and glade, your road
makes a winding descent into Bear River Valley. The rolling
hills have the look of the Scottish Highlands. Capetown Ranch,
before the river crossing, was once a stagecoach stop. Beyond
Bear River the road climbs Cape Ridge, passing a huge lily pond
west of the road.

The Mattole Road tops Cape Ridge at 980 feet, then descends
steeply, with wonderful views of the cape and the coast. You
approach sea level at the mouth of Singley Creek, ½ mile south
of the cape, 18 miles from Ferndale.

The road follows the level coast for 6 miles. For hikers, the
best all-tide access is 6 miles south at McNutt Gulch. If your visit
coincides with a low tide, the northern half of the beach may be
passable. You can reach it from the unnamed creek one mile

south of Singley Creek. Park at the north end of the bridge and walk 200 feet down the steep creek to the beach. At low tide you can walk north 1¼ miles to the foot of the cape, or south to Devil's Gate.

You can also reach the beach from three parking spots at Devil's Gate, 20 miles from Ferndale, but you need a medium tide to walk north or a low tide to go far south. Excellent tidepools in this area were rich with marine life until the April 25, 1992 earthquake. The temblor uplifted the entire coast from Cape Mendocino south to Punta Gorda up to four feet. Now the tidepools at Devil's Gate are barren, except for a few sea vegetables and turban snails. Scientists are studying how long it takes for various species to repopulate the pools.

You cross three more creeks as you drive south from Devil's

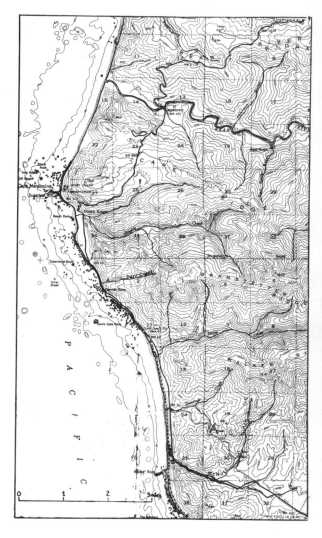

Gate. The third is McNutt Gulch, where the road turns inland to climb the gulch on its way to Petrolia. At M.23.3 (24.5 miles from Ferndale) a path leads through the fence to the dunes and beach. You can walk north for 4 miles along the beach, with inspiring views of the rugged Cape and 323-foot Sugarloaf Island. Steamboat Rock, Hell Gate and hundreds of lesser rocks provide breeding areas for seabirds and Steller sea lions. From the McNutt Gulch trail, you can also walk south for up to 3 miles, depending on the tide.

Continuing on Mattole Road, you enter Petrolia in 5 miles. A store and cafe offer provisions, while a steepled church and an old wooden schoolhouse add charm to this pastoral hamlet named for California's first oil boom. Occurring in the 1860s, the boom died after little success.

One mile beyond the store you cross the Mattole River and come to Lighthouse Road, which provides access to the Lost Coast's 25 miles of wilderness beach (see Trail #47).

Mattole Road turns east along the river for which it is named. In 6 miles, A. W. Way County Park lies on the right on a big bend of the river. The park is truly AWAY from the cares of the world. It provides swimming and fishing in the Mattole and picnic and camp spots for reasonable fees.

If you follow Mattole Road 8 more miles, you come to the Honeydew Store, where Mattole Road and Wilder Ridge Road meet. The store, a popular local hangout, is open 9 to 5, Monday through Saturday. It is 23 miles farther on the Mattole Road to reach Highway 101 at South Fork, in the heart of Humboldt Redwoods State Park. The steep, winding road takes one hour. Or you can drive south along Wilder Ridge Road for more access to the King Range (see Trails #48 through 53).

HUMBOLDT REDWOODS
STATE PARK

Northern California's largest state park (51,315 acres) stretches along Highway 101 for 40 miles, from south of Scotia on the north, to Phillipsville on the south. Most of the park's spectacular redwood groves are accessible by car or short walks. The 33-mile-long Avenue of the Giants brings visitors through grove after grove of virgin giants. This world-famous scenic drive is highly recommended, but to experience the essence of these primeval forests, hike into the backcountry away from Highway 101. The more zealous hiker can take a full day to climb to the top of Grasshopper Peak or get a permit to sleep overnight in the backcountry at one of five trail camps in the Bull Creek basin.

43.

HIKER'S GUIDE TO
THE AVENUE OF THE GIANTS

Every year three-quarter million visitors from around the world come to see the Avenue of the Giants, but many never venture more than ¼ mile from their cars. Although they see many beautiful redwoods, they never experience the grandeur and solitude of a redwood grove away from the sounds of roaring traffic. Yet numerous trails lie along Avenue of the Giants. For further information about these trails, refer to Humboldt Redwoods Trail Guide *(revised 1992), available at the park's Visitor Center for $2.*

On the north, the Avenue of the Giants begins at the Pepperwood exit from Highway 101, at M.46.1 (if you are following the Avenue from the south, read the listings from bottom to top). Stop and pick up a free Auto Tour brochure. Pass through the tiny town of Pepperwood. Leaving town you come to the following features at the markers indicated:

M.43.8. Drury and Chaney Trail on the west side of the road. The 2¼-mile semi-loop leads through virgin forest with a lush understory of lady fern, oxalis, star solomon seal, hazel and poison oak.

M.43.6. Percy French Loop Trail on west side of road. The ½-mile loop leads to dedicated groves and the Girdled Tree.

M.43.3. Freeway access.

M.40.0. The tiny town of Redcrest.

M.39.65. Freeway access. Then the milepost markers jump to

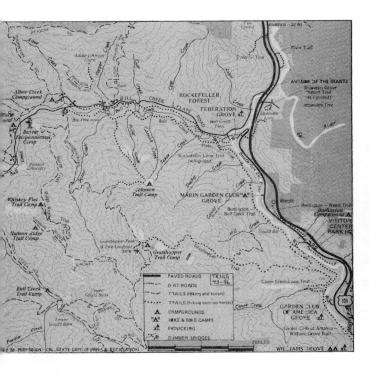

M.24.

M.22.12. Five Allens' Trail on west side of road. In its 2¼-mile round trip, the trail passes through a tunnel under the freeway and climbs 1000 feet. The trail through mixed forest provides an abundant huckleberry harvest in September.

M.20.8. Junction with Honeydew Road, which provides access to Trails #44-50, including the tremendous Rockefeller Forest. Freeway access going south.

M.20.5. Go east .1 mile to the Founder's Grove Nature Trail, one of the most beautiful and popular hikes in the park. The ½-mile loop is level enough for wheelchairs, although it gets a bit uneven on the second half. The Dyerville Giant was the tallest tree in Humboldt Redwoods State Park before it fell in 1991. Freeway access going north. Avenue of the Giants then crosses to the west side of the freeway.

M.19.6. Road on west leads to California Federation of Women's Clubs Grove, with a short trail and a picnic area. In summer a bridge crosses the river to Lower Bull Creek Flats.

M.18.4. Gravel trail on west leads into Marin Garden Club Grove, location of the hike/bike campground.

M.18.0. Road on east leads to town of Weott and to freeway.

M.17.5. Parking on west for Gould Bar—fishing and swimming.

M.16.6. Burlington Campground (year round) to the east. Between campsites 24 and 25 the Burlington Beach Trail follows

DISTANCE: Various trails from ½ mile to 6 miles in length.

TIME: Thirty minutes to all day.

TERRAIN: Varies from level to steep, all in virgin forest.

BEST TIME: Spring for wildflowers. Summer for swimming and seasonal bridges. Fall for autumn colors.

WARNINGS: Watch for poison oak, which grows extensively in Humboldt Redwoods State Park. Drive carefully and use turnouts.

DIRECTIONS TO TRAILHEAD: Avenue of the Giants leaves Highway 101 at Pepperwood (M.46.1) on the north, at Phillipsville (M.17.5) on the south. Various freeway access points in between.

FURTHER INFO: Humboldt Redwoods State Park (707) 946-2409, 445-6547.

Robinson Creek to reach the river in ¼ mile. You can fish year round (with a license) or spot wildlife at dawn or dusk. In summer the swimming is great, and a low-water bridge leads to miles of trails west of the river. Branching left off the Beach Trail is the Gould Grove Trail, which parallels the river for ⅝ mile and includes a self-guiding nature loop.

M.16.5. Humboldt Redwoods State Park Visitor Center includes a fine natural history museum and a store with postcards and nature guidebooks. Open year round.

M.15.0. Short loop trail to William Kent Grove on west.

M.14.73. Road on west leads to Garden Club of America Grove. In summer (May through September), a low-water bridge crosses the river, providing access to the beautiful Canoe Creek Trail, a 2-mile loop through virgin redwood forest in a steep stream canyon rich with wildlife. On the west side of the river, a trail north parallels the river to Bull Creek Flats (5¼ miles). The River Trail also runs south. Just north of Canoe Creek Loop, Grasshopper Trail heads west. This scenic hike climbs to Grasshopper Peak in 6 miles.

M.13.5. Road on west leads into Williams Grove, which has picnic tables and restrooms. In summer only, a bridge crosses the South Fork of the Eel and connects with the Children's

Forest Loop Trail, a 2⅜-mile round trip through both young- and old-growth forests. In one mile the Avenue of the Giants passes through the town of Myers Flat. There is access to the freeway as you pass under Highway 101 and head east.

M.11.7. Hidden Springs Campground on left (open May to September). A trail leaves from the campground and goes west to Williams Grove, 1¾ miles. A short trail to Hidden Springs Beach is opposite the campground entrance.

M.10.5. Bolling Grove, dedicated in 1921, was the first grove purchased for the park. Across Elk Creek, a short trail follows the stream.

M.6.80. Town of Miranda.

M.4.83. Freeway access.

M.2.27. Franklin Lane Grove marks the southern end of Humboldt Redwoods State Park. A short trail leads into the grove, where there is a picnic area. In one mile the road passes through Phillipsville, then passes the Chimney Tree and Hobbittown before joining Highway 101.

44.

BULL CREEK FLATS
THROUGH HEART OF IMMENSE FOREST

Bull Creek acquired its name in the 1860s as the hinterlands of Humboldt County opened to settlement. A settler who lived on the Eel River became one of the first white men to explore Bull Creek when one of his bulls wandered from the herd. He named the pristine creek hidden among immense redwoods after the animal that led him there. Bull Creek was settled in the next decade but the settlers had difficulty with raids by Indians, mountain lions and grizzly bears.

In the summer of 1917, three prominent conservationists, Madison Grant, Henry Osborn and John Merriam, drove the new Redwood Highway through Humboldt County. Camping at Bull Creek, they heard the sounds of logging filtering through the immense redwoods around them. They returned home determined to preserve the tall trees in parklands. In 1918 they established the Save-the-Redwoods League. In 1921 the League purchased its first grove, now a part of Humboldt Redwoods State Park.

John D. Rockefeller Jr. brought his family to see Bull Creek Flats in 1930. Rockefeller's two-million-dollar donation to the League in 1931, matched with state funds, purchased 9000 acres at Bull Creek.

As logging accelerated after World War II, the headwaters of

DISTANCE: Up to 8 miles or more round trip.
TIME: One to 4 hours.
TERRAIN: Mostly level through forest of immense redwoods.
ELEVATION GAIN/LOSS: One way: 200 feet+/240 feet-. Round trip: 440 feet+/440 feet-.
BEST TIME: Spring for wildflowers. Nice anytime.
WARNINGS: Watch for poison oak.
DIRECTIONS TO TRAILHEAD: Leave Highway 101 at South Fork/Honeydew exit (M.36.1 from north, M.35.5 from south). Go west on Mattole Road to Grasshopper Road on left in 5.4 miles. Trail on left side of Grasshopper Road 250 feet from pavement.
FURTHER INFO: Humboldt Redwoods State Park (707) 946-2409, 445-6547.

Bull Creek were heavily logged. With the record rains of 1955, the creek became a raging silt- and gravel-filled torrent 300 feet wide, washing away 50 acres of Bull Creek Flats and toppling 525 trees. Such dire effects of upstream logging led to state acquisition of virtually the entire Bull Creek Basin, bringing Humboldt Redwoods State Park to its present size. Though upper Bull Creek still shows logging scars, the forest slowly recovers, aided by reforestation and stream restoration.

The following trail explores the virgin forests of Bull Creek. It provides a cool, shady respite from the heat of summer. In winter, however, the virgin forest is like an icebox, though no less beautiful. Whenever you hike it bring a sweater or heavier protection.

This description starts at the trail's west end, .2 mile west of the turnoff for Albee Creek Campground. (You may join the trail at its one-mile point by going over the all-year bridge across the creek at the Big Tree Area.) In summer a low-water bridge provides access to the east end of the trail from Lower Bull Creek Flats, allowing you to start there or make a loop with the north shore trail.

Your trailhead is on Grasshopper Road, just 250 feet south of Mattole Road. Head east beneath redwoods to ten feet in diameter. The trail meanders the flood plain along Bull Creek; sections may be wet or muddy after rains. You soon approach the cutbank above the edge of the flood plain.

At ¼ mile you climb the cutbank, now right beside the creek.

Climb to a view of the creek, then quickly drop back to the flood plain. The trail winds through forest with an understory of tanoak, huckleberry, sword fern and salal.

At ½ mile you again climb the cutbank. From a clearing near the top, you have a fine view of Bull Creek 60 feet below. On the opposite bank tower immense redwoods. Your trail then descends by seven short switchbacks to the flood plain at ¾ mile, encountering the largest trees yet.

Continue along the flat through a blowdown area where wind and age have brought down many giants. You climb over some logs and pass under and through others. Your trail meanders, encountering ever larger redwoods. Just before one mile you come to the Flatiron Tree. Its amazing shape demonstrates a leaning redwood's ability to buttress itself. This tree is seven feet thick on one side and 17 feet thick on the broad side.

Stay left and quickly come to the creek and the year-round bridge at the Big Tree Area. A picnic spot lies across the bridge. To continue along the Bull Creek Flats Trail, stay on the south side of the creek, coming to the impressive Giant Tree, at 353 feet the tallest tree in the park. Then veer right, returning to deep forest.

As you meander the level flood plain, notice the variety of plants growing on the forest floor: sword fern, bracken fern, redwood sorrel, iris, trillium, salal and calypso orchid. Some trees support healthy vines winding around their trunks— most of it is poison oak: beware!

At 1¼ miles you pass a giant redwood root ball on your left, then approach a small creek. You soon cross Squaw Creek on a rustic bridge atop a fallen log. Another 300 feet brings you to the junction with the Johnson Camp/Grasshopper Peak Trail (see Trail #45). Go left on the Bull Creek Trail.

Your path contours past a rest bench, then a burl-encrusted giant. You again approach the cutbank at 1½ miles. Notice that the trees are smaller where the ground steepens. At 2 miles you cross Miller Creek on another fallen redwood with railings. The redwood forest thins, allowing a few Douglas firs to intrude. By 2⅛ miles the forest is exclusively redwood again.

Before 2¼ miles you enter a natural clearing where two old bends of Bull Creek have been bypassed by the present creekbed. This spot makes a pleasant rest stop. The trail approaches the bank of Bull Creek before plunging back into dense forest, passing large redwoods.

At 2½ miles the trail crosses tiny Connick Creek, then follows it for a few hundred feet. As your path cuts through a blown down redwood, notice that the tree is nearly six feet in diameter here, 150 feet from its base. Our senses are easily overwhelmed by the immensity of this forest!

At 2⅞ miles pass between two redwood giants leaning on each other for support. For ½ mile the trail traverses an area where standing water collects in winter and spring. The dense forest opens up somewhat at 3⅝ miles, where sword ferns blanket the forest floor. At 3⅞ miles cross Tepee Creek. Follow the creek to its confluence with Bull Creek at 4 miles.

Now the trail becomes more difficult to follow. A steep cutbank rises on the right, with Bull Creek directly on the left. Pass along the base of a slide beside the creek. At 4¼ miles, the trail climbs a steep, gravelly slide and rises 80 feet to plunge back into the forest. It is less than one mile from the first slide to the summer bridge at Lower Bull Creek Flat, but ask about conditions before walking east from the mouth of Tepee Creek, especially in winter. Turning back at the mouth of Tepee Creek still makes an 8-mile round trip from Grasshopper Road, 6 miles from Big Tree Area.

45.

GRASSHOPPER PEAK

TREES, TIE HACKS AND VISTAS

This report follows the Johnson Camp Trail from Big Tree Area to the rustic cabins of Johnson Camp, then joins Grasshopper Road to climb Grasshopper Peak, at 3379 feet the highest point in Humboldt Redwoods State Park. We describe the shortest, most direct route to the peak, open only to hikers. If you want to ride horses or mountain bikes to the summit, follow Grasshopper Road (starts one mile to the west) for the entire trip, a longer but less steep route. A third route, the most scenic way to the peak, is accessible only in summer. It leaves from Garden Club of America Grove (see Trail #43).

To reach the peak on a day hike, leave early and take lunch and plenty of water. Plan seven to ten hours round trip for the steep hike. An overnight trip, whether you camp at Johnson or Grasshopper Camp, gives you time to linger at the summit and explore the surrounding countryside.

Park at the Big Tree Area, cross the bridge over Bull Creek and follow the trail east for ⅜ mile to the Johnson Camp Trail junction. (The mileages given at the junction are correct, not those at Bull Creek.)

Take the right fork south, starting to climb in 200 feet. You will gain 1400 feet in elevation in the 2 miles to Johnson Camp, so the climb is steady and often steep. At first you head southwest,

but by ¾ mile your trail climbs southeast. The virgin forest continues almost to the camp, but the redwoods are mostly under eight feet in diameter, sharing the forest canopy with madrone and Douglas fir.

Your trail levels briefly, then climbs gradually from one m le. At 1¼ miles you can briefly see the steep face of Grasshopper Peak ahead to the south. Continue your steady climb with occasional steep stretches until the 2-mile point. Then, after a brief downhill stretch, the trail contours, with a few short climbs. You may hear the sound of Miller Creek on your right. Veer right at 2¼ miles and head west to Johnson Camp at 2⅜ miles.

The camp sits south of the trail. Four primitive cabins cluster around a spring at the headwaters of Miller Creek. This shady spot amidst second-growth redwoods housed "tie hacks," men who split redwoods into railroad ties. It was active from about 1920 into the 1950s. Today the facilities include the four cabins, tent sites, a chemical toilet, and a redwood tub for a cool bath on a warm summer day. Mosquitoes thrive in this pleasant spot, so

GRASSHOPPER PEAK VIA JOHNSON CAMP:

DISTANCE: 10½ miles round trip from Big Tree. 13½ miles via Grasshopper Road (mountain bikes and horses). 4¾ miles round trip to Johnson Camp.

TIME: Full day or overnight.

TERRAIN: Contours through virgin forest, then climbs ridge to Johnson Camp, old road to top of peak.

ELEVATION GAIN/LOSS: Round trip to Johnson Camp: 1360 feet+/1360 feet-; to Grasshopper Peak: 3340 feet+/3340 feet-.

BEST TIME: Spring is ideal, but any clear day is good.

WARNINGS: Watch for extensive poison oak. Long, steep trail. If climbing peak as a day hike, leave early, take water and lunch. Permit required to camp at Johnson or other backcountry camps.

DIRECTIONS TO TRAILHEAD: Leave Highway 101 at South Fork/Honeydew exit (M.36.1 from north, M.35.5 from south). Go west on Mattole Road 4.5 miles to Big Tree Road on left. Mountain bikers and equestrians must use Grasshopper Road, on left at 5.4 miles.

FEES: Johnson Camp and other backcountry camps: $3/night/person.

FURTHER INFO: Humboldt Redwoods State Park (707) 946-2409, 445-6547.

be sure to bring plenty of repellent.

Do not be confused by the maze of old trails and skid roads around the camp. Your trail continues west, descending to cross a small creek, then contouring to meet Grasshopper Road at 2½ miles. (It is 4.2 miles back to Bull Creek Flats Road if you go right.)

Turn left onto the broad road and climb. At 2¾ miles you climb steeply, but most of the grade is moderate. You are halfway to the top of Grasshopper Peak (in both miles and elevation). Views open up to the west. Just beyond 3 miles, you cross another small stream that flows in winter and spring.

At 3⅜ miles your trail turns sharply left and heads northeast. Climb steadily by long switchbacks through young forest. At 3¾ miles you pass a redwood stump at least 16 feet in diameter. This and other giants here were cut 80 to 100 years ago; on some stumps you can see the springboard cuts where the fallers put planks to stand on.

Beyond 4⅛ miles a stand of virgin redwoods is alongside the road, somehow missed by the axemen. At 4⅜ miles the steadily climbing road bends right and heads straight toward the summit.

At 4½ miles you come to the best view yet. Kings Peak (4087 feet) is to the southwest. From here to the summit the soils consist of small, fractured light-color rock, just like the soils of the Kings Crest.

About 5 miles from the trailhead, you meet the turnoff to Grasshopper Camp. Bear left to the camp, right to climb the peak. It is less than ½ mile of level walking to the camp, on the border between forest and meadow. The Grasshopper Trail from Canoe Creek meets the road near the camp. (The bridge across the Eel River on that trail is summer only.) The final ¼ mile to the peak climbs only 160 feet but seems like more. You can see the lookout tower with ⅛ mile to go.

At the top, you are rewarded with a 360-degree view of forest, mountains and sea. To the southwest is Kings Crest with its peaks from right to left: Blue Slide, Shubrick, Kings, Saddle and Horse. South-southwest is a notch where you can see the ocean on a clear day. From southeast to east sit the snowy summits of the Yolla Bollys: Hull, Sanhedrin, flat-topped Black Butte, Anthony, South and North Yolla Bolly, Black Rock and Four Corners Rock, the latter almost due east. South Fork Mountain runs miles north from there. In the foreground are the vast forests of Humboldt Redwoods State Park, the Eel River and Highway 101. To the north-northwest a plume of smoke marks Eureka when it is clear enough. And to the west are several ridges and peaks which extend all the way to Cape Mendocino (beyond view).

If you are on a day hike, be sure to leave enough time to hike the 5¼ miles back to Big Tree or 6¾ miles down Grasshopper Road before dark. Luckily, it is a downhill run.

46.

SQUAW CREEK RIDGE
BACKPACKING BULL CREEK BASIN

Squaw Creek Ridge and the rest of Bull Creek Basin provide varied opportunities for day hikers, backpackers, equestrians and mountain bikers. The shortest route to Squaw Creek Ridge is described below, the first mile open only to hikers. If you want to ride horses or mountain bikes along the ridge, you must start at Grasshopper Road. That route climbs ⅝ mile, then goes to the right on Squaw Creek Ridge Road, climbing ⅝ mile, then contouring for one mile to meet the trail described below.

To stay at Baxter or Hamilton Barn Environmental Camps or at any of the trail camps, you must first register at Park Head-

An old road heads south past bay laurel trees, poison oak, hazel, wild rose and pioneer apple trees, coming to Baxter Camp in ⅛ mile. The camp sits in a redwood grove beside Bull Creek. Just beyond the camp, a sign points left for the trail to Squaw Creek Ridge Road and Whiskey Flat Camp.

The trail climbs steeply, then eases to ¼ mile. Climb steeply again to an old skid trail. You follow the skid, climbing south-southeast. Before ⅜ mile your trail bends left and makes a steep, winding ascent through tanoak forest. Beyond ½ mile the climb becomes moderate. Pass a dogwood tree at ¾ mile. Your trail bends left beyond ⅞ mile and soon comes to Squaw Creek Ridge Road.

Turn right on the wide road, climbing south past large redwoods to level at one mile. Contour to 1¼ miles, then climb gradually to a saddle on the ridge at 1⅜ miles, where big redwoods grow with Douglas firs, tanoaks, madrones, huckleberries and irises.

Make an easy ascent along the ridge to 1⅝ miles, then descend to another saddle. Follow the ridge southwest as ceanothus, wild rose and salal join the understory. Beyond 2 miles you continue along the ridge with short ups and downs.

After a straightaway you start the last big climb to Whiskey Flat Camp. The climb eases at 2¼ miles, then steepens as your trail bends left into virgin forest. Climb and wind to 2½ miles, then descend into a grove of large redwoods, where rare western yew also grows.

Your road climbs to 2¾ miles where it enters Whiskey Flat Camp. In this beautiful spot redwoods of ten-foot diameter tower over woodwardia and sword ferns, salal, redwood sorrel and a babbling brook. A faucet at the camp entrance provides sweet water. The camp was named for a Prohibition-era still located here.

You can use Whiskey Flat Camp as a base for exploring the surrounding wilderness. It is 5½ miles to Grasshopper Peak, an 11-mile round trip with far less elevation change than from the Big Tree Area.

Another option is to use a different trail camp each night. From Whiskey Flat Camp, it is a steady climb to Hanson Ridge Road in 1⅝ miles, 2¼ miles to Hanson Ridge Camp with its wonderful views. From Hanson Ridge Road junction, it is 4 miles via Preacher Gulch Road to Grasshopper Camp, 7 miles to Johnson Camp. You can also descend to Bull Creek Trail Camp, then follow Bull Creek to the main road, but the lower part of Preacher Gulch Road has been closed by a big slide, so you must now descend via South Prairie or Grieg Road. The options are many but you must plan ahead to get the required camping permits. All camps mentioned, except Johnson Camp (hikers only), are accessible to hikers, equestrians and mountain bikers.

SQUAW CREEK RIDGE:

DISTANCE: 5½ miles round trip to Whiskey Flat Camp (add 1¾ miles each direction from Grasshopper Road).

One way to Hanson Ridge Camp: 5 miles.

To Grasshopper Camp: 8¼ miles.

TIME: To Whiskey Flat: 1 to 2 hours. Park backcountry ideal for 1- to 3-night backpack trips.

TERRAIN: Climbs to and traverses ridges. Possible peak climb or descent along stream canyon.

ELEVATION GAIN/LOSS: From Baxter Camp or Grasshopper Road to Whiskey Flat: 1630 feet+/120 feet-.

From Whiskey Flat to Hanson Ridge Road junction: 520 feet+/160 feet-.

To Hanson Ridge Camp: add 240 feet+/100 feet-.

From Hanson Ridge junction to South Prairie Road: 860 feet+/760 feet-.

To Bull Creek Road and Camp: add 1200 feet-.

Preacher Gulch Road to Grasshopper Camp: 1320 feet+/340 feet-.

From Grasshopper Camp to peak: add 300 feet+.

BEST TIME: Spring and fall. Summer is hot, but Whiskey Flat Camp is always cool.

WARNINGS: Watch for extensive poison oak. Permit required to camp at Whiskey Flat and other backcountry camps. No fires in backcountry.

DIRECTIONS TO TRAILHEAD: Exit Highway 101 at South Fork/Honeydew (M.36.1 from north, M.35.5 from south). Go west on Mattole Road for 5.4 miles to Grasshopper Road (starting point for horses or mountain bikes), 6.4 miles to Baxter Camp Road. (Environmental Camp and trailhead for hikers only.) Park on the east side of the road where Baxter Camp trail heads south.

FEES: Environmental Camps: $7-9/night. Trail camps: $3/person/night.

FURTHER INFO: Humboldt Redwoods State Park (707) 946-2409, 445-6547.

OTHER SUGGESTION: LOOK PRAIRIE TRAIL (on north, 4.3 miles from highway) climbs to a pioneer barn with a grand view (1⅞ miles round trip). Mountain bikers can make an 11-mile loop by continuing steeply up Look Prairie Road to go left on Peavine Road along the ridge, then descending Thornton Road to Albee Creek. JOHNSON PRAIRIE TRAIL (on north, 4.6 miles from highway) climbs through prairie to a pioneer grave (1⅝ miles round trip).

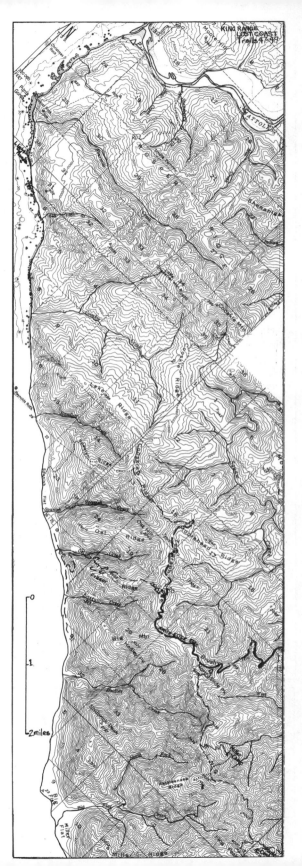

KING RANGE
LOST COAST
Trails 47-49

THE LOST COAST
KING RANGE NATIONAL CONSERVATION AREA

Imagine 25 miles of wilderness beach backed by steep bluffs and cliffs rising to ten peaks over 2000 feet and cut by fifteen year-round streams. If you like such wild rugged country, plan a trip to the Lost Coast.

The King Range is the largest area of wilderness on the Pacific Coast between Olympic National Park and Point Reyes National Seashore. Popularly known as the Lost Coast, the 60,000 acres of King Range National Conservation Area include the wilderness coast, the steep mountains and canyons of the King Range, and the 4000 acres of Chemise Mountain Primitive Area. About 37,000 acres of the King Range are currently being considered for formal wilderness designation. The Wilderness Society and the California Wilderness Coalition are lobbying for the largest wilderness area possible. The final decision will not come until at least 1994, when Congress will examine the various proposals for wilderness status for the King Range and make the choice. You can get a free map of the area's roads and trails from the Bureau of Land Management office in Arcata or Ukiah.

47.

MATTOLE RIVER SOUTH
ALONG THE LOST COAST

Most people enter this wild coast from the north or south end. Though these approaches avoid significant elevation change, the trek is not easy. Walking in strong winds over loose sand and uneven rocks demands hiking boots for backpackers. Three other trailheads reach the middle portion of the Lost Coast, all involving substantial elevation change: Spanish Ridge, Smith-Etter Road and Buck Creek Trail. Consider them for shorter trips or as part of a loop only if you are in good shape.

Of the north and south trailheads, the mouth of the Mattole River on the north provides the most pristine approach. You may be exposed to strong winds for the 3-mile hike to Punta Gorda Lighthouse. Unless you time your hike with the tide as you pass Sea Lion Gulch, you must scramble over crumbling cliffs to stay out of the surf. The 1992 earthquake made the tidal passage there even tighter than it was before. Walking becomes easier as you pass the deep canyons of Cooskie, Randall and Spanish Creeks.

Prevailing winds blow from northwest to southeast. So the

MATTOLE RIVER SOUTH:

DISTANCE: 25 miles one way, or round trip of your choice.

TIME: Three to 4 days for entire hike. 4-hour day hike to Punta Gorda Lighthouse.

TERRAIN: Mostly level beach and headland, backed by precipitous cliffs and deep canyons. Some rough rock hopping.

BEST TIME: Spring. September and October next best.

WARNINGS: Get a campfire permit at any BLM office or state fire station. Purify water, especially Cooskie Creek north and in Shelter Cove area. Watch for timber rattlers, especially near wood piles. Isolated country with no services. Difficult beach walking in soft sand and over rocks. Two or three points difficult or impassable at high tide.

DIRECTIONS TO TRAILHEAD: Exit Highway 101 at South Fork/Honeydew (M.36.1 from north, M.35.5 from south). Go west on Mattole Road for 23 miles to Honeydew, then right on Mattole Road for 14 miles to Lighthouse Road, just before Petrolia. Go left on Lighthouse Road to its end at the beach near the mouth of the Mattole River.

FURTHER INFO: Bureau of Land Management, Arcata (707) 822-7648 or Ukiah (707) 462-3863.

common lore is that you hike the Lost Coast from north to south, with the wind at your back. But unless you intend to go the whole 25 miles, you will likely have the wind against you in one direction or the other.

If you enter from the south via Shelter Cove (see Trail #52), keep in mind that the beach is open to vehicles for the first 3 miles, an incongruous intrusion on the solitude of this place. Beyond the vehicle closure lies the most spectacular part of the Lost Coast, a narrow beach backed by high cliffs and steep canyons with lush vegetation and wildflowers.

Wherever you approach the Lost Coast, you will find solitude and physical grandeur to challenge your spirit, and a wondrous diversity of plant and animal life growing right to the ocean's edge. Be careful, watch for rogue waves, and treat the wilderness with respect.

From the end of Lighthouse Road, walk west to the tide line, then head south along the broad, dark sand beach. The firm sand just above the water provides the best walking, except where a firmly packed jeep trail follows the base of the bluffs. Sheep graze the steep grasslands on your left.

Before one mile the first of many year-round creeks cascades down the steep, grassy bluff. The beach gets rockier to the south. Stay on the beach to avoid a huge slide on the bluff caused by the 1992 earthquake. Tidepools and sea stacks lie offshore. Beyond 1½ miles the broad beach narrows. Beyond a small point, several seasonal streams drop to the beach.

At 2½ miles an old ranch road winds steeply up the bluff. You immediately round Punta Gorda as the lighthouse comes into view. From here you can walk on a firm roadbed. You pass two cabins near Fourmile Creek at 2⅝ miles. After the ford, continue on a firm track across the grassy bluff, passing more dilapidated ranch buildings.

At 3 miles a path forks left to Punta Gorda Lighthouse ruin. The light station helped ships navigate this fogbound, rugged coast from 1911 to 1951. It was built after the wreck of the *SS Columbia* claimed 87 lives here in 1907. Today only the squat light tower remains, the keeper's quarters and fog signal house having been razed by BLM in 1970. The wind usually roars and whistles through the concrete tower.

You cross several small creeks in the next ½ mile as you follow the old jeep road along the coast. After the creek at 3½ miles, you can climb a hill to stay on the road, or you can return to the beach. On the road you have another chance to return to the beach at 3¾ miles. Either way, you come to steep Sea Lion Gulch at 4 miles. Sea Lion Rocks lie just offshore, home to three dozen Steller sea lions and many cormorants and pelicans. The steep mouth of the creek provides shelter from the wind, views of the sea lions and wildflowers.

The beach narrows after the gulch. At 4½ miles beach passage may be blocked at medium to high tide. If necessary, you might scramble over crumbling rock and mud slides on a steep, rough detour above the surf. You would do better to wait for the tide to drop below +1.0 foot, when the beach is passable. (Keep in mind that the tides here occur about 30 minutes earlier than the times for the mouth of the Mattole.) When the tide is out, uneven-sized rocks on the beach slow your progress.

You pass a barn and cabin above the beach at 4¾ miles. Then walking becomes easier at the base of steep cliffs. At 6 miles you come to the broad, deep canyon of Cooskie Creek. A sweat lodge of driftwood sits beside its mouth. Sheltered camps lie within ¼ mile upstream. Fishing is fair for trout to nine inches. You should purify drinking water. Private property lies about one

mile upstream.

Continuing southeast, you must boulder-hop for a few hundred feet. Then footing improves as the beach widens. You pass small waterfalls and two narrow spots to 7 miles. From 7¼ to 7¾ miles, the cliffs above the beach have massive landslides. At 7½ miles large, uneven rocks on a steeply slanting beach make rough walking. The bluffs, however, are worse, cut by many little canyons. Beyond 7¾ miles loose sand and gravel slow progress.

About 8 miles from the trailhead, Reynolds Rock lies offshore. You pass a point showing greatly twisted rock strata. The geological folding continues to the mouth of Randall Creek at 8⅝ miles.

Narrower and more wooded than Cooskie Creek, Randall Creek also provides fair fishing. A pleasant camp lies a short walk upstream on the north side of the creek.

A road along the bluffs south of the creek provides firm footing. Just 250 feet from Randall Creek, the Spanish Ridge Trail meets your road. Then your path climbs the rolling grassland at the base of the steep bluffs. At 8⅞ miles you cross a small stream where watercress grows. Offshore rocks line this stretch of coast. Near 9¾ miles a mostly level footpath crosses the lower bluff. Or you can walk the old road, which leads up and down along the upper bluff. You pass two more streams jammed with wildflowers, the second with watercress and mint.

At 10¼ miles the grassy headlands get broader and flatter as you come to the north end of Spanish Flat. If it is not too windy these lush grasslands provide good camping. At 10½ miles another spur climbs Spanish Ridge. You walk the broad grassy flat, once the site of a sawmill. The lumber was hauled to market by ship. Wildflowers lie scattered through the grasslands. Woodwardia ferns grow at the base of the steep bluffs.

At 11⅜ miles you come to the broad flood plain of deep Spanish Creek Canyon. Several campsites lie in or near the canyon. Continue over mostly level grasslands. You pass an old corral, then come to pioneer Paul Smith's cabin, 12 miles from the trailhead. It overlooks a broad sandy beach.

At 12⅜ miles you cross Oat Creek. The creek cascades down its twisting, rocky gorge. Swallows dip and soar overhead. Mimulus, iris, sticky monkeyflower, columbine, yarrow, paintbrush, cow parsnip, penstemon and lupine grow in the sheltered canyon. You meet the Smith-Etter Road at 13 miles (see Trail #48).

The road continues southeast along the coast, crossing the broad, gravelly wash of Kinsey Creek in ¼ mile. It leads along grasslands below steep bluffs, passing the Etter cabin at 14 miles. The headlands narrow as a sandy track heads for Hadley Creek (also known as Big Creek), which you cross at 14⅝ miles. Dense forest in the deep, shady canyon shelter pleasant campsites.

Your trail continues in loose sand along a narrow beach. At 14⅞ miles the beach is backed by high sand dunes stacked against a steep grassy hill. A trail climbs the steep headlands to the south. It provides better walking than continued slogging in the sand. At 15 miles the faint double track is obliterated by a slide, but a narrow trail continues. Back on the grasslands the trail becomes vague; stay high on the headlands below steep bluffs. You cross a stream choked with watercress at 15⅛ miles. Then your trail descends to meet a gently rolling grassland, soon returning to an obvious dirt road.

You cross a small creek at 15¾ miles and come to Big Flat, which stretches along the coast for over a mile. The first of many Indian shell middens lies beside the road. It is unlawful to disturb these archaeological sites. The road provides easy walking for your sand- and rock-weary soles. As Big Flat broadens to its widest point, the road draws away from the shore. At 16¼ miles your path crosses a landing strip used by the residents of the house ahead.

As you approach the canyon of Big Flat Creek, watch for the small timber rattlesnakes that live on the flat and in the rocky wash of the creek. Other animals frequenting Big Flat include bear, deer, fox, badger, rubber boa snake (harmless) and various lizards. Douglas firs and cypresses grow along the edge of the flat.

After paralleling the runway, your trail forks. The roadbed continues along the runway, then heads into the canyon, where the most protected campsites lie among trees alongside the broad, gravelly wash. If you are continuing south or want to camp at Miller Flat, take the trail that forks right, crosses the runway, and follows the edge of the alder and willow forest near the beach. It passes two camps around 16¾ miles. The second one has a driftwood shelter tall enough to stand up in, with a nifty flag. From here you can look up Big Flat Creek Canyon to 4087-foot Kings Peak. Then you cross Big Flat Creek. Stay right of the trees on the far side. Watch for rattlers!

You come to Miller Flat, broader and more wooded than Big Flat. Wild rose, chemise, gooseberry, red alder and poison oak grow near the creek. Several campsites lie near the trail. More sheltered camps are in the forest to the northeast. Your trail turns east, climbing gradually up the broad flat, a favorite browse for deer. Easy walking across Miller Flat brings you to 17⅝ miles, where a short descent drops you back on the beach at 17¾ miles.

You again walk the beach at the base of steep bluffs. On your right lie many offshore rocks and tidepools. After a small, unmapped creek, the beach becomes very rocky. You round a small point at 18⅜ miles as the beach gets narrower.

Ahead lies another stretch where progress may be blocked at a tide of +4.0 feet or more. The rugged cliffs above have many small creeks, seeps and springs, supporting hanging gardens of wildflowers in spring and early summer. The narrowest point lies just before Shipman Creek at 18¾ miles.

Beautiful Shipman Creek has camps in the driftwood on either side of its mouth. The deep wooded canyon is a treat to explore. At low tide you can visit the rewarding tidepools west of its mouth. You are 6¼ miles from Shelter Cove.

You walk a broad beach until 19½ miles, where you cross a small creek. Round a point where the beach turns rocky and narrow. Pass Buck Creek at 20 miles and meet the Buck Creek Trail, which climbs 3300 feet in the 2½ miles to Kings Crest Trail (see Trail #51—OTHER SUGGESTION).

Many more creeks tumble down the cliffs on your way to Gitchell Creek at 21½ miles. A campsite sits beside its mouth. But the vehicle users allowed this far north on the beach from Shelter Cove have degraded the place with trash.

After another mile of sandy beach, you can follow a dirt road along the bluffs. At 23½ miles is the mouth of wooded Horse Mountain Creek, where the road returns to the beach. Big rocks lie along the beach at 23⅞ miles, before another steep creek. The beach broadens as you turn south, heading straight for Point Delgada. As you walk the beach or bluff road along the base of the rugged Kaluna Cliff, your thoughts may turn to the cold beer or ice cream available in Shelter Cove. You cross Telegraph Creek at 25 miles and come to the parking area.

176

48

SMITH-ETTER ROAD
TO BEACH

STEEP SHORTCUT TO HEART OF LOST COAST

This is the shortest hiking route into the heart of the Lost Coast. Although it entails a longer drive on dirt roads to get to this trailhead, the extra effort by car allows you to hike just 4 miles to reach the middle section of the Lost Coast, 12 miles from the north and south trailheads. Remember that you must climb 2400 feet in elevation to return to your car from the beach.

The Smith-Etter Road was reopened to vehicle traffic in spring, 1987. When the road is open, April 1 to October 31, you can drive nine steep, winding miles on the Smith-Etter Road, park at the locked gate and hike to the beach.

The locked gate blocks Smith-Etter Road at its junction with the Telegraph Ridge Road. Park near the gate, being sure not to block traffic on Telegraph Ridge Road (which you can drive northwest for 2½ miles to the Spanish Ridge Trail).

Behind the gate your route follows the Smith-Etter Road northwest, then west, below the summit of Telegraph Ridge. On your left the steep drainage of Kinsey Creek drops to the ocean far below. The trail climbs slightly for ½ mile. Beyond ¼ mile big Douglas firs grow where a little gully crosses the road. This pleasantly sheltered spot has room to camp on flat ground on either side of the road. When the wind dies down you can hear the roar of the surf.

At ½ mile your climb levels atop Kinsey Ridge, which you follow to the beach. A wide spot on the ridge marks ¾ mile. The trail descends steadily from there. The low, brushy vegetation allows views northwest into deep Oat Creek Canyon and grassy Oat Ridge and Spanish Ridge beyond.

At one mile you have another view of the beach at the mouth of Kinsey Creek. Then your trail leaves the ridgetop, bending right to descend along its north face. Beyond 1½ miles you regain the top of the ridge as it descends steeply toward the shore. Wildflowers along the road include bush lupine, wild rose, sticky monkeyflower, Douglas iris, morning glory, thistle and pennyroyal.

The road starts a series of long switchbacks at 1¾ miles. These descend into a dark forest of Douglas fir and live oak. Return to the ridge briefly at 2¼ miles, then switchback right to its north side. Many birds frequent this area. Poppy, coastal manroot and poison oak grow on the road shoulders.

At 3 miles you come to the westernmost bend in the road, high above the mouth of Oat Creek. Switchback sharply left here and descend steeply southeast. The wilderness coast stretches magnificently before you. The broad shoal of Big Flat lies 4 miles away. Far beyond it Point Delgada extends into the Pacific. You can see the Etter cabin to the south and Paul Smith's cabin not far to the north. The point where the road comes to the beach is also visible, still 800 feet below.

At 3¼ miles you switchback right and descend by five more steep switchbacks to the beach, 3¾ miles from the locked gate. Sticky monkeyflower, rattlesnake grass and beach morning glory grow at the junction.

From the junction a road runs south to Kinsey Creek in just ¼ mile. Big Flat is 4½ miles, while the southern trailhead at Shelter Cove lies 12 miles to the southeast.

Along the coast to the north, Paul Smith's cabin lies at the foot of Oat Ridge in one mile. Spanish Flat is 1¾ miles away. It is 10 miles to the Punta Gorda Lighthouse, 13 miles to the northern trailhead at the mouth of the Mattole River. See Trails #47 and 52 for more details on the Lost Coast.

49.

KINGS CREST NORTH
FROM SMITH-ETTER ROAD TO KINGS PEAK

The Kings Crest Trail traverses the high ridge of King Range National Conservation Area. One of the more rugged hikes in the area, Kings Crest Trail provides spectacular views of the wilderness coast to the west. The route connects with spurs to designated campsites at Rattlesnake Ridge, Miller and Maple camps, or you can dry-camp along the trail. After 5⅝ miles the trail reaches the 4087-foot summit of Kings Peak, where the views are unsurpassed. The trip to the peak is ideal for a backpack trip of one or two nights. It can also be done as a long, rigorous day hike of 11¼ miles. Experienced backpackers may make a 27-mile loop, continuing south beyond Kings Peak to descend the steep Buck Creek Trail, walk the beach, then ascend Smith-Etter Road to the trailhead.

You will often have the Kings Crest to yourself. Carry water since there is none along the main trail and the sources at Miller and Maple Camp may dry up by summer. The Smith-Etter Road may be closed in wet weather, limiting access to the trailhead.

The trail starts by climbing 200 feet on an old jeep road to a flat clearing with views east. Your trail then descends along the east face of North Slide Peak with fine views of the rugged ridge you follow southeast to Kings Peak. The path descends an open,

DISTANCE: 11¼ miles round trip to Kings Peak, 12½ miles with
Maple Camp loop; 10 miles one way to Buck Creek Trail.

TIME: Best as an overnight, though possible as long day hike.

TERRAIN: Up and down along a rugged ridge to top of Kings Peak.

ELEVATION GAIN/LOSS: One way to peak: 2210 feet+/1380
feet-. Round trip: 3590 feet+/3590 feet-. Round trip with
Maple Camp loop: 3800 feet+/4250 feet-.

BEST TIME: Spring is best. Summer or fall also good.

WARNINGS: Isolated country, no services. Watch for timber
rattlers. May be snow on trail in winter or early spring. Road
to trailhead may be closed in rainy season: November to
March.

DIRECTIONS TO TRAILHEAD: Follow directions for Trail #48,
except that you come to the trailhead at 7.5 miles on Smith-
Etter Road.

FURTHER INFO: Bureau of Land Management, Arcata
(707) 822-7648 or Ukiah (707) 462-3873.

brushy slope to ½ mile, then descends gradually along a shaded section.

At ⅞ mile make a big bend left and cross another barren stretch to the end of the old jeep track at one mile. A broad spot on the trail sits in a saddle of the ridgetop, a level spot for a dry camp. The trail turns east, climbing steadily for ⅛ mile to a summit where one-leaved wild onion grows.

Make a short, steep descent to 1¼ miles. Then your path contours for nearly ¼ mile before climbing steeply again along the razor ridgetop. More than a dozen steep, short switchbacks wind up a north face of the ridge. Meet the Miller Camp Trail at 1¾ miles, which forks left and descends 800 feet in 2 miles to the camp and a spring.

After the junction, your trail turns south and descends through burned forest, the result of a fire that you will see much evidence of along the rest of the route. You soon return to the ridgetop. Two miles from the trailhead, you come to a saddle with great views along the razor ridge and west to Shubrick Peak and into Hadley Creek Canyon. In spring wildflowers sprinkle the steep slide below you.

The next ⅜ mile offers some of the easiest walking in the King Range. Contour along the leeward side of the ridge, then climb gradually to meet the south end of the Miller Camp Trail beyond 2⅜ miles (one mile to Miller Camp on vague tread).

Kings Crest Trail climbs by six switchbacks through forest where Oregon grape, waterleaf, gooseberry and bear grass thrive, coming to a knob on the ridgetop at 2⅝ miles. Make a shady descent, followed by a short uphill to 2⅞ miles, where a shady dry camp sits astride the trail. Descend, then climb to the 3-mile point, where you meet the Rattlesnake Ridge Trail, marked by a plastic sign. The spur drops steeply south to a camp and reliable water source in ¾ mile.

The Crest Trail climbs steeply by seven switchbacks to a summit of 3620 feet at 3¼ miles. Then you descend steeply through a brushy area for ¼ mile. The trail follows the ridgetop up, down, up and down again in the next stretch with frequent views of Big Flat Creek and the blue Pacific 3000 feet below.

From 3⅞ miles you leave the ridgetop to climb steeply again. At 4⅛ miles the trail becomes easier, contouring through a pleasantly shaded forest of Douglas fir, crossing steep slopes prone to slides. Around 4½ miles you have views of the Mattole Valley and the Yolla Bolly and Trinity Mountains.

Your trail climbs a bit, then crosses a talus slope before 4¾ miles. Return to the ridgetop briefly at a saddle with breathtaking views of the steep and rugged surrounding country. The headwaters of Big Flat Creek lie just ¼ mile to the south and 1000 feet below.

The trail climbs, then descends through fir and hardwood forests along a steep slope, then ascends steeply to a junction at 5⅛ miles. On the left the Lightning Trail (see Trail #50) descends 2 miles to its trailhead, with a spur branching right to reach Maple Camp in ⅝ mile. On the right the Kings Crest Trail continues (see Trail #51) for 5¾ miles to end at Saddle Mountain Road. Turn right for the top of Kings Peak as well, ascending 600 feet in ½ mile to the summit. Trail #50 has a detailed description of the fantastic view from the peak.

50.

LIGHTNING TO KINGS PEAK
STEEP BUT SHADY ROUTE

The Lightning Trail offers the shortest hike of the three routes to Kings Peak, with the easiest road access as well. It is the most accessible in winter, although the King Range Road may also be closed by slides in the rainy season. This route has two other advantages: it is the shadiest route, ideal in hot weather; it is the shortest route to Maple Camp, which has water in winter, spring and early summer. Although the route ascends 2000 feet to Kings

DISTANCE: 2½ miles to peak, 1⅞ miles to Maple Camp.

TIME: At least 3 hours to top and back.

TERRAIN: Ascends brush-and-forest-covered ridge to summit of Kings Peak.

ELEVATION GAIN/LOSS: Round trip: 2000 feet+/2000 feet-.

BEST TIME: The best year-round trail to the peak, still nicest in spring.

WARNINGS: Watch for timber rattlesnakes and ticks. Isolated country with no services. Best to carry water in dry season when water sources are not reliable.

DIRECTIONS TO TRAILHEAD: FROM NORTH: Leave Highway 101 at South Fork/Honeydew exit (M.36.1 from north, M.35.5 from south). Follow Mattole Road west for 23 miles to Honeydew and junction with Wilder Ridge Road. Turn left and go 5 miles to junction with Horse Mountain Road. Turn right and go 3 miles on steep, winding Horse Mountain Road to junction with King Range Road. Take sharp right and go 6.6 miles to Lightning Trailhead.

FROM SOUTH: Leave Highway 101 at Garberville (M.10.8). Take Briceland Road from Redway (2.8 miles north of Garberville on Redwood Drive). Go 18 miles, then turn right onto unpaved Horse Mountain Road (aka Kings Peak Road). Follow this for 9.5 miles to junction with King Range Road, where you turn left and go 6.6 miles more to trailhead.

FURTHER INFO: Bureau of Land Management, Arcata (707) 822-7648 or Ukiah (707) 462-3873.

OTHER SUGGESTION: Two pleasant campgrounds are located on Kings Crest Road, TOLKAN CAMP and HORSE MOUNTAIN CAMP (respectively 3.8 and 7.0 miles from Shelter Cove Road).

Peak, it is well graded and pleasant.

The Lightning Trail ascends a high bank on the left side of King Range Road, just beyond a big curve left and a wide spot where you can park. Head southeast, coming to a garbage can and a trail register in 100 feet. Sign in, please. The trail climbs through a hardwood forest of madrone and tanoak, with huckleberry in the understory.

Your path soon switchbacks left and heads east on faint tread. The trail steepens, climbing moderately through a series of lazy switchbacks. Just beyond ⅛ mile you pass through a sunny clearing surrounded by manzanita.

Climb steadily along a hardwood-covered ridge. At ¼ mile you pass an old Douglas fir and veer to the left The trail runs southeast, then south, climbing the ridge with occasional switchbacks.

By ½ mile a steep drop lies on the right. Continue your climb, meandering in and out of virgin Douglas fir forest with much bear grass and salal as you approach the sound of a stream. Beyond ⅝ mile, a right fork leads to pretty Big Rock Camp, beside a stream with big, moss-covered rocks and Douglas firs eight feet in diameter.

Climb steeply by many switchbacks for the next ¼ mile. At ⅞ mile you switchback left and head southeast onto the relatively cool and wooded north side of the ridge. Regain the top of the ridge briefly at one mile, then climb west through the forest. After a straight, uphill stretch, your trail switchbacks left at 1⅛ miles. Salal and Oregon grape cover the forest floor.

You soon return to the dry ridge, where manzanita and canyon live oak mix with the fir forest. Climb the ridge, passing through a thicket of spiny whitethorn ceanothus, which has fragrant white flowers in May. At 1⅜ miles you climb through a dense forest of young Douglas fir.

Just 1⅝ miles from the trailhead, you come to a junction where gooseberry grows. The left fork leads to Maple Camp in ¼ mile (shady camp by a stream) and to Kings Crest Trailhead in 6 miles. Take the right fork northwest. It is one mile to the top of Kings Peak, 5½ miles to the Smith-Etter Road.

The trail continues to climb through forest and brush fields where white-veined shinleaf and tall prince's pine grow in the understory. As you meet the Kings Crest Trail at 2 miles, make a sharp left for the top of Kings Peak. The trail climbs by switchbacks, then follows a brushy ridge to 2¼ miles, where you turn right on the trail to the summit.

Climb a jagged ridge, with views down the west face of the peak to Big Flat and the ocean far below. Indian warriors brighten the way in spring with their bold, dark red flowers. Reach the summit less than ¼ mile from the turnoff. Suddenly you come out on top of the world.

The top consists of a 30-feet-by-40-feet semi-flat area, dropping off steeply on all sides. To the west the ocean glimmers in sunlight. Infinite waves roll toward the shore, reflecting light and heat over chilly ocean depths. Purplish streaks far offshore mark the deepest water, beyond which a snow-white fog bank often obscures the horizon.

The rugged King Range stretches northwest, ending just beyond view at Cape Mendocino, westernmost point in California. To the northeast lie the Trinity Mountains. The jagged Trinity Alps rise to 8000 feet beyond the lower Trinitys. On the clearest of days you can see the round bulk of Lassen Peak (10,487 feet) to the east-northeast, 141 miles away. Directly to the east, at half the distance, the 7000-foot peaks of the Yolla Bollys show in sharp relief.

As you look south down the coast, Saddle Mountain looms in the foreground. Shelter Cove juts seaward to its right. South of Shelter Cove fall (in order) Chemise Mountain, Mistake Point, Cape Vizcaino, Bruhel Point, then the white sands of Ten Mile Dunes. The sawmill smokestack marking Fort Bragg may be seen to the right of the dunes, with Point Arena stretching seaward beyond.

Take a moment to reflect on the geology of this place. Directly west of Kings Peak is Big Flat, 4000 feet below (just 3 miles as the crow flies). The San Andreas Fault lies just offshore. Over eons, as the onshore tectonic plate moves south, it collides with the Pacific plate moving north. This immense and powerful collision has uplifted these rugged mountains.

From the peak you can return to the Lightning Trailhead in about one hour.

51.

KINGS CREST SOUTH
SADDLE MOUNTAIN TO THE TOP OF THE WORLD

Since the first edition of this book, the Bureau of Land Management has closed the last 3.1 miles of Saddle Mountain Road to vehicles and added it to the Kings Crest Trail. This more than doubles the old trail distance to Kings Peak, making the Kings Crest Trail a total of 10⅞ miles between its southern and northern trailheads. The road closure enhances both the aesthetics and the difficulty of the trek to Kings Peak. Now if only Congress would get around to designating this a wilderness area, the magnificent King Range would truly be protected.

From the new trailhead, the Kings Crest Trail follows the old Saddle Mountain Road, then the trail along the high ridge of the King Range to the top of Kings Peak. At 4087 feet, the peak is the highest point along the Northern California coast. Brush fields alternate with fir forests in this steep, rugged country. This route to the peak is a pleasant overnight hike (or a strenuous, 11-mile day hike) climaxing in spectacular views. Be sure to read the DIRECTIONS TO TRAILHEAD to prepare you for the drive to the starting point.

The Legend of Kings Peak claims that a Manila galleon was wrecked on the Lost Coast. Survivors or Indians carried away its

184

KINGS CREST SOUTH:

DISTANCE: 10¾ miles round trip to Kings Peak, 11⅝ miles with Maple Camp loop; 5¾ miles one way to Lightning Trail junction, 10⅞ miles to Smith-Etter Road.

TIME: Best as an overnight, but can reach Kings Peak as a long day hike.

TERRAIN: Climbs a high, rugged coastal ridge to the top of Kings Peak; continues up and down along the ridge to Smith-Etter Road.

ELEVATION GAIN/LOSS: One way to peak: 2480 feet+/1420 feet-. Round trip 3900 feet+/3900 feet-.

BEST TIME: Clear weather. Spring is best; September and October next best.

WARNINGS: Isolated country without services. Last 3.6 miles of road are steep and rough, prone to washouts in winter. No water available on trail. Watch for ticks and timber rattlesnakes. May be snow on trail in winter, early spring.

DIRECTIONS TO TRAILHEAD: Leave Highway 101 at Garberville (M.10.8) from the south (or Redway at M.14.6 from the north). Take Redwood Drive to Redway, then Briceland Road west for 18 miles (steep and winding, but paved). Go right on unpaved Horse Mountain Road (aka Kings Peak Road) for 6.5 miles. Then turn left on Saddle Mountain Road, marked "Kings Crest Trail." The driving gets rough here. While most cars can make it to the trailhead, consider Lightning Trailhead as the "better road" alternative if your car has low clearance, a weak transmission or bad tires, or if you visit in winter. If you take the high road, drive slowly and alertly as it is steep, winding and poorly maintained. In one mile you top Horse Mountain Ridge. Go right, coming to Kings Crest Trailhead at 3.6 miles. The broad parking area on the right has room for a rudimentary camp but no water.

FURTHER INFO: Bureau of Land Management (707) 822-7648, Arcata or (707)462-3873, Ukiah.

OTHER SUGGESTION: BUCK CREEK TRAIL forks left at ⅞ mile up the Kings Crest Trail. It descends 3300 feet to the beach at the mouth of Buck Creek in just 2½ miles. It is the shortest and steepest route to the beach from Kings Crest. Not recommended for a stroll to and from the beach. Experienced backpackers may choose to make a 29-mile CREST TO COAST LOOP: descend to beach at Buck Creek, head north for 9 miles, where you climb east on the Smith-Etter Road for 6 miles. Then take Kings Crest Trail for 10⅞ miles to return to Kings Crest Trailhead. Trails #47, 48, 49 and 51 provide further detail. You might do it in the opposite direction, but the climb from the beach to Saddle Mountain may conjure thoughts of an eternity in hell.

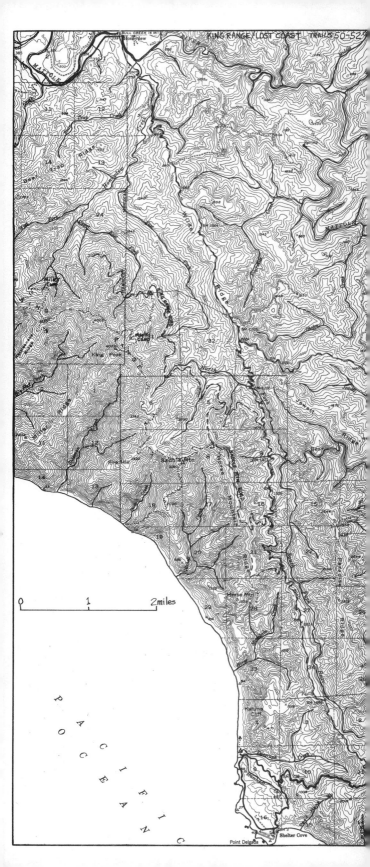

gold, jewels and spices to a cave and hid them. Years later an earthquake sealed the cave and obliterated all traces of it. My own favorite treasure is the view from the peak.

From the new trailhead, your trail descends west to a trail register (sign in, please). Then descend south on the old road through mixed forest of Douglas fir, tanoak and madrone. After a view south along the coast, the track climbs west as sugar pine joins the forest. The road switchbacks left at ⅛ mile, then right on a steady ascent.

Around ⅞ mile Buck Creek Trail forks left, climbing south before descending steeply to the beach (see OTHER SUGGESTION). The Kings Crest Trail descends gradually west. Beyond 1¼ miles you descend moderately, winding along the crest with views down to the mouth of Buck Creek and ahead to Kings Peak.

At 1⅝ miles your track bends right and resumes climbing. Live oak joins the forest, with whitethorn and coffeeberry in the understory. The route offers more vistas south along the coast until you switchback to the right around 2⅛ miles and pass a dry camp.

Ascend moderately north with views east to the Yolla Bollys. Beyond 2¾ miles the road switchbacks right, then left to climb gradually. Descend west from 3 miles, coming to the old trailhead at 3⅛ miles.

Descend gradually north as the trail narrows. For the next ¼ mile you descend through mixed forest of Douglas fir, sugar pine and hardwoods. Bear grass and spiky Oregon grape grow in the understory. The trail contours to 3½ miles, then descends past madrone, tanoak, canyon live oak and scattered fir.

You soon see the glimmer of the ocean through the trees on your left. To the north lie the steep slopes of Kings Peak, scarred

187

by a massive landslide. Before 3¾ miles the trail starts to climb. Soon gnarled, gravity-defying canyon live oaks on the left afford views of the sheer drop to the headwaters of Shipman Creek. You might notice the massive roots of a tenacious Douglas fir down slope.

Now the climb starts in earnest, making ten switchbacks through madrone and oak forest. At 4⅛ miles a clearing provides the best views yet to the east and south.

For another ⅛ mile, you climb through manzanita brush fields with broadleaf ceanothus (can be unpleasant on a warm day). Then your climb eases as the trail plunges into cool mixed forest. At 4½ miles the trail levels on a brushy ridge. Views open up to the ocean far below and Kings Peak to the northwest.

Your trail returns to the east side of the ridge and climbs north. At 4⅝ miles you can see Wilder Ridge below you, dotted with houses and barns. The Mattole River Canyon lies beyond the ridge. Beyond that, the parallel ridges of the Coast Range, bisected by the Eel River Canyon, stretch to the horizon.

Your climb steepens around 4¾ miles. You switchback twice to regain the brushy ridgetop. At 4⅞ miles you pass cabin-sized boulders surrounded by Fremont silktassel as the tread turns rough briefly. The Trinity Alps may be visible to the northeast beyond the very long and straight South Fork Mountain. Just up the trail you have views down the ocean side of the ridge. Make a steep, winding climb to a broad flat covered with low manzanita.

At 5 miles a steel sign marks the junction. The right fork descends ½ mile to Maple Camp, in a shady canyon beside a creek that rushes in winter and spring, and to Lightning Trailhead (2½ miles, 1000 feet below). Take the left fork. This leads to another junction at 5⅛ miles. From the junction you can see the simple shelter on the east face of Kings Peak. If you go left, the summit lies a brisk ¼ mile up the trail, 200 feet more in elevation. The thrilling view from the top is described in Trail #50.

Take the right fork to continue along the Kings Crest Trail. It climbs gradually west, then north across the east face of the peak. It soon descends, returning to the ridge and rejoining the peak trail by 5⅜ miles. Look northwest for a view along the rugged north end of the Kings Crest.

The trail descends north along the brushy ridgetop, then climbs east to 5½ miles. Descend through chaparral, then drop by seven switchbacks to another junction at 5¾ miles. The Lightning Trail on the right (see Trail #50) offers the last chance for Maple Camp.

Go left for the Kings Crest Trail. It descends to 6 miles, then contours along the ridgetop briefly, then across the shady east and north slopes of Peak 4005. You return to the ridgetop again around 7 miles. Climb, then contour along the ridge to 7⅜ miles. Climb steeply for ¼ mile, then descend steeply by six switchbacks. You return to the ridgetop and meet the Rattlesnake Ridge Trail at 7⅞ miles.

The spur down Rattlesnake Ridge has been reworked recently. It descends moderately along the ridgetop for ½ mile, then turns steep and brushy (marked with pink flagging) for ¼ mile to reach a camp and a year-round water source in a gravelly swale at the headwaters of Big Flat Creek. BLM may eventually open the trail all the way to Big Flat.

Kings Crest Trail continues northwest along the main ridge. It passes the Miller Camp spur at 8½ miles on its way to the Northern Trailhead at 10⅞ miles. See Trail #49 for details of the north half of the trail.

52.

SHELTER COVE NORTH
LOST COAST, SOUTH END

The subdivision of Shelter Cove sprawls over the steep, grassy bluffs of Point Delgada. It sits like a mirage, surrounded by the rugged wilderness peaks and canyons of the King Range. In the northwest corner of the subdivision, Beach Road ends at Black Sands Beach, the southern trailhead for the 25 miles of wilderness beach called the Lost Coast. If you have forgotten anything, Shelter Cove has two small general merchandise stores.

The first 3½ miles of beach are open to motorized vehicles, a sad commentary on the Bureau of Land Management's policy for

SHELTER COVE NORTH:

DISTANCE: Up to 25 miles; 5⅛ miles to Buck Creek, 6¼ miles to Shipman Creek, 8 miles to Big Flat.

TIME: One or more days.

TERRAIN: Level beach walking.

BEST TIME: Spring or fall.

WARNINGS: Watch for timber rattlers and rogue waves on beach.

DIRECTIONS TO TRAILHEAD: Follow directions in Trail #51, but stay on Shelter Cove Road about 21 miles. As you descend to Shelter Cove, take first right, Ridge Road, which ends at trailhead.

FURTHER INFO: Bureau of Land Management, Ukiah (707) 462-3873; Arcata, (707) 822-7648.

this pristine wilderness. Still, on a typical weekday, hikers may find little or no motorized traffic. This trailhead allows you to reach some of the most spectacular areas of the Lost Coast in an overnight hike. The virgin canyon of Shipman Creek lies just 6¼ miles from the trailhead. Miller Flat and Big Flat are about 2 miles farther.

You walk north on the broad beach, quickly crossing Telegraph Creek. At ⅛ mile a hard-packed road on the bluffs parallels the beach. It climbs a short, steep hill sprinkled with wildflowers and soon descends to a campsite at the top of the beach at ⅜ mile. Although the road climbs the bluff again, it soon ends at a rough crossing of the creek that comes off the steep face of Kaluna Cliff. Hike the broad beach north, crossing another creek at 1⅛ miles, beyond which big rocks stand on the beach.

At 1½ miles you come to Horse Mountain Creek, a deep wooded canyon with a mouth bracketed by steep, grassy slopes. The beach tapers to its narrowest point at 1¾ miles, then broadens. Before 2 miles a primitive road runs along the bluffs again. You can follow the bluff road for ½ mile, as the coast bends northwest. A washout near 2½ miles forces you to return to the beach.

Pass Gitchell Creek at 3½ miles, where you leave the ORV area. The broad beach narrows at 4⅛ miles. You continue along the base of steep cliffs with many cascading streams. At 4⅝ miles the beach tapers to a point that may be impassable at very high tide. Walk the narrow, rocky beach to Buck Creek at 5⅛ miles. The Buck Creek Trail climbs east from the south side of the creek (see Trail #51).

Continuing along the beach, you quickly come to another rocky, narrow section of beach. It should be passable at all but the highest tide. The narrow beach continues past many off-shore rocks. The high cliffs on your right have many springs and hanging gardens of wildflowers.

At 5½ miles a creek cascades to the beach, just short of a rocky promontory. It plunges 1600 feet in its short, ¾-mile course. Offshore lies the deep submarine trench of Delgada Canyon, which is 450 feet deep just ½ mile from shore. Beyond the rocky point, the beach becomes very broad.

You come to Shipman Creek 6¼ miles from the trailhead. Huge piles of driftwood lie in the protected mouth of the wooded canyon, which has camps on both sides. Clear pools and water-falls lie upstream, while wildflowers thrive on the grassy bluff east of its mouth.

To continue along the beach, you need a tide lower than +4.0 feet. The narrow beach is backed by 10-foot cliffs topped by steep, grassy bluffs. Beyond 6⅝ miles the beach gets wider, though steep cliffs still tower overhead. At 7¼ miles a painted rock covered with iceplant marks a path that climbs onto rolling and grassy Miller Flat. You come to Big Flat Creek at 8 miles. The base of the Smith-Etter Road lies 4 miles beyond. For details of this area and the north end of the Lost Coast, see Trail #47.

53.

HIDDEN VALLEY
TO CHEMISE MOUNTAIN
TO WHALE GULCH
CONTINUING ALONG THE LOST COAST

Much of this old pack trail has recently been reconstructed. It connects the northern and southern sections of the Lost Coast Trail. You can now start backpacking at the mouth of the Mattole River, walk 25 miles along the beach to Shelter Cove, then hike or hitchhike 3 miles of paved road to Hidden Valley Trailhead. From there it is a 28-mile hike to the Usal Trailhead, 6 miles north of Highway 1. The 4½ miles south from Hidden Valley Trailhead provide excellent walking. But the next 2½ miles descend the ridge steeply to the mouth of Whale Gulch.

You can also start this hike from pleasant Wailaki or Nadelos

HIDDEN VALLEY TO CHEMISE MOUNTAIN TO WHALE GULCH:

DISTANCE: 8⅝ miles one way to Needle Rock Visitor Center; 7 miles one way to Whale Gulch, 5 miles round trip to Chemise Mountain.

TIME: Three to 5 hours.

TERRAIN: Contours through chaparral to a lush meadow, climbs along edge of forest to ridge, which you follow to its summit. Descends ridge to mouth of deep canyon on the coast, climbs, then contours to Needle Rock.

ELEVATION GAIN/LOSS: One way to Whale Gulch: 1170 feet+/ 2880 feet-. Round trip to Chemise Mountain: 1040 feet+/ 1040 feet-.

BEST TIME: Spring. Summer and fall are also good.

WARNINGS: No water on trail until Whale Gulch. Watch for timber rattlers and poison oak. Nearest year-round facilities at Shelter Cove. South end of trail is very brushy; wear or carry long pants. Stay on trail and off private property.

DIRECTIONS TO TRAILHEAD: Leave Highway 101 at Garberville (M.10.8) from south or at Redway (M.14.6) on the north. Take Briceland Road from Redway (2.8 miles north of Garberville on Redwood Drive) for 17 miles. Go left on Chemise Mountain Road for ¼ mile to trailhead on right.

FURTHER INFO: Bureau of Land Management: (707) 822-7648, Arcata; (707) 462-3873, Ukiah.

OTHER SUGGESTION: A shorter, easier route to CHEMISE MOUNTAIN leaves from Wailaki Campground, 1.5 miles south of Hidden Valley Trailhead on Chemise Mountain Road. WHALE GULCH can be reached from Briceland Road in Sinkyone Wilderness State Park.

Campgrounds. This shortens the trip to Chemise Mountain or Whale Gulch by 1¼ miles.

Walk past the gate heading southwest on an old road. Young Douglas fir mix with alder, bay laurel, hazel, and thimbleberry. Wild mint grows in the middle of the road. You will notice the harsh devastation of a forest fire on the left. This hike winds in and out of the area burned by the Chemise Mountain fire of 1973.

At ⅛ mile the road swings left and crosses a tiny, slow-flowing creek. In spring the purple shades of bush lupine, Douglas iris, and ceanothus brighten the path.

You quickly come to a lush green meadow stretching for ½ mile up a valley surrounded by chaparral and fire-scarred forest.

Poppy and lupine sprinkle the heavenly meadow of Hidden Valley in the spring. Views of the blue Pacific lie to the west and south. In the upper end of the valley, an apple orchard marks the site of an old ranch.

At ¼ mile your road forks. Take the left fork; the right fork continues into Hidden Valley. Climb moderately with views of the valley and the ocean beyond. Before ½ mile you come to the upper end of the apple orchard. Your trail switches left and heads north, climbing steeply away from the road. As you climb by several steep, short switchbacks, you are rewarded with views of Hidden Valley.

Climb into unburned forest, then descend briefly back into the burn. The ascent resumes, entering hardwood forest at ¾ mile. It changes to fir forest by ⅞ mile. Then your steep climb winds to gain the ridge at one mile.

The ridge soon becomes brushy. Descend the ridge to 1¼ miles, where you return to forest. Climb briefly, only to descend

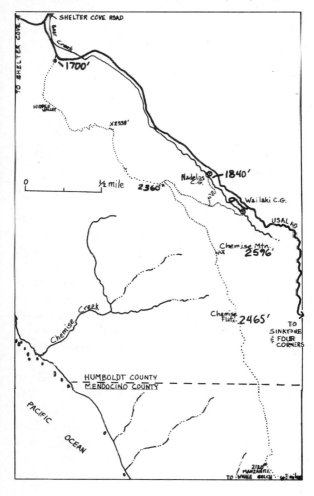

again, with ceanothus along the trail. Your trail levels at 1⅜ miles, then makes a steep, short climb to 1½ miles. Another level stretch leads to another short climb.

Climb steeply to 1¾ miles, then level at the junction with the trail from Wailaki and Nadelos Campgrounds. Turn right for Chemise Mountain and Whale Gulch. You climb gradually, heading south to gain the ridgetop.

In ⅝ mile your climb brings you to a sign marking the 2596-foot summit of Chemise Mountain on your left. A narrow, brushy trail winds to the very top in about 150 feet. The side trip is worthwhile because the brush opens to present fine vistas in all directions. Immediately to the south, Chemise Mountain drops off into the deep canyon of Whale Gulch, the route of the rest of this trail. The Sinkyone Wilderness and precipitous Anderson Cliffs lie just beyond. On a clear day you can spot at least 13 different coastal ridges to the south. The high peaks of the Yolla Bolly Mountains are to the east.

The main trail heads south along the ridge. The ridgetop trail continues south to the secondary peak of Chemise Flat at 2¾ miles.

The trail south descends briefly, then climbs to a brushy knob on the ridgetop at 2⅞ miles. Then you descend gently on a rocky, well-cleared path until 3⅛ miles. Your trail descends steeply, then moderately along the west side of the ridge before it climbs to a top at 3¼ miles where bay laurel grows. You descend again with more views south.

You can hear the distant roar of surf as you climb to another top at 3¾ miles. Then a shady portion of trail descends along the ridge before climbing briefly to the top called Manzanita at 4 miles from your trailhead. A USGS bench marker beside the trail indicates an elevation of 2120 feet. This is a good place to turn back if you are day hiking. From here the trail descends steeply to sea level in less than 3 miles.

What the heck, you say? Let's go! You can reach the beach in an hour. Your trail descends southeast. By 4¼ miles you enter cool, mature Douglas fir forest. You leave the ridge to descend steeply into a gully by switchbacks, then contour to return to the ridge at 4⅜ miles.

The trail descends steeply along the ridge, then levels briefly at a grassy clearing, a sign of what lies ahead. Your trail bends left and descends through mixed forest before climbing to another knob on the ridgetop at 4¾ miles. Your trail levels along the shady ridgetop, then descends gradually beyond 5 miles before leveling again. Wild rose, Douglas iris, sugar stick and huckleberry grow beneath the dense forest canopy.

Before 5½ miles you make a brief steep descent, then climb along the crest of the razor ridge, with grasslands to the west. This quickly brings you into a grassy clearing, with excellent views south into the Sinkyone Wilderness. Descend, then climb through the grasslands, then descend steeply through the forest for ⅛ mile. At 5⅞ miles you again descend through grasslands sprinkled with poppy, yarrow, redwood sorrel, tall brodiaea, buttercup, purple bush lupine, sticky monkeyflower and paintbrush. You soon meet a road from the left that the trail follows, climbing to a flattop on the ridge at 6 miles. An unfinished hip-roofed building sits beside the trail. Horses are not allowed beyond this point. From here you should stay on top of the ridge or on its west face; private property lies to the east.

Enjoy the easy descent through the grasslands. The trail will soon turn steep and brushy. At 6¼ miles you return to the forest as you descend steeply along the narrow ridge. As you pass the bench marker called Red Hill (elevation 1418 feet), you can see a private house below on the left. Stay on the razor ridge to avoid the private property.

Beyond the house the trail steepens. Watch for poison oak from here to the bottom. At 6⅜ miles the trail veers left and follows the east side of the ridge through hardwood forest. Return briefly to the ridge. Then, at 6½ miles, the trail descends east by switchbacks. Slink pod and hazel grow on the forest floor. The broad cleared path descends steeply, zigzagging toward Whale Gulch Creek.

At 6¾ miles your trail comes to a shady, slippery ford of the creek. Rock-hop across the creek, then follow the well beaten trail climbing east by switchbacks, then winding south through small gullies. You ascend to a summit and an overlook of Whale Gulch Creek.

Descend toward two small lakes, 7 miles from the Hidden Valley Trailhead. The trail soon climbs southeast, coming to Jones Beach Environmental Camp at 7⅝ miles. Three campsites are around a eucalyptus grove beside a small creek. It is one mile farther south to Needle Rock Visitor Center, where you must register if you wish to camp.

If you plan to continue on the Lost Coast Trail to Usal, you must walk the dirt road south for 2¾ miles to its end at Orchard Creek. From there it is 16¾ miles to Usal. See Trail #54.

SINKYONE WILDERNESS STATE PARK

Located in the extreme northwestern corner of Mendocino County, the Sinkyone (sing-key-own) preserves a sample of the rugged wilderness that once existed all along California's North Coast. Though the Sinkyone was settled in the 1860s and was logged and ranched for much of the next century, it now stands as a largely pristine wilderness. The state park was established in 1976.

The Sinkyone Wilderness State Park (7407 acres) is unlike any other park in the state. It can be reached only by isolated, unpaved mountain roads that are often impassable in winter. You must hike at least 200 feet to camp in the northern half of the park. The Visitor Center, where you can sleep for $10 per night, is located in a rustic old ranch house with no electricity or telephone.

The Sinkyone was named for the tribe that originally inhabited this rugged country. They were the southernmost of the Athapascan language tribes on the coast. Known for their backwoods skills, the Sinkyone tribe was small and loosely organized. They were quickly overrun by white settlers.

On the brighter side, a four-legged group of Sinkyone natives have recently been relocated in the park. At last count 29 Roosevelt elk live within park boundaries. If you meet elk on the trail, give them plenty of room, especially in rut season in September. The half-ton bulls may resent sharing their territory. When agitated, they can run as fast as 35 mph.

For more trails in Sinkyone Wilderness State Park, see The Hiker's hip pocket Guide to the Mendocino Coast.

54

NEW LOST COAST
HEART OF THE SINKYONE

*The New Lost Coast Trail traverses the most spectacular portion
of the Sinkyone, a rugged untamed country. You pass remnants
of century-old homesteads and logging camps, even walk through
a ghost town abandoned in 1960. But most signs of habitation
have been erased by the harsh climate and lush vegetation.*

*This trail, completed in 1986, does not show on USGS topo
maps. The California Coastal Trails Foundation publishes* Trails
of the Lost Coast, *the best mapping of the trail to date. On the
ground, the trail is adequately marked. Map and compass are still
recommended, as is hiking with a friend. You must register to
camp along the trail. The cost is $3 per person per night.*

From the road-end the trail crosses Orchard Creek on a small
footbridge. The nearly level trail parallels the creek through
lush, riparian vegetation. At ⅛ mile a spur forks left to Railroad
Creek Environmental Camp. Before ½ mile you come to the site
of Bear Harbor Ranch, where Bear Harbor Environmental Camp
lies near the beach.

The Lost Coast Trail heads east along a creek, passing a corral
and trail register. Grasslands give way to forest as you begin to
climb. At ⅞ mile you cross the creek. Then you switchback to
the right and climb steadily out of the canyon. Before 1¼ miles
your trail joins the first of many old logging roads it follows. It
climbs to grand views of the rugged coast.

At 1½ miles the trail switches away from one logging road
and promptly joins another. Redwood, huckleberry, wild rose,
iris and slink pod grow along the path. You top a ridge, then
descend into Duffys Gulch. The trail leaves the logging road and
joins a portion of the original Humboldt Trail, built in 1862 when
the coast to the south was opened to homesteading. Settlers
from Mendocino had to ride or walk the trail to Eureka to
register their land claims.

As you descend east into Duffys Gulch, you spot virgin
redwoods. The trail switchbacks down to the creek crossing,
passing ancient redwoods ten feet in diameter, grand fir,
Douglas fir, bay laurel and bigleaf maple.

Take a minute to quench your thirst, fill your canteen, and
marvel at the virgin beauty of this place. Along the creek grow
five-finger, woodwardia, leather, sword and lady ferns. Pacific
waterleaf and saxifrage thrive in this moist habitat, as does
poison oak, which you should watch for. You have come 2¼

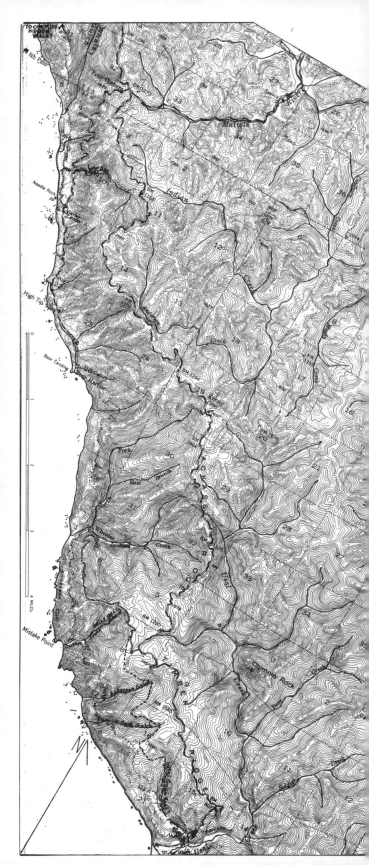

miles from Orchard Creek.

At 2¾ miles you leave the forest for steep coastal grasslands. Your trail traverses the grassy bluffs through a series of small gullies and rises. Paintbrush, buttercup, blue-eyed grass, lupine and golden poppy add color as the roar of surf rises from below.

You soon plunge into the first of several dark forests along the ridge. After more grasslands, you enter another fir forest as you wrap around a sinkhole on your left. Notice the dense vegetation growing in its shelter. Pass a gnarled, wind-topped redwood, then come to more grasslands.

You come to a nice stand of redwoods at 3¼ miles. Your trail switchbacks left and climbs to the ridge. Climb steeply along the narrow ridge to its top (elevation: 1000 feet), passing trillium, iris, redwood sorrel, one-leaved wild onion, slink pod, miners lettuce, toyon and columbine. You parallel an old fence before descending steeply east, then south. Climb steeply again to another top, then descend more switchbacks before climbing to a third top at 3¾ miles. From here you can look east into the heavily wooded canyons of Jackass Creek, site of the logging ghost town of Wheeler.

Descend gradually along the east side of the ridge through forest. Then you switch sharply right and descend bluffs of low brush and grass with foxglove, tall brodiaea, blue-eyed grass, sticky monkeyflower, beach strawberry and poison oak.

Parallel the edge of a forest around 3⅞ miles. At 4⅛ miles your trail leaves coast and ridge to descend southeast by a series of long switchbacks.

You soon pass two large redwoods surrounded by smaller redwoods, then descend into a fern-filled gulch. Come to big trees at the bottom of the canyon. This is known as School marm Grove, named for the Wheeler schoolhouse once located nearby. A campsite sits beneath two large redwoods in a clearing beside the North Fork of Jackass Creek. A second campsite lies 200 feet downstream, near the creek crossing. A spring is in the gulch to the west.

Wheeler was established in 1950, one of the last company logging towns and probably the newest ghost town in the west. The town lasted 10 years, abandoned as improved roads allowed the logs to be hauled to larger mills. Wheeler housed 32 families who harvested the timber, worked in the sawmill, and hauled the cut lumber to Willits by truck. The modern town had electricity, telephones and a water system.

The trail into "town" crosses the creek on a large log, remnant of an old bridge. Then the trail heads south on the old road, passing crumbling foundations, rusting logging relics and side streets. Domesticated plants grow wild here: foxglove, spearmint, red hot poker and alyssum. About ¼ mile from the creek

NEW LOST COAST:

DISTANCE: One way: 16¾ miles to Usal; 4½ miles to Wheeler, 9⅜ miles to Little Jackass, 11¾ miles to Anderson Gulch.

TIME: Up to 3 days.

TERRAIN: Many ups and downs over rugged coastal ridges and through canyons.

ELEVATION GAIN/LOSS: To Wheeler: 1440 ft.+/1440 ft-. Bear Harbor to Usal: 5300 feet+/5300 feet-.

BEST TIME: Spring. Summer and fall are next best.

WARNINGS: Isolated country far from towns and services. Timber rattlesnakes, ticks, poison oak, stinging nettles all occur along trail; watch for them. You must have a permit to camp overnight on the trail. Camping allowed only in designated areas.

DIRECTIONS TO TRAILHEAD: Exit Highway 101 at Garberville (M.10.8) on the south or Redway (M.14.6) on the north. Take Briceland Road from Redway (2.8 miles north of Garberville on Redwood Drive). In 12 miles go left through Whitethorn. In 4.5 more miles you come to the junction known as Four Corners. Go straight, descending a steep and narrow, winding dirt road (impassable to RV's or trailers, may be closed after heavy rains). Pass the Visitor Center in 3.6 miles. Then continue 2.5 miles to trailhead at end of road.

FEES: $3/person/day.

FURTHER INFO: Sinkyone Wilderness State Park (707) 946-2311, 247-3318.

crossing, you come to the heart of town. The sawmill was located here at the confluence of the two forks of the creek.

The trail crosses the creek and heads south, paralleling the beach at 4⅞ miles. A large grassy flat and a lagoon lie between the trail and the beach. High cliffs guard the dark sand beach at both ends.

The trail turns southeast and climbs a grassy gulch where the bosses lived. At 5⅛ miles you come to a wildflower garden at the top of the cleared portion of the gulch. The trail climbs steeply through dense brush, then into tall forest. At 6¾ miles you climb by several switchbacks to top a ridge at 800 feet elevation.

Descend along the border between forest and grasslands. At 7¼ miles a vernal pool lies west of the trail. Continue your descent into a hanging valley of grasslands sprinkled with wildflowers. At 7½ miles you approach the creek at an elevation of 450 feet. Be careful as you cross it because stinging nettles cover deep holes in the creek; one false step and they will sting you.

Then your trail climbs east, following the south fork of the creek. At 7⅝ miles you switchback right and climb a ridge at the top of Anderson Cliff by a dozen switchbacks. Several of the westernmost switchbacks have side trails that lead to the top of Anderson Cliff for magnificent views.

The long climb ends as you gain a grassy ridge at 8⅜ miles (1100 feet elevation). An old jeep road on your left climbs to meet the Wheeler Road. After a brief level stretch, your trail descends gradually east, then steeply south toward Little Jackass Creek. At 8⅞ miles you veer left and descend by several switchbacks through grasslands with great views. You might hear a herd of sea lions barking on the beach below. Wildflowers brighten the way: foxglove, paintbrush, yarrow, monkeyflower, poppy and brodiaea.

Come to the floor of the canyon at 9¼ miles, near an old corral, all that remains of a pre-1900 logging camp. An outhouse at the junction serves two adjacent campsites. The magnificent beach lies about ⅛ mile west, bordered by sea caves and the towering Anderson Cliff. A herd of sea lions sometimes lives on the south end of the beach. Please stay at least 200 feet from the wild animals.

The main trail heads up the canyon, crossing the creek at 9⅜ miles. In another 500 feet, you come to the upper camp with two more sites near the creek beneath large redwoods and maples.

The trail south starts climbing immediately, crossing the creek and ascending along it before switching right. Ascend steadily by six switchbacks into the upper canyon, a checkerboard of clearcuts and virgin stands. At 10¼ miles the trail meets an old road. Follow it east, then south above Northport Gulch. The road contours, crossing a small creek at 10½ miles, then passing whole hillsides of sticky monkeyflowers.

Beyond 10⅞ miles you come to a broad landing where the road turns northeast. Your trail leaves the road here, descending south, with views down to the mouth of Northport Gulch. Switchback left, then descend steeply by eight switchbacks into Anderson Gulch. At 11¾ miles you reach the camp, with a view down to the mouth of Anderson Gulch.

Descend two more switchbacks to a ford of the creek. Climb steeply to precipitous, grassy headlands above the rugged shore. Then descend to fern-filled Dark Gulch, which you follow upstream, crossing the creek at 12⅞ miles.

Now you make one last long ascent, climbing 900 feet in 1¼ miles to just below the 1320-foot summit of Timber Point. Your trail meanders south through the forest, crosses a seasonal creek, then descends to grasslands at 15¼ miles. An unusual red and green brodiaea called chinese firecracker grows beside the trail in spring.

You follow the ridge southeast, with great views of the coast to the south and the wooded canyons of Hotel Gulch and Usal Creek to the east. In the last ⅞ mile, you descend east by 20 switchbacks to Usal Road, 16¾ miles from the northern trailhead.

55.

PIONEER MEADOW LOOP
A DYING MEADOW AND RUSTING RELICS

Water is the focus for the 975-acre Benbow Lake State Recreation Area. The South Fork of the Eel River winds through the park, offering steelhead fishing in winter. In summer the river is dammed to form Benbow Lake, which provides swimming, fishing, canoeing (rentals available) and sailboarding. The park also has several miles of hiking trails for exploring the wooded ridges in a big bend of the river, as well as the shorelines of lake and river. You seldom see many people once you leave the trailhead.

During most of the year you must start your hike from campsite 11. (In winter the gate may be closed at campground entrance, requiring an additional ⅜ mile walk—if you can ford the river.) Only in summer is the upper loop of the campground open, which allows you to start at campsite 73. From campsite 11, head north to parallel the chain-link fence near the freeway. As you walk through grasslands scattered with oaks and firs, you may see pretty yellow globe lilies flowering in spring. The trail passes under the freeway, coming to the upper campground. As

PIONEER MEADOW LOOP:

DISTANCE: 2¾- or 3⅝-mile loop (from campsite 11).

TIME: One or 2 hours.

TERRAIN: Climbs wooded canyons and ridges above Benbow Valley to a dying meadow, then descends.

ELEVATION GAIN/LOSS: 640 feet+/640 feet-. Add 200 feet +/- to ridge.

BEST TIME: Spring for wildflowers, summer to jump in the lake.

WARNINGS: Watch for poison oak and rattlesnakes.

DIRECTIONS TO TRAILHEAD: Leave Highway 101 at Benbow exit. From north (M.8.5) go left. From south (M.8.35) go right. Then go right again for one mile. Turn right at campground entrance, cross the river, and drive to north end of campground. Trail leaves from campsite 11 in off season, campsite 73 in summer.

FEES: Day use/parking: $5/vehicle. Car camping: $12-14/night.

FURTHER INFO: Benbow State Recreation Area (707) 923-3238, 247–3318.

the trail forks, you can go left along the fence to meet the Otter Trail, which follows the South Fork upstream. The described route takes the right fork west through the campground, passing the restroom at ¼ mile, then following the road for 200 feet to the real trailhead beside campsite 73.

The Pratt Mill Trail heads uphill past large redwoods, then bends right and passes through second-growth forest. At ⅜ mile you descend into a moist gully, then climb by switchbacks to a junction at ⅝ mile. Go left here. (You will return on the right fork.) In 150 feet you meet the Pioneer Trail, where you go right.

The Pioneer Trail climbs west on an old skid road. Just beyond ¾ mile, the unmarked Ridge Trail branches left. (You can add ⅞ mile and an exhilarating climb to this 2¾-mile loop by taking the Ridge Trail, which climbs to a 973-foot peak with fine views, then loops back to the Pioneer Trail.) Continuing straight on the Pioneer Trail, you make a winding contour through small gullies.

At 1⅛ miles the Pioneer Trail veers right, where the ridge loop returns to meet it. Descend gradually for 300 feet, then descend by switchbacks into virgin redwood forest. At 1⅜ miles your trail levels and comes to Pioneer Meadow. This is not so much a meadow as a grassy glade overgrown with large black oaks. Virgin redwoods and Douglas firs surround it. An uncommon place in the redwood forest, it makes a pleasant blanket-picnic spot.

The trail follows the eastern edge of the meadow. At 1½ miles you descend north by steep switchbacks. As your descent eases, you can see the inviting blue-green waters of Benbow Lake below. You soon meet the Pratt Mill Trail, which is a rutted road at this point.

Go right on Pratt Mill Trail, climbing briefly, then descending, with views of Benbow Inn across the lake. Follow the shore of the lake through a forest of large redwoods. At 1¾ miles Pratt Mill Trail leaves the road, veering right. In 100 feet you come to the site of Pratt Redwood Mill. An old boiler and drive wheels sit rusting beneath virgin redwoods. How incongruous that a redwood sawmill was shaded by these big trees!

The trail continues southeast on the old mill road and climbs a steep hill. At 2 miles you come to an overlook high above the shore of the lake, with the picnic area and Benbow Inn on the opposite bank. Then your trail veers away from the lake, climbing steadily. As your climb eases, you reach the junction with the campground loop at 2⅛ miles. Go left here, returning on the path you started out on. You come to campsite 73 at 2½ miles. It is another ¼ mile back to campsite 11.

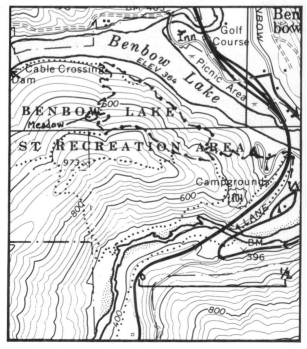

56

TANOAK SPRINGS
DURPHY CREEK LOOP

EXPLORING RICHARDSON GROVE STATE PARK

The Sinkyone tribe had a winter village on the South Fork of the Eel River near the present southern park boundary. The village of Kahs'chosoningibe had six houses constructed of slabs of redwood bark. The people of the village spent about six months of each year there, catching salmon and other fish. They lived near the coast for the rest of the year.

The Tanoak Springs/Durphy Creek Loop is the longest hike in 1414-acre Richardson Grove State Park. It explores a high ridge and a stream canyon in the southwest quadrant of the park. Other trails are listed in OTHER SUGGESTION.

The trail heads southwest beside campsite 58. (In summer, unless you are camping here, you must park in Day-Use area and walk ⅜ mile up to the trailhead.) You climb gradually through mixed forest of redwood, Douglas fir, tanoak and madrone to a fork in 150 feet. Go left on the Lookout Point Trail, heading southeast. This trail climbs gradually, following the top edge of the river canyon. Soon you switchback to the right and climb up and around a steep side canyon. Cross it at ¼ mile and climb east.

In 300 feet you come to Lookout Point, where you have a fine view of the river and highway snaking below. Then climb gradually southwest. As you pass under a power line, the trail steepens, becoming gradual again beyond ⅜ mile.

You soon pass back under the wires and come to a fork. (You can turn right for a short 1¼-mile loop.) Our described trail goes left, meeting the Tanoak Springs Trail in 300 feet. Go right and head northwest. (The left fork descends ½ mile to reach Hartsook Inn.) Tanoak Springs Trail climbs gradually at first, then winds and climbs steeply to gain the top of the ridge at ¾ mile. Douglas irises and tiny calypso orchids grow along the trail in spring.

You climb steeply between level stretches along the ridge to 1¼ miles, where the trail runs sidehill on the steep north slope. Descend to a saddle, climb again to 1⅜ miles, then contour along the ridgetop to 1½ miles. Large madrones, tanoaks and Douglas firs grow along this part of the ridge.

Your trail stays on the ridgetop, climbing, descending to another saddle, then climbing into a young forest of firs at 1⅝

TANOAK SPRINGS/DURPHY CREEK LOOP:

DISTANCE: 4⅛-mile loop (add ⅜ mile from Day-Use area).

TIME: Two to 3 hours.

TERRAIN: Climbs up to and along a wooded ridge, then descends a creek canyon.

ELEVATION GAIN/LOSS: 950 feet+/950 feet-.

BEST TIME: Spring for wildflowers. Nice anytime.

WARNINGS: Watch for poison oak and ticks along the trail. Carry water because the spring may be dry or fouled by animals.

DIRECTIONS TO TRAILHEAD: Turn west off Highway 101 at M.1.73 into Richardson Grove State Park. Go .1 mile to fork. Then go right to Madrone Campground, coming to trailhead in .4 mile, just past campsite 58. In summer, unless you are camping here, you must park in Day-Use area: go left at fork, then .3 mile to parking near river.

FEES: Day use/parking: $5/vehicle. Car camping: $12-14/night.

FURTHER INFO: Richardson Grove State Park (707) 247-3318.

OTHER SUGGESTION: HARTSOOK TRAIL climbs ½ mile from Hartsook Inn (M.0.89) to meet main trail at Lookout Point. WOODLAND TRAIL offers an easy 1.6-mile loop through the northern portion of the park. In summer you can cross seasonal bridges over Eel River to reach the TOUMEY-BIG SPRINGS LOOP (2 miles).

miles. Then contour along the ridgetop.

Beyond 1¾ miles your trail switches right and makes a winding descent to meet the spur trail to Tanoak Springs at 1⅞ miles. Walk the 350 feet to the springs, where a lush patch of woodwardia ferns thrives in the cool and wet.

Returning to the main trail, turn left and descend through thickets of huckleberries. The trail makes a steep and winding descent into the canyon of Durphy Creek. At 2⅜ miles you hear the creek gurgling below as big Douglas firs line your path. Descend by about ten more switchbacks to 2¾ miles, where you head east, fifty feet above Durphy Creek.

The trail follows the shady, north-facing south bank of the creek. The cool, moist bank shelters iris, redwood sorrel,

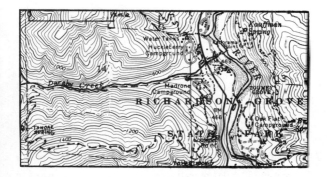

saxifrage, bay laurel and many ferns: sword, horsetail, woodwardia, maidenhair and five-finger. Just before 2¾ miles, you have easy access to the creek.

Your trail descends steps to a bridge at 3⅛ miles, then quickly crosses two more bridges over side streams. Gooseberries grow here. The trail follows Durphy Creek, alternating between drier and wetter microclimates. Interior live oaks with prickly leaves grow in the drier spots, while ferns, redwood sorrel and even a few western yew trees grow in the moist spots.

At 3¼ miles you draw near the creek again, but it quickly drops deeper into the canyon. Cross two more bridges around 3⅜ miles, then return to redwood forest. At 3½ miles a 12-foot-diameter redwood stands to the left of the trail.

You then descend by short switchbacks to Durphy Creek Rest at 3⅝ miles. A short spur leads to a small redwood grove in a level spot between creek and trail, where a bench provides a picnic spot. Trilliums, redwood sorrel and calypso orchids grow beneath the big trees.

The main trail crosses two more side streams, climbs briefly, then descends through a rocky area to reach the creek bed again. From there a broad trail climbs away from the creek, coming to the paved park road in 250 feet, just before your 4-mile point.

To return to the Madrone Campground trailhead, turn right on the paved road and climb the hill into the campground. Follow the road to campsite 58 for a total loop of 4⅛ miles. (If you parked in the Day-Use area, turn left on the paved road and descend to your car.)

CALIFORNIA COASTAL TRAIL
BECOMING REALITY IN DEL NORTE, HUMBOLDT
& NORTHERN MENDOCINO COUNTIES

The California Coastal Trail is a proposed 1600-mile system of interconnected beach and coastal range trails running the length of the spectacular California coast from Oregon to Mexico.
-California Coastal Trails Foundation

The California Coastal Trail is a work-in-progress, with an estimated 750 miles of trail already in place, providing public access. Although only the most avid coast hikers will hike the California Coastal Trail (CCT) in its entirety, its establishment will greatly expand coastal access for millions of hikers and coast lovers.

The northernmost segment of CCT is one of the most complete. Roughly 120 nearly continuous miles of the trail exist from Northern Del Norte County through Redwood National Park and beyond to Humboldt Bay. Partial segments of CCT exist from the bay south into Mendocino County. This report catalogs the current status of CCT development, from north to south.

From the Oregon border you can walk south along open beach through Pelican State Beach and Kamph Memorial Park to the mouth of the Smith River. Through hikers, having no way to cross the river at its mouth, must detour inland on Highway 101 and Fred Haight Drive. After crossing Smith River on the Highway 101 bridge, one may turn west on Lake Earl Drive, then Moseley Road to enter Lake Earl public lands either via Pala Road or Kellogg Road. South of the river CCT continues along the beach or through the dunes of Lake Earl State Park and Wildlife Area (see Trails #1 and 2). You must register before arriving to stay at the Environmental Camps off Kellogg Road.

South of Lake Earl you can walk the beach around Point St. George to follow Pebble Beach Drive into Crescent City. One might shorten this segment by following the Dead Lake Trail southeast to Riverside Drive, then walk streets into town. From Crescent City, you can follow the bike path to the Small Boat Basin, then walk south on Crescent Beach for two (or more) miles. The best route turns inland at Crescent Beach Picnic Area on two miles of new trail to Enderts Beach Trailhead.

The Coastal Trail runs south continuously from there for 18 spectacular miles to Klamath Overlook near Requa (see Trails #4, 6, 8 and 9). Campsites along the way provide off-road camping: Nickel Creek at one mile and DeMartin Camp at ten miles. Redwood Hostel, in a charming pioneer house, offers accommodations at the south end of the DeMartin Trail. ($9 per adult per night, half price for guests under 18 accompanied by a parent.)

To continue on CCT from Requa, the Klamath River is an obstacle, as it was to early travelers. It is 7 miles by car to the start of the Flint Ridge Section of CCT. The distance can be halved if someone ferries you across the Klamath.

The Flint Ridge Section of CCT (see Trail #10) heads west 4½ miles to the coast, passing Flint Ridge Camp ¼ mile from the west end. Then CCT follows the Coastal Drive for 4¼ miles to Carruthers Cove Trailhead (see Trails #11 and 12). A steep descent brings you to the beach at Carruthers Cove, where 3 miles of beach walking lie to the south. You must have a tide lower than +3.0 feet to walk the first mile. After you have synchronized with the tide, it is 2⅛ miles to Butler Creek Backpack Camp (you must register at Prairie Creek State Park *before* arriving). If you have not pre-registered, continue south 3¾ miles to the Gold Bluffs Hike/Bike Camp, where you register on the spot.

From Gold Bluffs Campground, it is 1¾ miles to Espa Lagoon, northern trailhead for the Skunk Cabbage Creek Trail (see Trail #21). That trail runs 5½ miles to meet Highway 101 at the current end of this length of CCT. If the tide is low enough to get around Mussel Point, an alternate route stays on the beach to the mouth of Redwood Creek. Contact Redwood National Park before attempting this section; ask if the beach is passable around Mussel Point and if Redwood Creek can be forded.

South of Orick, you can walk the beach past Freshwater Lagoon. A new segment of CCT from Stone Lagoon to Dry Lagoon will add 5 miles to CCT when completed in 1994. It passes a walk-in camp beside Stone Lagoon and Environmental Camps at Dry Lagoon. You may not be able to ford the seasonal outlets of Stone or Big Lagoons in winter or early spring. When the barrier beach is passable you can walk 6¼ miles from Dry Lagoon to Patrick's Point (see Trail #26).

After walking through beautiful Patrick's Point State Park (see Trails #27 and 28), you must walk Patrick's Point Drive to Trinidad, then Scenic Drive to Moonstone County Park at the mouth of Little River (see Trail #33).

From Little River to the mouth of Humboldt Bay lie 19 miles of beach and dunes (see Trail #34). You can walk onto the beach at Moonstone County Park, ford Little River, and walk the beach for 5 miles before you come to the mouth of Mad River. As the latter is usually too deep to ford, head east to cross the river on the Hammond Bridge. The designated CCT follows the Hammond Bicycle Trail on back roads to the city of Arcata. You may also return to the coast at Mad River County Park for another 14 miles of beach walking to the mouth of Humboldt Bay. Though you cannot cross the channel, the south spit on the other side begins another 9-mile beach walk to the mouth of the Eel River (see Trail #38). To get around the Eel River delta, through hikers must detour inland on county roads to Fernbridge, then follow State Route 211 to Ferndale.

South of the Eel, Centerville Beach provides 9 miles of beach and dune trekking (see Trails #39 and 40). The steep cliffs between False Cape and Cape Mendocino block passage south, but one might follow Mattole Road (see Trail #42) to reach the Lost Coast south of Petrolia.

The Lost Coast of the King Range may be the most famous stretch of CCT. It follows 25 miles of wilderness beach from the mouth of the Mattole River on the north to Shelter Cove on the south (see Trail #47).

From Shelter Cove, it is 3 steep miles on paved roads to the Hidden Valley Trailhead, starting point for a steep segment of CCT that climbs over Chemise Mountain, then descends into Mendocino County and Sinkyone Wilderness State Park (see Trail #53).

From Whale Gulch it is 1½ miles to the Visitor Center of Sinkyone Wilderness State Park. Then you walk 2¾ miles on unpaved Briceland Road to the New Lost Coast Trailhead, start of another 16¾-mile section of CCT (see Trail #54).

The above trails include almost 200 miles of coastal hiking, a great start for the California Coastal Trail. If you would like more information about CCT and what you can do to help, contact the California State Coastal Conservancy, 1330 Broadway, Suite 1100, Oakland, CA 94612 or COASTWALK, 1389 Cooper Road, Sebastopol, CA 95472.

CROSS REFERENCE LISTING
TRAILS SUITABLE FOR A PARTICULAR ACTIVITY

TRAILS FOR HANDICAPPED ACCESS
11. Coastal Drive and Short Trails
16. Elk Prairie—see OTHER SUGGESTION
20. Lost Man Creek
22. Lady Bird Johnson Grove Loop
28. Rim Loop—see OTHER SUGGESTION
43. Avenue of the Giants—see M.20.5: Founders Grove

Following may be passable under best conditions or with assistance:
29. Elk Head
36. Arcata Marsh—first loop

TRAILS FOR BACKPACKING
1. North to Yontocket & the Mouth of Smith River
3. Little Bald Hills
4. Last Chance Section, Coastal Trail
6. DeMartin Section, Coastal Trail
10. Flint Ridge Section, Coastal Trail
11. Coastal Drive and Short Trails
12. Carruthers Cove—see OTHER SUGGESTION
15. West Ridge to Butler Creek Camp
17. James Irvine (to Gold Bluffs Beach Hike/Bike Camp)
23. Redwood Creek
24. Tall Trees/Emerald Ridge Loop
45. Grasshopper Peak
46. Squaw Creek Ridge
47. Mattole River South
48. Smith-Etter Road to Beach
49. Kings Crest North
50. Lightning Trail to Kings Peak
51. Kings Crest South
52. Shelter Cove North
53. Hidden Valley to Chemise Mountain to Whale Gulch
54. New Lost Coast

TRAILS FOR MOUNTAIN BIKES
1. North to Yontocket & the Mouth of Smith River
2. Dead Lake Loop
3. Little Bald Hills
4. Last Chance Section, Coastal Trail
11. Coastal Drive
13. Ossagon—see OTHER SUGGESTION: 19-mile loop
14. Brown Creek—see OTHER SUGGESTION
20. Lost Man Creek
34. Mad River Beach—see OTHER SUGGESTION: Hammond Trail
35. Arcata's Redwood Park—see map

45. Grasshopper Peak—see map
46. Squaw Creek Ridge—see map: 11-mile loop
48. Smith-Etter Road to Beach

TRAILS FOR EQUESTRIANS

1. North to Yontocket & the Mouth of Smith River
2. Dead Lake Loop
3. Little Bald Hills
23. Redwood Creek—see OTHER SUGGESTION: 34 miles
29. Elk Head—see OTHER SUGGESTION
34. Mad River Beach
35. Arcata's Redwood Park—see map
38. Table Bluff County Park
39. Centerville Beach North
40. Centerville Beach South
45. Grasshopper Peak—see map
46. Squaw Creek Ridge—see map
47. Mattole River South
48. Smith-Etter Road to Beach
49. Kings Crest North
50. Lightning to Kings Peak
51. Kings Crest South
52. Shelter Cove North
53. Hidden Valley to Chemise to Whale Gulch
54. New Lost Coast

BEACH WALKS (OR RUNS)

1. North to Yontocket & the Mouth of Smith River
2. Dead Lake Loop
4. Enderts Beach—see also OTHER SUGGESTION: Crescent Beach
9. Hidden Beach
11. Coastal Drive—see Dad's Camp
19. Coastal Trail (and all of Gold Bluffs Beach)
21. Skunk Cabbage Creek (west portion)
25. Dry Lagoon to Big Lagoon—see also OTHER SUGGESTION: Stone Lagoon
27. Agate Beach
29. College Cove
30. Trinidad State Beach
32. Indian Beach
33. Other Trinidad Trails
34. Mad River Beach and Dunes
38. Table Bluff County Park
39. Centerville Beach North
40. Centerville Beach South
42. Cape Mendocino
47. Mattole River South—the ultimate!
52. Shelter Cove North

COMMON & SCIENTIFIC NAMES
OF PLANTS ALONG THE TRAILS

* alyssum, *Lobularia maritima*

anemone (wind flower),
Anemone deltoidea, A. lyallii

angelica, *Angelica hendersonii*

azalea (western azalea),
Rhododendron occidentale

baby blue eyes, *Nemophila
menziesii*

bay laurel, (California bay,
pepperwood), *Umbellularia
californica*

beach morning glory, *Calystegia
soldanella*

beach pea, *Lathyrus japonicus
var. glaber*

beach primrose, *Oenothera
cheiranthifolia*

beach strawberry, *Fragaria
chiloensis*

bear grass, *Xerophyllum tenax*

bedstraw, *Galium spp.*

bigleaf maple, *Acer macrophyllum*

Bishop pine, *Pinus muricata*

black crowberry, *Empetrum
nigrum*

black oak (California), *Quercus
kelloggi*

bleeding heart (western), *Dicentra
formosa*

213

blue dick, *Brodiaea capitata*

blue flag iris, *Iris purdyi*

blue gilia, *Gilia capitata*

* blue gum eucalyptus, *Eucalyptus globulus*

blue-eyed grass, *Sisyrinchium bellum*

blueblossom (California lilac), *Ceanothus thyrsiflorus*

Bolander's lily, *Lilium bolanderi*

bowl-tubed iris, *Iris macrosiphon*

bracken fern, *Pteridium aquilinum var. pubescens*

broadleaf ceanothus, *Ceanothus griseus*

brodiaea (tall brodiaea), *Brodiaea laxa*

brook foam, *Boykinia elata*

brooklime, *Veronica americana*

buttercup, *Ranunculus repens*

California blackberry, *Rubus vitifolius*

California lace fern, *Aspidotis densa*

California polypody, *Polypodium californicum*

California poppy (golden poppy), *Eschscholtzia californica*

California water hemlock, *Cicuta douglasii*

calla lily, *Zantedeschia aethiopica*

calypso orchid, *Calypso bulbosa*

canyon gooseberry, *Ribes menziesii*

canyon live oak, *Quercus chrysolepis*

cascara sagrada, *Rhamnus purshiana*

cattail, *Typha spp.*

chamise, *Adenostoma fasciculatum*

checker lily, *Fritillaria lanceolata*

chinese firecrackers, *Brodiaea ida-maia*

chinquapin, *Castanopsis chrysophylla*

clintonia, *Clintonia andrewsiana*

coast buckwheat, *Eriogonum latifolium*

coast lily, *Lilium maritimum*

coast silktassel, *Garrya elliptica*

coastal broom-rape, *Orobanche californica ssp. californica*

coastal manroot (wild cucumber), *Marah fabaceus, M. oreganus*

coastal nemophila, *Nemophila menziesii var. atomaria*

coffeeberry, *Rhamnus californica*

Columbia lily, *Lilium columbianum*

columbine, *Aquilegia formosa*

common juniper, *Juniperus communis*

coral root orchid, *Corallorhiza spp.*

cordgrass, *Spartina foliosa*

* cotoneaster, *Cotoneaster spp.*

cow parsnip, *Heracleum lanatum*

coyote brush, *Baccaris pilularis*

cream cups, *Platystemon californicus*

creek trillium, *Trillium rivale*

* creeping myrtle, *Vinca minor*

cypress, *Cupressus spp.*

dandelion, *Taraxacum officinale*

death camas, *Zigadenus venenosus*

deer fern, *Blechnum spicant*

deer oak, *Quercus sadleriana*

Del Norte pea, *Lathyrus delnorticus*

Del Norte wallflower, *Erysimum menziesii ssp. eurekense*

dogwood (Pacific), *Cornus nuttalli*

Douglas fir, *Pseudotsuga menziesii*

Douglas iris, *Iris douglasiana*

duckweed, *Lemna minima*

dune tansy, *Tanacetum douglasii*

elderberry (red), *Sambucus callicarpa*

* English daisy, *Bellis perennis*

Eureka lily, *Lilium occidentale*

evergreen huckleberry (California huckleberry), *Vaccinum ovatum*

evergreen violet (redwood violet), *Viola sempervirens*

fairy bells, *Disporum smithii, D. hookeri*

false lily of the valley, *Maianthemum dilatum*

false solomon's seal (fat Solomon's seal), *Smilacina racemosa*

fawn lily, *Erythronium oregonum*

fiddleneck, *Amsinckia intermedia*

* filaree (redstem storksbill), *Erodium cicutarium*

fireweed, *Epilobium spp.*

five-finger fern, *Adiantum pedatum var. aleuticum*

* foxglove, *Digitalis purpurea*

Fremont silktassel, *Garrya fremontii*

fringe cups, *Tellima grandiflora*

giant horsetail, *Equisetum temateia*

giant trillium, *Trillium chloropetalum*

godetia (farewell to spring), *Clarkia spp.*

gooseberry, *Ribes roezlii*

grand fir, *Abies grandis*

gum plant, *Grindelia stricta*

hairgrass, *Deschampsia cespitesa ssp. holciformis*

hairy cat's ear, *Hypochoeris radicata*

hairy honeysuckle, *Lonicera hispidula*

hairy manzanita, *Arctostaphyos columbiana*

hairy star tulip, *Calochortus tolmiei*

hazel (California), *Corylus cornuta var. californica*

hedge nettle, *Stachys bullata*

hen and chicks, *Dudleya farinosa*

* Himalayan blackberry, *Rubu procerus*

* holly, *Aquifoliaceae aquifolium*

huckleberry oak, *Quercus vaccinifolia*

huckleberry, *Vaccinum spp.*

* iceplant, *Mesembryanthemum spp.*

Indian pink, *Silene californica*

Indian plum (osoberry), *Oenleria cerasiformis*

Indian warrior, *Pedicularis densiflora*

inside-out flower, *Vancouveria planipetala*

Jeffrey pine, *Pinus jeffreyii*

johnny tuck, *Triphysaria eriantha*

kinnikinnick (bearberry), *Arctostaphylos uva-ursi*

knobcone pine, *Pinus attenuata*

knotweed, *Polygonum paronychia*

lady fern, *Athyrium filix-femina*

laurel, *Umbellularia californica*

leather fern, *Polypodium scouleri*

leopard lily, *Lilium pardalinum*

licorice fern, *Polypodium glycyrrhiza*

lupine, *Lupinus latifolius, L. littoralis, L. nanus, L. polyphyllus, L. variicolor, L. rivularis*

madrone, *Arbutus menziesii*

manzanita, *Arctostaphylos spp.*

miners lettuce, *Montia perfoliata*

* mint, *Mentha sp.*

miterwort, *Mitella ovalis*

monkeyflower, *Mimulus guttatus ssp. litoralis*

* Monterey cypress, *Cupresssus macrocarpa*

* Monterey pine, *Pinus radiata*

morning glory, *Calystegia sp.*

mouse-ear chickweed, *Cerastium arvense*

ninebark, *Physocarpus capitatus*

northern dune tansy, *Tanacetum douglasii*

ocean spray (cram bush), *Holodiscus discolor*

oenanthe, *Oenanthe sarmentosa*

one-leaved wild onion, *Allium unifolium*

Oregon crab apple, *Malus fusca*

Oregon grape, *Berberis nervosa, B. aquifolium*

* ox-eye daisy, *Leucanthemum vulgare*

Pacific silverweed, *Potentilla egedei var. grandis*

Pacific waterleaf, *Hydrophyllum teniupes*

paintbrush, *Castilleja latifolia, C. affinis, C. foliolosa, c. hololeuca, C. wightii*

* pampas grass, *Cortaderia selloana*

pearly everlasting, *Anaphalis margaritacea*

* pennyroyal (western), *Mentha pulegium*

penstemon, *Penstemon spp.*

pickleweed, *Salicornia virginica*

piggyback plant, *Tolmiea menziesii*

pinemat manzanita, *Arctostaphyllos nevadensis*

plantain, *Plantago spp.*

* poison hemlock, *Conium maculatum*

poison oak, *Toxicodendron diversiloba*

poppy, *Eschscholzia californica*

Port Orford cedar, *Chamaecyparis lawsoniana*

prince's pine (pippsissewa), *Chimaphila umbellatum*

raspberry, *Rubus leucodermis*

* rattlesnake grass, *Briza maxima*

rattlesnake plantain, *Goodyera oblongifola*

red alder, *Alnus rubra*

* red hot poker, *Kniphofia uvaria*

red huckleberry, *Vaccinium parvifolium*

red trillium, *Trillium chloropetalum*

red-flowering currant, *Ribes sanguineum*

redwood lily, *Lilium rubescens*

redwood sorrel, *Oxalis oregana*

redwood, *Sequoia sempervirens*

rein orchid, *Habenaria elegans var. maritima*

rhododendron, *Rhododendron macrophyllum*

rush, *Juncus sphaerocarpus*

salal, *Gaultheria shallon*

salmonberry, *Rubus spectabilis*

sand verbena, pink, *Abronia maritima*

sand verbena, yellow, *Abronia latifolia*

saxifrage, *Saxifraga spp.*

* Scotch broom, *Cytisus scoparius*

scouring rush, *Equisetum hyemale*

scythe-leaved onion, *Allium falcifolium*

* sea fig (ice plant), *Mesembryanthemum chilense*

* sea rocket, *Cakile maritima*

sea thrift, *Armeria maritima var. californica*

seaside daisy, *Erigeron glaucus*

sedge, *Carex spp.*

self heal, *Prunella vulgaris*

serviceberry, *Amelanchier alnifolia*

shooting star, *Dodecathon hendersonii*

shore pine, *Pinus contorta ssp. contorta*

Siberian miners lettuce (candyflower), *Montia sibirica*

silky beach pea, *Lathyrus littoralis*

silver beachweed, *Franseria chamissonis ssp. bipinnatisecta*

silverleaf phacelia, *Phacelia argentea*

Sitka spruce, *Picea sitchensis*

skunk cabbage, *Lysichitum americanum*

slink pod, *Scoliopus bigelovii*

snow queen, *Synthyris reniformis*

snowberry, *Symphoricarpus alba*

soap root, *Chlorogalum pomeridianum*

* spearmint, *Mentha spicata*

star solomon's seal (slim solomon's seal), *Smilacina stellata*

starflower, *Trientalis latifolia*

sticky monkeyflower, *Mimulus aurantiacus*

stinging nettle, *Urtica lyallii*

sugar pine, *Pinus lambertiana*

sugarstick, *Allotropa virgata*

sundew, *Drosera rotundifolia*

sword fern, *Polystichum munitum*

tanoak, *Lithocarpus densiflorus*

tarweed, *Madia madioides*

thimbleberry, *Rubus parviflorus*

thistle, *Cirsium brevistylum*

tooth-leaved monkeyflower,
Mimulus dentalus

trail plant, *Adenocaulon bicolor*

trillium, *Trillium ovatum*

twin flower, *Linnaea borealis*

twinberry, *Lonicera involucrata*

twisted stalk, *Streptopus amplexifolius*

vanilla leaf (deer foot), *Achlys triphylla*

vetch, *Vicia angustifolia*

vine maple, *Acer circinatum*

watercress, *Nasturtium officinale*

wax myrtle (bayberry), *Myrica californica*

western coltsfoot, *Petasites palmatus*

western dog violet, *Viola adunca*

western hemlock, *Tsuga heterophylla*

western redcedar, *Thuja plicata*

western wood anemone, *Anemone lyallii*

western yew, *Taxus brevifolia*

white-veined shinleaf, *Pyrola picta*

whitethorn, *Ceanothus incanus*

wild ginger, *Asarum caudatum*

wild mustard, *Brassica campestris*

wild rose, *Rosa sp.*

wild tobacco, *Nicotiana attenuata*

willow, *Salix spp.*

wintergreen, *Pyrola sp.*

wood fern, *Dryopteris arguta*

wood rose, *Rosa gymnocarpa*

woodwardia (chain) fern,
Woodwardia fimbriata

yarrow, *Achillea millefolium*

yellow globe lily (fairy lantern),
Calochortus amabilis

yellow mat, *Sanicula arctopoides*

yellow pond lily, *Naphar polysepalum*

yerba de selva, *Whipplea modesta*

* Introduced species

BIBLIOGRAPHY

Adams, Kramer, *The Redwoods*, Popular Library, New York, 1968.

Alt, David D. and Donald W. Hyndman, *Roadside Geology of Northern California*, Mountain Press Publishing Co., Missoula, Montana, 1975.

Becking, Rudolph, *Pocket Flora of the Redwood Forest*, Island Press, Covelo, California, 1982.

Brown, Joseph E., *Monarchs of the Mist*, Coastal Parks Assoc., Pt. Reyes, California, 1982.

California Coastal Access Guide, Fourth Edition, University of California Press, Berkeley, 1991.

California Coastal Resource Guide, University of California Press, Berkeley, 1987.

Chase, J. Smeaton, *California Coastal Trails*, Tioga Publishing, Palo Alto, California, 1987, reprint, originally published: Houghton Mifflin, Boston, 1913.

Chronic, Halke, *Pages of Stone: Geology of Western National Parks and Monuments: Sierra Nevada, Cascades and Pacific Coast, Volume 2*, Mountaineers, Seattle, Washington, 1986.

Coy, Owen C., *The Humboldt Bay Region 1850-1875*, California State Historical Association, Los Angeles, 1929.

Dawson, Ann, *Nature Bound Pocket Field Guide*, Omnigraphics Ltd., Boise, Idaho, 1985.

Dewitt, John B., *California Redwood Parks and Preserves*, Save-the-Redwoods League, San Francisco, 1982.

Grillos, Steve J., *Ferns and Fern Allies of California*, University of California Press, Berkeley, 1987.

Handbook of North American Indians, edited by William C. Sturtevant, Smithsonian Institution, Washington, D.C., 1978.

Hayden, Mike, *Exploring the North Coast*, Chronicle Books, San Francisco, 1982.

Hoopes, Chad L., *Lure of the Humboldt Bay Region*, Wm. C. Brown Co., Dubuque, Iowa, 1966.

Jepson Manual: Higher Plants of California, edited by James C. Hickman, University of California Press, Berkeley, 1993.

Keator, Glenn and Ruth Heady, *Pacific Coast Berry Finder*, Nature Study Guild, Berkeley, 1978.

Keator, Glenn and Ruth Heady, *Pacific Coast Fern Finder*, Nature Study Guild, Berkeley, 1981.

Kroeber, A.L., *Handbook of the Indians of California*, Dover Publications, New York, 1976.

Lewis, Oscar, *The Quest for Qual-a-wa-loo (Humboldt Bay)*, San Francisco, 1943, (no publisher cited).

Leydet, Francois, *The Last Redwoods and the Parklands of Redwood Creek*, Sierra Club, Ballantine Books, New York, 1969.

Little, Elbert, *The Audubon Society Field Guide to North American Trees, Western Region*, Alfred A. Knopf, New York, 1980.

Lyons, Kathleen and Mary Beth Cuneo-Lazaneo, *Plants of the Coast Redwood Region*, Looking Press, Los Altos, California, 1988.

McConnaughey, Bayard H. and Evelyn McConnaughey, *Pacific Coast,* Audubon Society Nature Guides, Alfred A. Knopf, New York, 1985.

Munz, Philip A., *California Spring Wildflowers*, University of California Press, Berkeley, 1961.

Munz, Philip A., *Shore Wildflowers of California, Oregon and Washington*, University of California Press, Berkeley, 1964.

Niehaus, Theodore F. and Charles L. Ripper, *Field Guide to Pacific States Wildflowers*, Peterson Field Guide Series, Houghton Mifflin, Boston, 1976.

O'Neill-Knight, Dusty, *Humboldt Redwoods Trail Guide*, Revised, Humboldt Redwoods Interpretive Association, Weott, California, 1992.

Peterson, Roger Tory, *A Field Guide to Western Birds*, Peterson Field Guide Series, Houghton Mifflin, Boston, 1990.

Petrides, George A. and Olivia, *A Field Guide to Western Trees*, Peterson Field Guide Series, Houghton Mifflin, Boston, 1992.

Randall, Warren R., Robert F. Keniston, Dale N. Bever and Edward C. Jensen, *Manual of Oregon Trees and Shrubs*, Oregon State University Bookstores, Corvallis, Oregon, 1988.

Ransom, Jay Ellis, *Complete Field Guide to North American Wildlife*, Harper & Row, New York, 1981.

Russo, Ron and Pam Olhausen, *Pacific Intertidal Life*, Nature Study Guild, Berkeley, 1981.

Schrepfer, Susan R., *The Fight to Save the Redwoods*, University of Wisconsin Press, Madison, 1983.

Spellenberg, Richard, *The Audubon Society Field Guide to North American Wildlfowers, Western Region*, Alfred A. Knopf, New York, 1979.

Watts, Phoebe, *Redwood Region Flower Finder*, Nature Study Guild, Berkeley, 1979.

Watts, Tom, *Pacific Coast Tree Finder*, Nature Study Guild, Berkeley, 1973.

Whitney, Stephen, *Western Forests,* Audubon Society Nature Guides, Alfred A. Knopf, New York, 1985.

Yocum, Charles and Raymond Dasmann, *The Pacific Coastal Wildlife Region*, American Wildlife Region Series, Naturegraph, Happy Camp, California, 1965.

Young, Dorothy King, *Redwood Empire Wildflowers*, Third Edition, Naturegraph Publishers, Happy Camp, California, 1976.

INDEX

ABOUT BORED FEET

We began Bored Feet Publications in 1986 to publish and distribute *The Hiker's hip pocket Guides*. If you would like to receive updates on trails included in our publications, send us your name and address, specifying your counties of interest.

We provide a retail mail order service specializing in books and maps about Northern California. Your purchases directly from Bored Feet support our independent publishing efforts to bring you more information about Northern California's spectacular natural beauty. Thanks for your support!

BORED FEET
P.O. BOX 1832
MENDOCINO, CA 95460
(707) 964-6629